W9-CEI-843

TITANIC

A fresh look at the evidence
by a former Chief Inspector
of Marine Accidents

TITANIC

A FRESH LOOK AT THE EVIDENCE
BY A FORMER CHIEF INSPECTOR
OF MARINE ACCIDENTS

———

JOHN LANG

Rowman & Littlefield Publishers, Inc.

SEAFARER BOOKS

To Joanna

for keeping me afloat for over 40 years

———

First published in the USA by:
Rowman & Littlefield Publishers, Inc.
4501 Forbes Blvd, Suite 200 · Lanham · MD 20706 · USA
www.rowman.com

A catalogue record for this book is available from
the Library of Congress, Washington, DC

Published in the UK by Seafarer Books Ltd
102 Redwald Road · Rendlesham · Suffolk IP12 2TE
www.seafarerbooks.com

A catalogue record for this book is available from the British Library

ISBN 978-1-4422-1890-1 hardback
eISBN 978-1-4422-1892-5

Photograph of icefield from SS *Carpathia*: Library of Congress/Science Photo Library.
Photographs of *Titanic, Californian* and *Carpathia*: Wikimedia Commons PD-Art.

Design, typesetting, maps and diagrams:
Louis Mackay / www.louismackaydesign.co.uk

Editing: Hugh Brazier

Proofreading: Eric Cowell

Text set digitally in Proforma

Contents

Photographs, maps and diagrams

Table

Foreword

A century after the world's most notorious marine disaster, we still have regular reminders that the sea remains a dangerous place, and that even aboard the most modern and best-equipped ships events can still conspire against those aboard, with disastrous consequences. But what we have today that was certainly not enjoyed by previous generations is an ability to investigate a marine accident with a high degree of forensic accuracy by professional investigators aided by voyage data recorder information from the ship's 'black box'.

After the whole world had been shaken by the loss of the 'unsinkable' *Titanic*, as with other marine disasters until quite recent times, the formal inquiries, taking place many months after the event, would have reached their conclusions with little really reliable assistance. Witness statements would often be contradictory and would reflect the inability of those who had been present to grasp the reality of what had been happening in the confusion of the emergency.

The passage of time would have dulled the recollection of survivors. Logbooks and other written records might well have been completed after the events rather than contemporaneously. The conclusions of the proceedings might reflect the ignorance of the judge or counsel and even the prejudices of the professional assessors. Even when everyone involved in an inquiry fulfilled their roles with good will and an open mind, the final report might well have been unable to properly establish the truth, and injustice could be reflected in the conclusions, resulting in wrecked reputations and lives ruined.

The best professional marine accident investigator will

bring to a casualty both independence and an ability to establish causation rather than blame. It is quite rare that there are clear-cut, single causes of an accident, and an objective, professional investigator will look beyond the most obvious conclusions such as 'human error', continuing to ask questions until the full picture emerges. Ideally, as with the UK system, the fact that the investigator is not gathering information that can form the case against a witness works in favour of the truth emerging. These are often complex cases which defy easy explanations, but the facts as established will be invaluable in preventing other similar accidents. This is so important, and represents the accident investigator's chief motivation.

John Lang, after a distinguished career in both the Merchant Navy and the Royal Navy, became the Chief Inspector of the Marine Accident Investigation Branch and did much to establish and secure the international reputation the MAIB enjoys today, where it has become a model for other maritime administrations. In his investigation of the sinking of the *Titanic*, he brings to this compelling story a fairness and objectivity that were lacking in the aftermath of the sinking, and he casts a fresh, seamanlike eye over the events of April 1912.

Michael Grey MBE
Former Editor of *Lloyd's List*

Preface

Following the sinking of the Royal Mail Steamer *Titanic* on 15 April 1912, the Lord Chancellor appointed Lord Mersey to act as the Wreck Commissioner to preside at the Formal Investigation tasked to investigate the circumstances of the loss. The Investigation sat for 37 days between 2 May and 3 July 1912, and published its report on 30 July, concluding that:

> The Court, having carefully inquired into the circumstances of the above mentioned shipping casualty, finds, for the reasons appearing in the annex hereto, that the loss of the said ship was due to collision with an iceberg, brought about by the excessive speed at which the ship was being navigated.
>
> Dated this 30th day of July, 1912
>
> MERSEY
> Wreck Commissioner

The Board of Trade asked the Investigation to provide answers to 26 specific questions, but only one sought to establish what the causes might have been. Question number 24 asked 'what was the cause of the loss of the *Titanic*, and of the loss of life which thereby ensued or occurred?' It went on to ask, 'What vessels had the opportunity of rendering assistance to the *Titanic* and, if any, how was it that assistance did not reach the *Titanic* before the SS *Carpathia* arrived?'

The answer was:

(a) Collision with an iceberg and the subsequent foundering of the ship.

(b) The *Californian*. She could have reached the *Titanic* if she had made the attempt when she saw the first rocket. She made no attempt.

In the report, the role of the SS *Californian* was singled out for special attention. At the end of the section that considered the actions of this ship, Lord Mersey made the following observation:

> When she first saw the rockets the *Californian* could have pushed through the ice to the open water without any serious risk and so have come to the assistance of the *Titanic*. Had she done so she might have saved many if not all of the lives that were lost.

Acknowledgements

Writing this book would not have been possible without the help and support of many friends and colleagues. It would be invidious to single out any one group for special mention but I can't, for one minute, forget the tireless encouragement and support that I have received from Seafarer Books whilst this book was being put together. Patricia Eve in particular has been the inspiration for so much that has been achieved and I cannot thank her enough. My thanks also go to Jed Lyons and his colleagues at Rowman and Littlefield. I owe my editor Hugh Brazier a huge debt of gratitude for all his hard work and forbearance with my missed deadlines and quirky approach to writing. I thank too the book designer Louis Mackay for his incredible ability to turn an idea into a diagram with seemingly effortless ease.

I owe much to the men and women of the Southampton-based Marine Accident Investigation Branch for everything they taught me during my five years as the Chief Inspector. They were inspirational then and still do a magnificent job today. The Branch richly deserves its reputation as one of the leading marine accident investigation organisations in the world.

There are others who have helped or encouraged me in different ways. I am grateful to Michael Grey for writing the foreword, and Richard Woodman for the words on the book's cover. They are among the few contemporary writers who draw attention to the forgotten world of ships, shipping and seafarers, and I am so grateful for their support. I thank Juliet Burn and for proofreading some of the text, Nick King from the Science Photo Library for his assistance with the *Californian* photograph, and Sarah-Jayne Wareham from Southampton Solent University for help with some photography.

There is also one source of information I must mention with particular gratitude, and that is the Titanic Inquiry Project, whose endeavours can be found on their website www. titanicinquiry.org. This contains the complete transcripts of both the US Senate Inquiry and the British Formal Investigation, and it proved to be of inestimable value in researching the material for this book.

I also thank Cambridge University Press for allowing me to quote from Professor James Reason's excellent book *Human Error*.

Prologue

There can be few people in the developed world who have not heard of the *Titanic* and how, on her maiden voyage across the Atlantic in April 1912, she collided with an iceberg and sank with the loss of over 1500 lives. Her sinking was one of the defining moments of the twentieth century, and her notoriety is such that some claim that, after God and Coca Cola, her name is the most easily recognised word in the English language. It has also been said that her name appears each day in at least one of the British newspapers. The 1997 James Cameron film of the same name was, for ten years, the most successful box office film of all time, and every time a passenger ship is involved in an accident there will be some survivors who declare their experiences as being 'just like the *Titanic*'. True to form, this is precisely what some claimed after the Italian cruise ship *Costa Concordia* capsized off the coast of Italy in January 2012. By a twist of fate this occurred within four months of the centenary of *Titanic*'s loss.

Until about twenty years ago I was probably no better informed about *Titanic* than most people. I had read and enjoyed Walter Lord's excellent book *A Night to Remember* and seen the film of the same name. As a professional mariner I was aware that her loss had led to a complete overhaul of the way safety at sea was administered and had resulted in a major change in the way international rules and regulations were drawn up. It took me a while, however, to realise that one of my earliest memories was part of *Titanic*'s legacy.

It was not long after the end of the Second World War that my father, a serving naval officer, was loaned to the Royal Australian

Navy and appointed to the new aircraft carrier HMAS *Sydney* shortly before she sailed from Britain to join the Australian Fleet in Sydney. His posting was an accompanied one, and my mother and her three children sailed out to join him. I was aged seven at the time and can still remember my excitement as we boarded the 20,000 ton Orient Line *Orontes* at Tilbury for the five-week voyage out via the Suez Canal. We sailed from Tilbury in April 1949, and I vividly remember mustering for lifeboat drill an hour or two after sailing. Even now I can recall my indignation at discovering that the lifeboat assigned to us didn't have a propeller. For days I had visions of having to row it in the event of our having to take to the lifeboats. Years later I was to learn that the whole process of lifeboat drills was a legacy of the *Titanic* disaster.

The voyage to Australia and our return in the then brand-new P&O Royal Mail Steamer *Himalaya* some months later made an enormous impression on me. By the time we arrived back in England I knew with total conviction that all I wanted to do in life was to go to sea and, one day, become the captain of a large, white-painted, passenger-carrying mail ship. It didn't quite work out that way, but on leaving the Nautical College Pangbourne aged 17, with seven O levels to my credit, I did indeed join the P&O Steam Navigation Company as a navigating officer apprentice. I spent the next three years sailing in cargo ships trading to both Australia and the Far East while acquiring the necessary knowledge and practical experience to become a ship's officer. At the end of my apprenticeship I obtained my Second Mate's Certificate of Competency – and I still look back on that achievement as one of the highlights of my working life.

Aged 20, I was on the threshold of making my career in the merchant navy when my attention was drawn to an advertisement seeking young men with at least five O levels to join the Royal Navy as seamen officers on a short service commission. Having thought about it for a week or two I decided to apply and, slightly to my surprise, was accepted. Shortly afterwards I found myself marching up the hill at Dartmouth to the Britannia Royal Naval College as a very new and somewhat apprehensive cadet in the Royal Navy. I was starting all over again, and instead of sailing as the fourth mate of a large passenger ship I was being told to get my hair cut three times in the space of 72 hours. I began to wonder what I had let myself in for

I soon began to enjoy naval life. I was extremely lucky with both my appointments and the people with whom I served. My first ship was a minesweeper based in the Persian Gulf and I later joined submarines. I subsequently transferred to the Navy's permanent list, qualified as a specialist navigating officer and served in a number of submarines. I qualified as a commanding officer and went on to command both a diesel and a nuclear-powered submarine. Promotions followed and I commanded a frigate before undertaking a number of staff jobs ashore. During my many years at sea I learned through experience and, like many, made a few mistakes. Bit by bit I added to my knowledge of the sea, ships, seamanship and seafarers, and acquired experience that was one day to become useful when considering the loss of the *Titanic*.

I came to know the North Atlantic well, experienced some bitterly cold nights, witnessed conditions of perfect visibility and even, on one occasion, found myself in command of a ship surrounded by ice. I learned the art of keeping a good lookout in the open air and, as a submariner, spent many a night keeping watch on the surface without radar or any other means of judging distance. I came to know only too well how fiendishly difficult it was to judge the range of single lights at night and, like most others, tended to underestimate their ranges. I discovered how too little sleep could adversely affect one's performance and how easy it was to make mistakes through working excessively long hours. I had furthermore formed a number of views about the qualities needed to become an effective ship's officer and, in one of the most rewarding appointments open to a naval officer, spent two years training and qualifying officers for submarine command. The course, known throughout the Royal Navy as the Perisher, gave me an insight into the qualities needed to be a good ship's captain.

My penultimate appointment in the Navy was Director of Naval Operations and Trade in the Ministry of Defence in London, and by virtue of being the senior navigating officer on the Naval Staff I became the navigation advisor to the Admiralty Board. My responsibilities included having to make recommendations on the action, if any, to be taken on individuals involved in serious accidents such as collisions and groundings.

My 33 years in the Navy ended in 1995. With no intention of retiring, I looked around for something new to do. I was, in time, greatly attracted by an advertisement I saw in a Sunday newspaper for a new Chief Inspector of Marine Accidents to head up the Southampton-based Marine Accident Investigation Branch (MAIB). The work involved investigating accidents to British-registered merchant ships, fishing vessels and leisure-sector craft anywhere in the world, and to any vessel involved in an accident within British Territorial Waters. Although I didn't have the precise qualities being sought, I felt my background and experience might be sufficient to be considered for it. I applied, and after a comprehensive selection process was delighted to be offered the appointment. I accepted with alacrity, but a technicality meant I couldn't take over immediately.

I therefore spent a few days with the highly regarded Air Accident Investigation Branch (AAIB) at Farnborough, learning how to investigate accidents, and also took the opportunity to bring myself up to date with the merchant shipping world. Since leaving the P&O I had always maintained my interest in the merchant service and had, whenever possible, taken passage as a supernumerary in a range of merchant ships. I was able to build on this experience in the few weeks I had available to me and, by the time I took up my new appointment, could look back on passages undertaken in a container ship, an oil tanker, a bulk carrier, several ferries, a light vessel tender, two sail training vessels and a large cruise ship. It was time well spent.

I took over as Chief Inspector in early 1997 and spent the early days learning as much as possible about how the MAIB investigated accidents and how reports were compiled and published. Whilst I already knew that the sole purpose of the organisation was to investigate accidents with a view to improving marine safety, I had little feel for how it was done.

As part of my initiation I asked my team which of the many accidents they had investigated had attracted the greatest public attention. To my surprise I was told it was a report about a ship called the *Californian* that had been widely blamed for not going to the aid of the *Titanic* on the night she foundered in April 1912. When the wreck of the *Titanic* was discovered by the American oceanographer Robert Ballard in 1985, its position was found to be 13 miles away from that given in the original distress signals. This difference was such that it gave rise to calls to reopen the investigation to establish once and for all whether the *Californian* could have been the ship that many believed was in sight of the *Titanic* when she sank and had failed to respond to the firing of rockets she had seen at the time. Although it was felt there were insufficient grounds to warrant a reopening of the Formal Investigation, the MAIB was tasked to re-examine the evidence to determine whether the *Californian* had been as close to the *Titanic* as many claimed. The evidence was re-appraised, and the report that emerged was the one that had attracted such widespread interest.

I found it a curious document. It made fascinating reading but I wasn't entirely sure I agreed with the conclusions and promised myself I'd take a look at the same evidence one day and see what I thought.

At about the same time the James Cameron film *Titanic* was released to wide acclaim, and I frequently found myself being asked about its authenticity and the accident itself. To learn more about what had happened in 1912, I decided to do some further research and discovered that the MAIB's library contained a hardback copy of the evidence given at the British Formal Investigation in 1912. You can now access this material online, but in 1997 it was a wonderful source of new information. Out of curiosity I began to dip into it from time to time. I also began to read one or two of the growing number of books on the subject and, before long, found myself comparing the conduct of the original inquiry with the way the MAIB was investigating accidents in the late 1990s.

In reading the many accounts about what happened I couldn't help but note that almost everyone relied heavily on the precise wording used by witnesses in response to the questions put to them during the original inquiries. This reliance on the quotes made me fundamentally uneasy, as I had already discovered that very few witnesses ever succeed in recalling events accurately and I had no reason to think *Titanic* survivors were any different. It is indeed possible that much of what was said never happened in the way the witnesses described. Today's investigator resists any temptation to quote witnesses when compiling a report but will take account of all the available evidence to establish what happened and why.

It also began to occur to me that nobody was approaching the accident from the viewpoint of someone whose only interest was to determine what happened without being interested in apportioning blame. It is this approach that defines the role of an accident investigator, who has to wade through evidence that is, typically, incomplete, inconsistent, incoherent and thoroughly confusing. Having done so, he then has to make sense of it all.

As I became better acquainted with the original evidence the more it began to occur to me that a modern investigator, using the techniques available today, might not necessarily agree with the original findings and might indeed draw different conclusions as to the causes. The thought persisted and I decided to pursue the matter further.

Both the United States Senate Inquiry and the British Formal Investigation were, in essence, public inquiries. Given the widespread interest in what had happened, it was inevitable. Although by no means universal, there is today a growing appreciation that the best way to learn from accidents is to have them investigated by a totally independent but government-funded marine accident investigation body. The MAIB is one such organisation. Following a serious accident it has primacy for the gathering of information and conducts its interviews in private. Any information derived is treated in confidence and this has the great advantage of encouraging witnesses to reveal what they know without fear of being disciplined by their employer or charged with a criminal offence. Statements are not made on oath and cannot be used in evidence against them. Sadly, this ideal is being undermined by a growing tendency for some marine administrations to bring criminal charges on the grounds that such draconian actions will deter others from making the same 'mistake'. It is a seductive argument but I take the opposite view and would far rather find out exactly what happened first and then look to means of preventing it happening again. Very often the best remedial actions stem from the underlying reasons, but these are often overlooked in a trial. I am not averse to criminal charges being brought in certain circumstances, but this should never be the first resort.

In looking at how the original investigations were conducted, I realised that those conducting the 1912 inquiries faced some formidable challenges. Many of those who would have been able to answer the most fundamental questions were victims of the disaster and had lost their lives. They included *Titanic*'s master Captain E J Smith, his first officer Mr William Murdoch and the Harland and Wolff chief designer, Mr Thomas Andrews.

Nearly all the evidence came from the survivors and from officials whose expertise had a bearing on what happened. Every witness had their own version of events to tell, and no survivor saw the same thing in quite the same way. Evidence collected through interviewing tends to be confusing and incoherent, and there is nothing to suggest that the *Titanic* inquiries were any different. To compound the difficulties, many promising lines of inquiry were never pursued, too many questions that should have been asked never were, and far too many potentially valuable witnesses were never called to give their account of what happened. I would, for instance, have given much to hear what some of the third class passengers who survived had to say. It didn't, furthermore, help that so many leading questions were put and that many of the questioners were unfamiliar with the maritime world. The biggest tragedy of all was that those conducting the inquiries failed to understand the significance of too many answers.

It went further than that. Survivors called upon to give evidence so soon after experiencing such a traumatic event would have been affected by it, and even the most reliable and conscientious witness would have found remembering exactly what happened extremely difficult. The more I looked at the original *Titanic* testimonies the more I reflected on the fragility of human memory. While some people are extremely good at memorising events, most of us forget things within minutes. How many of us, for instance, can accurately recall the content of a telephone conversation made moments earlier, let alone what happened last Sunday, or where we left the car keys?

In my experience most accident witnesses try very hard to remember events accurately, but even the best find it difficult to recall everything, and there is likely to be further deterioration if an experience is shared with someone else or the witness reads an account of the same event in a newspaper. This memory contamination is always present and, bearing in mind the time that elapsed between *Titanic* going down and the inquiries, it would have featured.

Some individuals make better witnesses than others. Those with nothing to lose tend to be reliable, but those whose future depends on the answers they give will be very cautious. The fear of losing one's job or having one's future jeopardised is always an obstacle to being completely open. There is also an assumption that the most experienced and knowledgeable witnesses give the most accurate accounts of what occurred. Curiously the exact opposite applies more often than not. Those in this category will often, quite unconsciously, give their versions of an event by recalling things that never occurred on that particular occasion, or describing what should have happened rather than what actually occurred. Scrutiny of the original *Titanic* evidence suggests that this may well have happened on several occasions. A passenger who knows nothing of the technicalities can, interestingly, make a better witness than a member of the crew. They may not use the correct terminology but their observations, seen through very different eyes, can be remarkably accurate.

I have found that witnesses rarely lie when giving evidence. It is, in fact, very difficult to do and is usually spotted. A witness who feels vulnerable can, however, very easily omit something, or become vague on a point of detail. When somebody says that something 'may' have occurred, it is often a sign that it did happen but they are reluctant to admit it. Every so often people try to falsify a document or chart after an event, or 'lose' something, but even these malpractices can be spotted without much difficulty. Needless to say, trying to falsify evidence is far more serious than whatever happened in the first place.

Among the most difficult things for people to remember are times and the correct sequence of events. When the *Titanic* sank few witnesses would have had the means of telling the time. Men did not wear wrist watches in the Edwardian era and few, I suspect, kept looking at their fob watches to record when things happened. There were clocks in public places but none on *Titanic*'s dark upper deck or *Californian*'s open bridge. My judgement is that the accuracy of both times and sequence of events given in the original narratives were very doubtful.

Any lingering doubts I might have had about the fragility of memory were neatly dispelled by three unrelated factors: a newspaper report, my totally unexpected involvement in someone's death, and my introduction to the 'black box' or the voyage data recorder.

British readers may be familiar with a TV series about motor cars called *Top Gear*. Some time ago one of the presenters, Richard Hammond, was seriously injured when the car he was driving crashed during filming. The event was widely reported and the following excerpt duly appeared in a daily newspaper:

> The BBC reported that two film crew members said they had seen him walk away from the crash and get into the air ambulance.

Anyone reading this would naturally assume this to be an accurate account of what happened. The witnesses reported what they had seen and I think most people would assume they must be right. Until you read the second part of the article:

> But a spokesman for the ambulance service said the presenter was unconscious when they got to the scene but regained consciousness in hospital.

Readers can draw their own conclusions as to which of the two accounts is probably the more accurate.

The second incident occurred whilst I was writing this book. In April 2011 I was one of a small number of people invited to a briefing and lunch on board a British nuclear-powered submarine visiting the same port from which *Titanic* had sailed almost exactly 99 years earlier, Southampton. We had been on board for just over half an hour and were talking to members of the ship's company when several loud pops were heard. I turned round to see a man, several feet away, holding a gun and looking at another man lying on the deck. Not knowing what was happening, I took my cue from the others present and cleared the area as rapidly as possible.

I then tried to make some sense of what I had just witnessed, and it occurred to me that I might be asked to recall everything. Aware of how difficult it can be, I decided to write it all down in a small notebook I happened to have on me. I made the entry within two to three minutes of the incident and started by carefully noting the time.

I learned later that a member of the ship's company, armed with a gun in his capacity as the upper deck sentry, had opened fire and killed one officer, injured another and narrowly missed two senior ratings. As a witness to much that had happened, I was interviewed three times that afternoon by the police and was able to refer to the notes I had taken. I was therefore mortified to discover that despite my precautions, I had already forgotten some important details. I also realised that my recollections of those things I had not written down were being influenced by what I had discussed with other witnesses immediately afterwards. I was asked, for instance, to say how many shots had been fired, and to provide specific details about the man I'd seen holding the gun. It came as a shock to realise I had absolutely no idea. It was the most extraordinary demonstration of how recall can be distorted in such a short space of time. If I couldn't recall some of the details so soon after the event, what chances, I asked myself, did the *Titanic* survivors have after days or even weeks?

My third and final example of how poor memory can be is linked to my introduction to the voyage data recorder (VDR), the maritime equivalent to the 'black box' or the flight deck recorder and cockpit voice recorder fitted in aircraft. From the time it first began to be fitted in ships during the 1990s it had already made a massive difference to the way accidents were being investigated and removed, at a stroke, the many inconsistencies and ambiguities that had prevailed previously.

The device has the ability to record automatically a number of ship operating parameters such as position, course, speed, the radar picture as displayed, VHF radio communications, alarms, status of hull openings, rudder angles, engine orders and responses and some weather parameters. It also records what people are saying in one or two key positions, including the bridge. Once the hard-disc memory is recovered and the data have been downloaded the investigator is presented with a remarkable record of precisely what happened. In the right hands this removes much of the doubt and ensures the precise timings of relevant features in any reconstruction.

To my mind, however, the most revealing feature to emerge from the VDR was the opportunity it provided to make a comparison between what a witness recalls and what actually happened. I discovered, as so many others have done, that the two versions of the same event were sometimes so totally different that it became difficult to reconcile the two. If this is true today, would it, I asked myself, have been any different in 1912?

By now my initial look at the original *Titanic* inquiries had made me realise that much of the evidence that we have always accepted and relied upon for so many years was very probably flawed. If so, it meant that, very possibly, every book that had ever been written about the *Titanic* was based on unreliable evidence. I equally knew there was no possibility of obtaining fresh material and that any further analysis would be based on precisely the same material as was used in 1912. The task now facing me was to take a far more critical view of exactly what was said, to analyse very carefully the different accounts of the same thing, and to use my experience and judgement as to the most likely course of events. I had no preconceived views as to what the outcome would be, but was very curious to see where the evidence might lead me.

My approach to the task was based on the philosophy that no accident is ever caused by a single event but by many, spread over time. I expected to find that the *Titanic* disaster would conform to this very general assumption, and that the analysis would reveal a single initiating cause, a very small number of key, or root, causes, and several hundred underlying or contributory reasons. I was not to be disappointed.

The initiating cause is very often something very simple and overlooked. Very often it is a decision taken at some crucial moment in the minutes or hours before the critical event.

Defining a root cause isn't easy, and there are many different

– and sometimes very complicated – explanations, but the one I found the easiest to understand was told to me when I first joined the MAIB. In essence, a root cause is something that is so fundamentally wrong that it lies at the heart of whatever happened. If whatever is wrong had been changed or designed differently beforehand, the incident or part of the incident would not have occurred.

An underlying or contributory cause, on the other hand, is something that might have influenced the outcome but would not necessarily have prevented it. The value of identifying the underlying causes is that they can become the most effective areas for making recommendations to prevent the same thing happening again.

Of all the challenges facing an investigator the most difficult is, arguably, the avoidance of hindsight. If it dictates the way conclusions are drawn the investigator will find it becomes impossible to identify the real reasons why things happen. I encountered many words of wisdom during my time as the Chief Inspector, but few matched those of Professor James Reason, formerly professor of psychology at the University of Manchester, who warned against allowing hindsight to explain human error:

> For those of us who pick over the bones of other people's disasters, it often seems incredible that these warnings and human failures, seemingly so obvious in retrospect, should have gone unnoticed at the time. Being blessed with uninvolvement and hindsight, it is a great temptation for retrospective observers to slip into a censorious frame of mind and to wonder how these people could be so blind, stupid, arrogant or reckless.[1]

The analysis process starts from the moment the investigation begins, but the good investigator will never close his mind to any number of possibilities. In the end, however, he has to make a judgement about what happened and the final report will reflect those views. No witness will be quoted but a narrative

---

1. Reason, James. *Human Error.* Cambridge University Press, 1991.

will emerge from an analysis of all the information provided. Some of it will have been discarded in the process, and seemingly minor points may have had far greater significance than at first realised. There are occasions when the investigator is struck by the complete lack of any information about something you feel sure should have happened. Rather than dismiss these gaps as a consequence of memory failure, it sometimes pays to explore the possibility that an expected action never occurred at all and could be very significant. I had reasons to suspect that there were a couple of occasions in the *Titanic* evidence when this occurred.

I also anticipated finding that the human factor would play a large part in any analysis. Even the most cursory glance at the circumstances indicated that many, many mistakes were made on board *Titanic* – but, using my instincts as an investigator, I hoped to go further than merely identify 'human error' and explore the reasons why people did things that, in retrospect, seemed so wrong.

By the time I came to relinquish my appointment at the MAIB after five interesting and rewarding years, I decided to follow up my early resolve and take another look at the original *Titanic* evidence through the eyes of an accident investigator. I was, among other things, very curious to find out whether I would agree with the conclusions reached in 1912. Would I, for instance, endorse the original finding that the 'cause of the loss was due to collision with an iceberg brought about by the excessive speed at which the ship was being navigated'? And would I also find that had the *Californian* reacted to the firing of rockets when first observed, and pushed through the ice to come to the aid of *Titanic*, she 'might have saved many if not all the lives that were lost'? That original criticism was a damning indictment of the *Californian* and her master, and it still polarises opinion to this day.

It seemed to me that the only way I could satisfy this curiosity was to do something about it and so, starting in about 2002, I began to trawl through the evidence and read many of the *Titanic* books that were beginning to appear on a regular basis. The one bit of new evidence that I could not ignore was the position and the images of the wreck following its discovery in 1985.

At the same time I began to wonder what an account of *Titanic*'s loss might look like if produced in the style of a twenty-first-century accident investigation report. At the original British Formal Investigation the court was required to answer 26 questions posed by the very organisation that the Inquiry should have been looking at, the Board of Trade. In today's world the investigator is not so constrained and seeks to determine what happened and why with a view to making recommendations to prevent the same thing happening again. It seemed to me that only two questions really mattered: 'Why did *Titanic* collide with an iceberg?' and 'Why did so many people lose their lives?' I felt that if both these questions could be addressed then all the lessons and recommendations to prevent the same thing happening again would flow from the answers.

It took me much longer than expected to go through the available evidence and, having done so, I make no secret of the fact that I don't have answers to all the questions. On many occasions I had to change a previously formed view when the evidence didn't fit but, as expected, I found a whole raft of reasons why the accident occurred. There was one very simple initiating cause, three root or key causes, and hundreds of small, and not so small, underlying reasons why it all happened – and it is these that are the most interesting and the most fertile for improving safety at sea. None of them is new, and there are no real surprises, but they are presented here in a way that has not, so far as I'm aware, been done before. To be fair to the original Formal Investigation, many of them were picked up in the form of recommendations, but for some curious reason they were not specifically identified as causes. I find that curious.

The result of this work forms the basis of this book. It is, first and foremost, a very personal view of what I think happened. It is not, most emphatically not, a new investigation. I make no pretence at being an expert on *Titanic*, and any reader expecting to find lengthy descriptions about the lifestyles of the passengers or explanations as to why I have favoured one interpretation of any one incident over another will be disappointed. I have written it in the format of a modern accident report but have made the deliberate decision to omit much of the technical detail and the many annexes that would normally be included in such a report. To do so would merely replicate what is already in the public domain, and I've no reason to change any of it. What it does contain is the factual account of what occurred, the analysis of the evidence and the conclusions, together with some personal afterthoughts.

I did feel, however, that to understand fully what happened in April 1912, and to wean the readers away from too much hindsight, it would help them to know a little about life in Edwardian England, the history of the North Atlantic and shipping in general. The book does therefore include a preliminary chapter on the background to what happened on *Titanic*'s maiden voyage and includes certain technicalities to enable the reader to understand better the circumstances under which *Titanic* operated those many years ago.

There is nothing very startling about my conclusions. Most have featured in other formats, but I hope that this version of the story will be of value for the way in which it shows how a modern marine accident investigator might present his findings were the loss of *Titanic* to be investigated today.

Background

Anyone seeking to form a view about the circumstances that led to the loss of the *Titanic* does so through the prism of life as we know it today with our prejudices, expectations, attitudes, custom and culture. Our familiarity with modern technology, 24-hour news coverage and instant communications makes it almost impossible to envisage life as it was in 1912. To fully understand the *Titanic* story and the circumstances of her loss, it helps to know something about life in the early years of the twentieth century. It is only by looking at the tragedy from the perspective of someone living in that era that we can even begin to understand what happened that fateful night and, perhaps more importantly, why.

The story of *Titanic* is essentially about one ship and several hundred people. It is essentially a maritime story, a British maritime story with a strong American element and a supporting cast of the many nationalities that were embarked on her first and only voyage. It has been told and retold many, many times and will be told again. This opening chapter attempts to provide, first, some background to everything that happened, and second, an introduction to the world of marine accident investigation.

The story starts, and finishes, with the Atlantic Ocean.

The North Atlantic

The Atlantic is the world's second largest ocean, only exceeded in size by the Pacific. It extends from the Arctic Ocean in the north to about 60° south, where it meets the circumpolar Southern Ocean. It is bounded on the east by Scandinavia, Europe and

Africa, and on the west by North, Central and South America. It derives its name from Atlas, one of the Titans of Greek mythology, who supported the heavens from the mountain range of the same name in northwest Africa.

The word *ocean* is derived from Oceanus, the river the ancient Greeks believed to circle the known world of the lands that embraced the Mediterranean. The river poured its waters through the gap we know as the Strait of Gibraltar, or the Pillars of Hercules – which in Roman times bore the warning to sailors *Non plus ultra* or 'nothing further beyond'. The wide open unknown beyond was known as the Infinite Ocean. It fell to the Phoenicians from the eastern Mediterranean to venture into its waters from about 1100 BC – but even they did not venture far from the west-facing coasts.

The Atlantic is divided into North and South by the equator, but it is the North Atlantic that concerns us most. Some 3000 miles across, it is, to the sailor, the most treacherous, the most troublesome and the most challenging of all the oceans. Not so long ago mariners referred to it as the Western Ocean. And some still do.

A significant percentage of the northern hemisphere's weather is determined by the Atlantic, with its substantial currents and the mixing of waters of different temperatures. The most significant current is the Gulf Stream, which originates in the Gulf of Mexico before breaking into the Atlantic around Florida to proceed up the eastern seaboard of the United States of America. Carrying a surge of warm water, it initially reaches a rate of nearly 5 knots, but by the time it passes Cape Hatteras, North Carolina, it loses some of its strength, tends to meander more and mixes more readily with the cooler water on either side of it. By the time it reaches the Grand Banks of Newfoundland it has become the much broader, slower-moving North Atlantic Drift as it heads eastwards towards Europe's west-facing northern countries. The warm air carried north on the Gulf Stream mixes with the cold winds blowing from the frozen north and, affected by the earth's rotation, produces deep low-pressure areas that in turn lead to ferociously wild weather and very high sea states. The warming influence of the Gulf Stream is, however, nature's greatest gift to many millions of people living in north-west Europe. Norway's coastline, for instance, remains ice-free throughout the year while the British Isles maintain an average temperature some 5 °C warmer than if no such influence existed. It ensures relatively mild winters, and summers lacking in extreme heat.

There are cold currents too. The cold Labrador Current that flows from Baffin Bay to the west of Greenland, along the coasts of Labrador and Newfoundland and into the Atlantic is the most relevant to the *Titanic* story. It meets the warm Gulf Stream in the relatively shallow waters of the Grand Banks to the south-east of Newfoundland to create some of the densest fogs known to the mariner as well as one of the richest fishing grounds in the world. From about April to August this south-flowing cold current carries quantities of field ice down from the Arctic and icebergs from the glaciers of Greenland into the transatlantic shipping lanes. The division between the two currents is marked by sudden changes in both sea and air temperature.

North Atlantic weather can be ferocious. After hurricanes in the Caribbean and adjacent seas, storms generated in the North Atlantic rank as the second largest source of loss in the insurance world. Gales develop at short notice and, from time to time, waves reach heights of 30 metres. Visibility can vary enormously. Fog, the seafarer's least-liked environmental condition, is commonplace in certain areas. Low cloud, driving rain, falling snow, flying spume and a long swell can all combine to prevent the sailor from maintaining the single most essential ingredient to ensuring safety, the keeping of a proper lookout. Yet, while the North Atlantic has this formidable reputation for generating bad weather, it can be supremely benign with calm seas and clear skies. By day the sun can beat down with unrelenting ferocity, and at night the stars can shine with an intensity rarely seen by observers ashore. The wind will sometimes fall away to nothing to create a flat, oily calm with perfect visibility. In the sailing-ship era windless days were unwelcome (at least for the seamen), but by the time steam arrived in the nineteenth century, such conditions were a welcome bonus for all concerned. Passages would be faster, wear and tear on the ships would be less and passengers would welcome the respite from the constant motion and the stuffiness of the accommodation spaces below decks.

A perennial problem facing all transatlantic seafarers in the age before radar and other electronic aids was the making of a landfall at night on an unlit coast or in poor visibility. Many ships would make a satisfactory crossing of the open ocean only to run aground in the final stages because their crews were uncertain of their position and did not realise they were so close to danger until it was too late. Factors that contributed to such a predicament were bad weather, fog, currents, the tide, poor steering or the inability to observe the sun and stars to fix the ship's position accurately in the final days of a crossing.

Ice in the North Atlantic

The ice found in the shipping lanes of the North Atlantic originates on the icecap of Greenland and forms over thousands of years. Eighty-four per cent of Greenland is covered in ice and, in places, it is 3400 m thick. This ice accounts for 10 per cent of the world's freshwater reserves.

Snow falling onto the icecap compresses into ice over the centuries and is then squeezed into a hundred or so tidewater glaciers that descend to the fjords punctuating the coastline of Greenland. Moving forward at some 20 metres a day, the glacier ice moves relentlessly downwards to sea level, where the action of the rising and falling of the tides breaks off great slabs of the accumulated ice in a process known as calving. The largest icebergs can weigh somewhere between 100,000 and 200,000 tons, with a length of over 150 metres and a height above the surface of over 60 metres. Typically about nine-tenths of an iceberg is under water, and its draught may be as much as 400 metres. In a typical year between 10,000 and 15,000 icebergs are calved.

Once an iceberg breaks free it will be carried by currents and weather around Baffin Bay, through the Davis Strait and into the Labrador Sea. Very few, however, survive the 1800-mile, two- to three-year journey into the North Atlantic. They will either ground or melt long before they reach the open sea and, in an average year, only some 150–300 will survive to enter the main shipping routes that cross the Grand Banks. Once they meet the warmer waters of the Gulf Stream they melt rapidly and may only last for a further two months. Icebergs drifting onto the Grand Banks will usually be accompanied by smaller bits of floating ice.

The iceberg 'season' falls between February and August each year, with the peak season occurring between March and May. The quantity is dependent on the severity or mildness of the winter the year before, with a mild winter producing the greatest quantity of drift ice. The limits of expected ice are marked on marine routing charts but, from time to time, icebergs have been observed much further afield. In 1926, for instance, one iceberg was observed some 150 miles to the northeast of Bermuda.

By far the biggest waterway on the eastern seaboard of North America, and one used by ocean-going vessels, is the St Lawrence Seaway. It freezes every year between October and April and, before the advent of the icebreaker it was only open for navigation for some six or seven months in the year, which meant that Canada's principal port on the east coast in winter was Halifax, Nova Scotia.

Mariners crossing the North Atlantic have always treated ice with respect, and know that the place they are most likely to encounter it is the vicinity of the Grand Banks, in spring and summer. To reduce the combined dangers of drifting ice and fog, the major shipping companies met in London in 1899, under the chairmanship of Mr Bruce Ismay, to agree a routing system whereby ships heading in opposite directions south of Newfoundland would be separated whilst keeping clear of the usual limit of ice for the time of year.

Given good visibility, mariners were confident of their ability to see any ice in sufficient time to take avoiding action. In such conditions very few shipmasters ever slowed down until the ice had been sighted. Ships did collide with ice from time to time, but the number of serious accidents was relatively small. In fog, however, ships would invariably proceed at slow speed with additional lookouts posted.

Ships, shipping and the North Atlantic

Shipping is, arguably, the oldest of all global industries. It precedes the concept of war at sea, is always evolving, is subject to extraordinary volatility, has its fair share of saints and sinners, and has to operate in an incredibly competitive environment. Ships and seafarers come in all shapes and sizes as they carry cargoes and people from one place to another across the seas and oceans of the world. They can be sailing in tropical seas under an unforgiving sun one week, and facing the ferocity of a hurricane or typhoon the next. They may have to spend days pitching into the unrelenting rollers of the Southern Ocean, the viciousness of a winter gale in the North Atlantic, or the short sharp seas of the North Sea with its unforgiving sand banks and manmade hazards all too close at hand. They face dense fog, falling snow, ice, sand storms, not to mention unrelenting commercial pressures as well as war and pirates. Those who go down to the sea in ships and do business in great waters have to live in an environment that is rarely still. Seamen acquire their skills through extensive training and, more importantly, years of hard-won experience. Some are masters of the traditional disciplines of navigation and seamanship while others devote their talents and dedication to engineering, electrotechnology and the ever-growing need to look after passengers and crew. At the same time there are many supporting industries ashore, including naval architects, ship builders, ship brokers, marine insurers and lawyers, surveyors, harbourmasters, pilots, lighthouse authorities, dockers, chandlers, college lecturers and many, many others.

From the earliest days of seaborne trade in the Mediterranean, Indian Ocean, China Seas and the islands of the Pacific, men have designed, built, managed and sailed vessels best suited to the prevailing conditions and the cargoes to be carried. A well-built, well-kept, well-manned and well-sailed vessel will earn money and, throughout history, successful ship ownership has been a profitable business. Having the right ship at the right time for a particular trade was the perpetual goal of all prospective owners and merchants. Fortunes could be made and, all too often, lost. A theme that has persisted throughout the years is the tendency for most, but not all, ship owners to reduce their operating costs by as much as possible to remain competitive in a ferociously competitive environment. The first secret of success has always been to have the right ship, at the right time and at the right price to capture a particular market. The second is to take whatever measures are necessary to avoid losing a ship in an accident.

For many hundreds of years the industry was largely unregulated, but even the most parsimonious ship owner had to acknowledge that a ship that fell apart at sea, or that was manned by an incompetent crew, was not conducive to the business of making money. Many things contributed to a change of attitude and led to the creation of safety regulations and international agreements – but it was the sinking of the *Titanic* in 1912 that had the greatest impact on changing attitudes to safety at sea.

The migration to North America

The catalyst for Europeans to venture cross the North Atlantic stems from the discoveries of what were thought to be the Indies by Christopher Columbus in 1492. Not long afterwards the discovery of mainland North America led to the single greatest event in world history, the mass migration of people across the huge Ocean Sea to the New World. It began at the end of the fifteenth century and slowly developed over the next 200 years. The ships were tiny but their endeavours led to the foundation of the most powerful nation the world has ever known.

By the eighteenth century people were crossing the Atlantic in the cargo-carrying merchant ships of the day. None were very big. Those over about 250 tons were usually ship-rigged with three masts, while those between 80 and 250 tons had two masts and were rigged as brigs. Cargoes being carried to America from England included clothing, household goods, ceramics, foodstuff and salt, while American exports embraced food such as wheat and corn, together with fibres, skins, dyes, tobacco and naval stores.

Regardless of ship size, crossing the Atlantic was hard work for the crews. Handling the sails was a backbreaking business, and the ability to shorten or set sail with every change in the weather as well as brace the yards to the best angle for sailing was a never-ending task. It had to be carried out by night without any form of illumination as well as by day. At the same time the crew had to mend the sails, tar ropes, maintain the ship, stop the many leaks, keep it clean, as well as steer and keep a good lookout. No matter what the time of year, the vagaries of Atlantic weather prevailed. In fine weather life was tolerable but in bad weather and in winter it could be very trying indeed. Heavy seas would curl inboard, sweep along the upper deck and carry away anything left unsecured. Any unsuspecting sailor who had failed to anticipate what was going to happen next was very liable to be swept overboard. Many were. Discipline on board was harsh, and conditions for the sailors were tough and very unpleasant.

Passengers undertaking the long transatlantic crossing had, in the meantime, to endure overcrowding, poor food, undrinkable water, little fresh air and disease. In poor weather they would be confined to the spaces below and battened down in the space between the main upper deck and the hold where there was little headroom. Because it was between decks it was known as the tween deck. Many would die on passage. And then, when they finally arrived at their destination, the newcomers found an unforgiving and demanding land where there was no substitute for hard work and commitment. They faced weather extremes, natives who were not always friendly and almost none of the infrastructure they had left behind.

The growing number of farming communities in the new colonies needed cheap labour. With very few 'free' men available the solution was to use indentured or bonded servants. To young men who were in need of work but were experiencing hard times in both the British Isles and on the continent after the Thirty Years War of the mid seventeenth century, the possibility of a new life in another country offered some hope for the future. In exchange for a free passage across the Atlantic and some other benefits such as clothing and food, they would agree to work for a number of years, usually between four and seven, without pay before being granted their freedom at the end. Between one-half and two-thirds of all immigrants arriving in America were indentured servants. Many of the rest were unfortunate young men who, having perhaps had too much to drink in the taverns of the ports used by ships bound for the New World, fell to the charms of some unscrupulous 'spirits'. These dubious characters used devious means to sign them up for a passage and 'help' them on board an outward-bound ship prior to sailing. They would wake up the next morning somewhat the worse for wear and already making for the open sea.

In a totally different category were convicts who had been sentenced for deportation (or penal servitude) for perhaps some relatively minor crime. They too were among those taking passage across the Atlantic

Many of the new arrivals were put to work in the tobacco fields of Virginia and Maryland. There, in the heat of the summer, they would spend long hours toiling away in conditions they were totally unaccustomed to, and under the supervision of overseers who could be every bit as cruel as the ships' officers they had encountered on passage.

Although life for the indentured servant was harsh, it was nowhere as bad as the treatment meted out to the growing number of black slaves. The slave trade had begun much earlier and owed its origins to a European taste for sugar. It was part of a much wider enterprise that became a major feature of trans-atlantic business over the next three hundred years. It involved ships sailing from their home ports in northern Europe filled with manufactured goods to the West African coast. Their holds would be filled with cargoes of textiles (a product much sought after by the Africans), brass and copper pots, cauldrons and jugs, china ware, hats, iron bars that could be melted down to become tools for agriculture, guns and gunpowder. All these would be exchanged for slaves who had been captured and collected by other Africans and then shipped across the Atlantic in what was known as the Middle Passage.

On arrival at their destination they would be sold in the slave markets to work in the West Indian island plantations. A relatively small percentage would be shipped on to the North American mainland. The ships would then load the products of the region such as sugar, rum, wood and other tropical produce for the market at home in England, Scotland and Europe. Known as the triangular trade, it was to become a valuable business, the catalyst for establishing the importance of ports such as London, Bristol and Liverpool and the basis for the creation of individual wealth. All at the expense of many millions of Black Africans who had no say in the matter at all. The first slaves to work on the mainland arrived at Jamestown in 1619, and by 1700 they were beginning to replace indentured servants in Virginia.

Between about 1630 and 1640 some 20,000 English crossed the Atlantic to start a new life in New England. Unlike the mainly male colonists who preceded them, they consisted largely of families. Among the others were the Scots, the Irish-Scots and a few from Germany, Holland and France. Colonial trade with Europe grew rapidly during the later part of the seventeenth century, and by the beginning of the eighteenth century the number of European settlers was about 300,000.

From 1651 English Navigation Acts restricted the use of foreign shipping for trade between England and its colonies. They sought to favour English shipping enterprises and prevent direct colonial trade with the Netherlands, France and other European countries. English and colonial ships therefore dominated the Atlantic traffic throughout the latter years of the seventeenth century and into the eighteenth By 1670 there were about 500 crossings each year, and by 1750 this had increased threefold. Outbound cargoes from England and Europe included manufactured goods such as copper, iron, coal, hops, household goods, tools, soap, textiles, agricultural and fish products, bullion, mail and people. Ships loading in America for the usually faster eastbound voyages carried timber, fish, furs, tobacco, indigo, rice, maize, tomatoes, sweet potatoes, grapes, peanuts, maple syrup and cotton. At the same time, reduced freight and insurance costs encouraged the carriage of all cargoes and the carrying of emigrants.

By the second half of the eighteenth century the number of emigrants from countries other than England began to grow as people attempted to escape from the religious persecution and political oppression that prevailed in parts of Europe. The Germans, in particular from the Rhine valley, were beginning to cross the Atlantic in ever-increasing numbers, and because Pennsylvania made a point of welcoming religious dissenters they would make for Philadelphia. Overall, however, migration levels were still relatively modest and it needed some new incentive or event to encourage very large numbers to brave the Atlantic crossing and settle in this land of opportunity. The events that were to provide the main catalysts for a surge in emigration were the Declaration of Independence on 4 July 1776 , the end of the American Revolutionary War in 1783, the Irish famine between 1845 and 1852, the end of the American

Civil War in 1865 and the Russian famine of 1891.

The Declaration of Independence led to a new interest in expanding westwards and within 30 years nine new states had been created around the Mississippi River and two to the west of New England. Freed from the constraints and interference of the British government, America came into its own. It started to expand in every direction and became a land where hard work, endeavour, enterprise, inventiveness and industriousness paid off. People continued to migrate across the Atlantic from Europe to seize the new opportunities being presented.

At the beginning of the nineteenth century the number of ships crossing the Atlantic was affected, to an extent, by the Napoleonic wars. Ships ran the risk of being harassed by the French and travelled in convoys. Trade improved after 1807 when the war between Imperial Russia and France came to an end and the first Treaty of Tilsit was signed. Among its many clauses was a provision for Russia to join the blockade against British trade. In effect this was Napoleon's way of mounting economic warfare against Britain. One consequence was to deny Britain its main source of timber from northern Europe, so an alternative had to be found. The solution was to import it from northern America. As a result the timber trade became immensely profitable and the number of ships engaged in it grew rapidly throughout the first half of the nineteenth century. Rather than return empty, they used the opportunity being presented to carry passengers in their holds and tween decks at a moderate cost, and this made emigration an attractive proposition for the poor. At the same time Great Britain's population was beginning to expand, putting even greater pressure on the country's ability to provide employment for all. The prospects of fertile, habitable and available land on the other side of the Atlantic became very attractive to many.

But Britain was incensed that America, a neutral country, was continuing to trade with France, and in 1807 introduced a series of trade restrictions to impede it. At a time when cotton had become the main crop of the southern United States and was being exported in growing quantities, to Liverpool in particular, any such restrictions were deeply resented in America, and this eventually led to an outbreak of war in 1812. The American merchant fleet had in the meantime rapidly expanded. On the outbreak of war Britain started to blockade the US coast, while warships and privateers on both sides attacked each other's merchant ships. The ending of this conflict and the defeat of Napoleon following the Battle of Waterloo in 1815 heralded a resumption of trade across the Atlantic just as agricultural prices collapsed in Britain. The impact hit the rural communities hard, and nowhere more so than in Ireland.

Despite the more favourable trading conditions, shipping was still a fairly ad hoc business. Sailing dates might be advertised but the captain would routinely delay setting sail until he had sufficient cargo and passengers to make a profit, and the weather was suitable. This meant that potential passengers might have to wait for days before they knew when the ship would depart. As many as five or six hundred could be packed into one ship at a time, with numbers sometimes exceeding one thousand.

The Americans, who were beginning to dominate the passenger-carrying sector of North Atlantic traffic, felt that an alternative to the 'go-when-ready' arrangement was not only desirable but feasible. A group of New York textile importers, led by the cotton broker Jeremiah Thompson, conceived the idea of a more reliable service whereby a number of ships sailing under coordinated management would sail on scheduled dates to designated destinations. The idea was first advertised in 1817 and became a reality in January 1818 when a company called the Black Ball Line initiated the first regular transatlantic liner service between New York and Liverpool with four three-masted sailing ships. All built in New York, they measured about 110 feet (33 metres) long and 300–500 tons, and soon earned a reputation for speed and reliability. Although the actual passage time was still dependent on the weather, the average time for a westbound crossing was between about 35 and 40 days (and possibly much longer) while an eastbound one before the prevailing weather took about 23 days. Any delay on passage was compensated for by a faster turn-around at the end of the voyage. The system worked, and the Black Ball Line's success with a ship sailing on the first of each month regardless of the weather or the amount of cargo being carried soon attracted competition. The Red Star, Black Star, Blue Swallowtail, and Black X began to emerge from 1822 to herald the golden age of American transatlantic transport. The service appealed not only to passengers travelling there and back but also to those only going one way, the emigrants.

The new ships brought into service got bigger and better, and the facilities for passengers steadily improved. The best by far were American. Their superiority was recognised by the British, and in 1837 a parliamentary committee noted that

> the American ships frequenting the ports of England are stated by several witnesses to be superior to those of a similar class among the ships of Great Britain, the commanders and officers being generally better navigators and more uniformly persons of education than the commanders and officers of British ships of a similar size and class trading from England to America.

American packet boat captains had a well-deserved reputation for excellence and many became very well known. The Western Ocean packets were driven hard and, while never as fast as the better-known clipper ships, they were every bit as effective and built up a strong following. They could point further into the wind than earlier types, could maintain a good average speed in most conditions, and had an outstanding safety record.

The British meanwhile had over 25,000 vessels at sea, but most were very small. About 2000 were engaged in the timber trade with British North America, and many of these were adapted to the carrying of emigrants.

The crews were drawn from many countries, especially Britain and Scandinavia. The transatlantic trade with its endlessly challenging weather did not, surprisingly perhaps, appeal to the 'Yankees' or American sailors, who preferred the longer voyages to Asia and the Pacific ports via either Cape Horn or the Cape of Good Hope. The fo'c'sle hands that shipped before the mast fell into one of two categories: the hard-bitten, tough, uncompromising sailors with extensive experience of the North Atlantic, known as the 'Packet Rats', and the shang-haied or unsuspecting landsmen who knew nothing of the sea but were victims of scheming crimps and others in the seaports of America, England and elsewhere. They would be shipped on board with little concept of what they had let themselves in for.

The early packet ships were rarely larger than 1500 tons and were fitted with two, sometimes three, decks. By the late nine-teenth century they were well established with, on average, one departing from New York for Liverpool, London or Le Havre every two days or even more frequently. There were two classes of passenger travel – cabin and steerage – with a few ships offer-ing second class as well.

Those travelling in cabin accommodation would enjoy a sizeable main cabin for eating and recreation, usually aft, with individual staterooms leading into it from either side. Much was made of the way the accommodation was presented and, far from it being very basic, effort was made to attract the dis-cerning passenger by fitting out public spaces with fine join-ery. Mahogany, rosewood, satinwood and birds-eye maple were used in at least one packet, 'with delicate carved pilasters and capitals edged with gold leaf' to provide the finishing touches. Passengers had the freedom of the deck in good weather, enjoy-ing reasonable food and the ear of the captain. Among the more descriptive accounts of passengers travelling in the cabin class was provided by one of the most outspoken critics of the day, Miss Harriet Martineau, who visited the United States in 1834. Departing Liverpool in August, she said of her fellow passengers:

> Our number was twenty-three ... the company assembled was, with two or three exceptions, so exceedingly agreeable, and so wonderfully

congenial, considering how accidentally we were brought together, that we mingled completely as one party. We had among us a Prussian physician; a New England divine; a Boston merchant with his sprightly and showy young wife; a high spirited young South Carolinian, fresh from German University; a newly married couple, whose station was not exactly discoverable while on board, but who opened a public-house soon after their arrival in New York; a Scotch Major, whose peculiarities made him the butt of the young men; an elderly widow lady, 'of no particular age', but of very particular placidity and good humour; and a youth out of Yorkshire, who was leaving his parents' roof for the first time alone, and who was destined to never return to it. The number was made up by English and American merchants – young men so accustomed to pass between Liverpool and New York that a voyage was little more than an expedition to Primrose Hill is to a cockney.

Second-class passengers travelled in slightly less comfort. They had smaller cabins but still ate well enough.

The conditions for those packed below decks were, by the standards of today, horrific. In the early days the only facilities provided by the ship were fires to cook food and water to drink. The term 'steerage' stems from the practice whereby the poorest passengers were originally carried in that part of the ship through which the steering lines linking the rudder with the helm would pass. Steerage passengers had to bring their own food and cooking utensils, for a passage of unknown duration. More often than not their supplies were inadequate for the length of the voyage. Their personal belongings, if any, would be carried in a cloth or a blanket tied at the corners.

At sea in rough weather those travelling in the steerage class would be battened down below decks and starved of fresh air in confined spaces with inadequate headroom. They had to endure seasickness, disease, rat infestation and total boredom. In many ships the death toll was depressingly high. Travelling steerage was, however, the only means by which the poor and underprivileged could hope to cross the cold, grey, menacing North Atlantic to a better world beyond.

The motives for crossing the Atlantic in the nineteenth

century were very similar to those that had prevailed earlier. Poverty at home, religious persecution, political unrest, hunger and even war were among the many incentives to leave behind the land and people they knew. It was not, however, just a desire to escape that underpinned this growing migration of what became thousands of people every year as the century unfolded – it was opportunity. Opportunity to work hard and reap the benefits of the effort put in. Opportunity to worship in the manner they chose. And opportunity to choose those destined to govern. America provided, at last, a place for the poorest of all and the most persecuted, the victims of famine and the Jews of Europe. During the ten-year period from 1825 to 1834, an average of 32,000 Europeans emigrated to North America each year.

Between the end of the Napoleonic wars and 1845 over a million of those emigrating from Britain were Irish. But if steerage was bad for the ordinary emigrant, including those from Ireland, it was infinitely worse for the victims of the Irish potato famine that began in 1845 and lasted for five to six years. The famine was devastating and, combined with other economic and political developments, including a deteriorating relationship with the British government, it led to a humanitarian crisis of the first order. Once the impact of the harvest failure in 1845 became evident, unscrupulous landlords looked for ways to evict tenants from their cottages. The half-starved occupants found themselves homeless, with few clothes, no money and little means to go elsewhere.

One solution to the rapidly growing problem was for the landlords to pay for the starving masses to be shipped across the Atlantic to Canada in British ships of dubious quality and reputation. Others paid their own fares but sought the cheapest option, often through dishonest agents in the ports. Fares were cheaper in British vessels, as the American ones were better regulated, provided more and consequently charged higher fares. Furthermore, the Americans were reluctant to accept people from impoverished Ireland. There was, however, a seasonal problem with migrating to Canada. The St Lawrence Seaway iced up between October and April, restricting the season for the transportation of Canadian-bound emigrants across the Atlantic.

Over the next five years about a million Irish fled to North America in the most appalling conditions imaginable. The standard route was to ship, first, to Liverpool and then embark in one of the merchant ships bound for Quebec and the immigration point of entry on the St Lawrence River, Grosse Isle. In view of the numbers involved, however, an increasing number of ships, known as coffin ships, sailed direct from Irish ports such as Dublin, Newry, Galway, Limerick, Londonderry, Sligo, Cork and Cobh. Many of the vessels involved were small, and at one stage one in every six was wrecked on passage.

Although ever more stringent Passenger Acts were introduced to set minimum standards for the provision of accommodation and facilities, the conditions on board were indescribably awful. The regulations stipulated that very basic rations were to be provided on the voyage but the meagre quantities served out were barely enough to prevent starvation. It was, furthermore, cooked in the most haphazard way, which often resulted in stomach ailments and dysentery. Seasickness affected almost everyone and the vomit, combined with human excrement from diarrhoea, only added to the misery of life below decks.

Disease flourished. Many of those travelling boarded while suffering from typhus, and the death rate on passage could be high. Some 7000 people died of typhus on passage in 1847 alone, and the victims were thrown over the side without any form of last rites. The deaths were, however, often offset by the high number of children born on passage and the ever-present hope that they would eventually disembark to the promise of a better life. After several weeks at sea they would find themselves sailing up the St Lawrence Seaway to anchor off Grosse Isle where, to their dismay, they found their ordeal was far from over. Before being allowed ashore emigrants were subjected to a quarantine inspection that might take days to complete. The number of ships arriving in the famine years was such that the shore authorities could not cope, and the passengers sometimes had to wait for days before they could land. At the end of May 1847, 40 vessels carrying over 14,000 emigrants were waiting to be cleared. This number grew throughout the summer until the line of anchored ships extended to several miles long. Inevitably this led to further deaths and Grosse Isle eventually became the largest burial ground outside Ireland for victims of the Irish potato famine. Over 70 per cent of those who survived the voyage did, however, make their way across the border into the United States.

The second event to have a major impact on transatlantic travel was the fitting of an auxiliary steam engine in a sailing ship. On 24 May 1819, the sailing ship *Savannah* departed the Georgia port of Savannah, first for Liverpool and then on to Stockholm and St Petersburg. She carried little cargo but filled the holds with 75 tons of coal. She completed most of the voyage under sail but used the engine from time to time when there was insufficient wind. Her passage took $29^{1}/_{2}$ days but was not, by any stretch of the imagination, an economic success.

The second ship to experiment with steam propulsion was a Quebec-built, schooner-rigged vessel called the *Royal William*. After undertaking a number of voyages under power from Quebec to Halifax and back, and to other ports in Nova Scotia, it was found almost impossible to operate her at a profit. The decision to sell her in Europe was taken and, in August 1833 she sailed from the port of Pictou in Nova Scotia for London with seven passengers and a small amount of cargo including a harp. Twenty-five days later she arrived off Gravesend on the London River, having steamed nearly all the way. Although she did resort to sail on a few occasions it was the first transatlantic crossing under power. The entire venture was watched and monitored with unusual care and interest by one of her co-owners, a Halifax merchant named Samuel Cunard.

The *Royal William* never returned across the Atlantic, and the vessel earmarked to make the first steam-powered passage to America was the Great Western Steamship Company's 1700-ton wooden paddle steamer *Great Western*. Designed by the great Victorian engineer Isambard Kingdom Brunel to initiate a new steamship service between Bristol and New York, she was launched at Bristol in July 1837, just days after the 18-year-old Princess Victoria of Kent had ascended the British throne. The *Great Western* sailed to London to be fitted out before returning to Bristol in March 1838 for her maiden voyage to New York. Before reaching Avonmouth, however, fire broke out in her engine room and delayed her departure. Suddenly presented with an opportunity to be the first to operate a steam-powered service across the Atlantic, the Great Western Company's great rival, the British and American Steam Navigation Company, chartered the Scottish-built 700 ton paddle steamer *Sirius* to achieve the distinction. Designed to operate between London and Cork, she was almost too small for the task and had insufficient space on board to embark sufficient coal. Part of her passenger accommodation was removed to make way for additional fuel bunkers, and when she eventually sailed from Cork on the morning of 4 April 1838 she had 450 tons of coal embarked. Carrying 44 passengers and some cargo, her westward passage was beset with heavy seas, gales, sleet and snow but she made the crossing in 15 days at an average speed of 8.03 knots. Despite embarking additional coal for the voyage she very nearly ran short and her crew was forced to burn cabin furniture, a mast and some spare yards in order to complete it. When she arrived in New York on 22 April she received a very warm welcome. She had crossed the Atlantic in record time.

The *Great Western*, meanwhile, was doing her best to make up for lost time. She sailed for New York four days later than the *Sirius*, made good progress and steadily gained on her rival to arrive in New York only twelve hours behind and with 200 tons of coal still remaining. Her achievement meant she captured the speed record for a crossing from the *Sirius*, which had held it for less than a day. She had carried just seven passengers.

The *Great Western* was to become the first ship to settle to a regular steamship service and her achievement heralded a completely new era in transatlantic travel. The transition to steam did not happen overnight, however, and the sailing packet, followed by the faster clipper ships, remained the preferred way to travel for many years yet. Although steamships could make two voyages to every one of a sailing ship, they were expensive to build and, in the early days, a large part of the space on board was taken up by the engine room and the carriage of coal. In the early days steamers could not compete with sail on cost but, bit by bit, they became more efficient. The average passage time for the early steamers westward bound on the North Atlantic run was 15 days, and 14 days for the return passage.

The name most closely connected with the development of the North Atlantic steamship was the Halifax-born entrepreneur Samuel Cunard. A part owner of the *Royal William*, he saw the potential of the new type of ship and travelled to England in 1838 to make a bid for the rights to run a transatlantic mail service between Great Britain and both Canada and the United States. His bid was successful and he was awarded the contract.

As in the past, and as was to become increasingly the case in the future, the right to carry mails gave a ship owner a significant advantage over any competition. With the contract agreed, Cunard founded the British and North American Royal Mail Steam Packet Company, and in 1839 he commissioned Robert Napier of the Clydeside shipbuilding firm of Wood and Napier to build three paddle ships of about 1200 tons.

The mail contract was signed on 4 May 1839 and the first vessel to enter service was the 230-foot (70-metre) *Britannia*. Capable of steaming at 8.5 knots, she sailed from the River Mersey on 4 July 1840 carrying mails, cargo and 63 passengers for Halifax and Boston. Among those embarked were Samuel Cunard and the Bishop of Nova Scotia. Twelve days and ten hours later she arrived safely at Boston before continuing to Halifax. On her return voyage she made good an average speed of 11 knots. The venture, while not profitable, was a success and set the pace for the future of transatlantic travel. The one-way fare to Halifax was 35 guineas, including wines and spirits. Her accommodation included a 'ladies only' saloon. Not everyone, however, enjoyed the experience of steamship travel. One passenger on an early westbound voyage was Charles Dickens. He was seasick for most of the voyage and likened the experience to travelling in a 'gigantic hearse'. He returned home in a sailing ship but felt the voyage had been too long.

For the next 60 years the pattern for transatlantic travel had been set. Steam ships became more efficient, they became larger, their construction and mode of propulsion evolved and they became more regulated. The sailing ship continued to provide an alternative, but slower, mode of travel and the cheaper fares remained an attraction for the less well-off emigrant. The factors in a ship that appealed to the cabin class passenger were looks, speed and comfort, and with each passing year the shipping companies vied with each other to provide ships that were pleasing to the eye, fast, and comfortable.

Although his was not the only steamship company on the North Atlantic, Samuel Cunard set the pace initially – but by 1847 he was being challenged by the American-owned Oceanic Steam Navigation Company, which had been awarded the US European mail contract. Its first ship was the 1750-ton wooden paddle steamer the *Washington*, which was claimed to be the most beautiful ever built. This opinion was not universally held, one British correspondent, seeing her arrive in Southampton, said she was 'about as ugly a specimen of steamship building as ever went through this anchorage' and 'one which seemed to roll along rather than steam through the water'. The *Washington* was not a great success, but it did draw attention to the merits of using New York rather than Boston as the American terminal for mail and passengers. This in turn persuaded Cunard to approach the British government to seek a new mail contract to operate a Liverpool to New York service one week and a Liverpool to Halifax and Boston service the next. The first steam packet ship to sail from Liverpool to New York was the Cunard-owned *Cambria* on 1 January 1848. Although sailing ships continued to play a part on the North Atlantic, the overwhelming advantage of the steamship was its ability to maintain some form of schedule.

The three shipping companies to dominate the North Atlantic passenger trade in the later years of the nineteenth century were the Cunard and White Star lines of Britain and the Inman line of the United States.

With the increasing number of passengers travelling across the Atlantic the importance of safety began to take on a greater significance. In 1843 the British parliament appointed a Select Committee to enquire into shipwreck following a disastrous three-day period in January that year when 240 ships had been wrecked with the loss of 500 lives. As a result various recommendations were made to improve the safety of steamships carrying passengers, as well as to develop the network of lighthouses, lightships and beacons. Within two years the Board of Trade established voluntary examinations for masters and mates and, in 1850, when the Marine Department of the Board of Trade was established, provision was made for the exams to be made compulsory. By 1857 the Board of Trade introduced a code of signals for merchant ships. The Merchant Shipping (Amendments) Act of 1864 required foreign-going steamships to carry qualified engineer officers on board and laid down rules for the prevention of collision at sea. The need for safety was not lost on the passenger-carrying companies, and the Cunard Line, in particular, focused on it.

A feature of passenger-ship evolution in the second half of the nineteenth century was the way that competition led to constant improvements in the way passengers were treated. With each new generation of ship the passengers were better off.

Each new class of ship was designed to be better than the last, and better than the rival companies' ships. Iron replaced wood as the main form of construction. It needed less maintenance, and iron-built ships could carry more cargo. The paddle wheel gave way to the more efficient propeller. Passenger accommodation moved from being aft to amidships where the vibration was markedly less and the pitching effects were less noticeable. The number of masts was reduced and, with improved propulsion and the introduction of the twin screw, the need for yards and sails eventually vanished for ever.

Facilities for passengers, meanwhile, continued to improve. Electric light was introduced, as was steam heating. Individual space increased, the food got better and ships began to get larger and faster. Great interest was taken in speed. Competition to be the fastest ship carrying passengers between Europe and America became intense with, at various times, British, French, American and German ships vying for the privilege. The trophy awarded to the ship holding the record for a crossing was known as the Blue Riband.

One company that held the Blue Riband on a number of occasions was one of Cunard's principal rivals: the White Star Line.

The White Star Line

The Aberdeen White Star line was founded in 1845 by two 25-year-olds, John Pilkington and Henry Threlfell Wilson. Trading as Pilkington and Wilson, they chartered their first ship in 1846 and by 1849 had three ships providing a service between Liverpool and the eastern seaboard of the United States. Following the discovery of gold in New South Wales, they extended their business to embrace the carriage of passengers and cargoes from England to Australia from 1850. But by 1867 the company was in financial difficulties, and it went into liquidation a year later.

In 1868, 30-year-old Thomas Ismay of Liverpool purchased the name of the company for £1000 from the liquidator. He had already made his mark in shipping circles, having founded the successful T H Ismay and Company, carrying cargo and passengers to both Australia and South America. Seeking to develop a transatlantic business using steamships to carry immigrants to the United States of America, he approached the Liverpool financier Gustavus Schwabe for support. This was offered on the condition that he was to build all his new ships at the Harland and Wolff shipbuilding yard in Belfast. Mr Schwabe was the uncle of Gustav Wolff, one of the partners in the firm. Mr Ismay agreed, and the first order for a new steamship was placed with the Belfast shipbuilder in July 1869. The 3707 grt *Oceanic*, incorporating many innovative features, was launched in August 1870 and commenced her maiden voyage on 2 March 1871.

Over the next 20 years both the size and speed of White Star liners increased significantly. By 1874 the first *Britannic* and the *Germanic* measured over 5000 grt and were capable of 16 knots. By 1890 the new *Teutonic* and *Majestic* measured 10,000 grt and, with twin screws, were capable of crossing the Atlantic at 20 knots. By 1877 the White Star Line was sharing the much valued mail contract with its main rival the Cunard Line.

Thomas Ismay retired from the firm of Ismay, Imrie & Company in 1892 but retained the chairmanship of the White Star Line. He died in November 1899 and his son J Bruce Ismay, already on the board of Ismay, Imrie & Company, succeeded him as chairman and managing director of the White Star Line. By the end of the nineteenth century the decision was taken to focus the business on providing a service that relied more on the size of ship and on comfort rather than on speed, and when the *Celtic* was introduced into service in 1901 she was the first ship to exceed 20,000 tons but only had a service speed of 16 knots. By contrast, the smaller Cunard liner *Lucania*, built in 1893, could make 22 knots.

In 1901 Bruce Ismay was approached by the American financier and banker John Pierpont Morgan, who was seeking to establish a monopoly of shipping on the North Atlantic and wanted to buy the Oceanic Steam Navigation Company (the White Star Line). In 1902 Bruce Ismay agreed to the sale to the International Navigation Company Ltd of Liverpool, and together with the British and North Atlantic Steam Navigation Company, the Dominion Line, the American Line, the Red Star Line, the Atlantic Transport Line and the Leyland Line became part of the American-owned International Mercantile Marine Company.

By 1912, the White Star Line owned 29 steamers, including the first two of a new class of 45.000 passenger steamships of the *Olympic* class built at Harland and Wolff. A third was to follow later. A feature of this new class was that they would offer infinitely better facilities for steerage class passengers, and even though they would still be accommodated at the ends of the vessel and on the lower decks, they would no longer be accommodated in large open-plan dormitories but in cabins with between two and ten berths in each. The term steerage was dropped and replaced by the designation third class.

The *Olympic* had been ordered in 1908 and her keel was laid in December that year. She was launched on 20 October 1910, handed over on 31 May 2011 and commenced her maiden voyage from Southampton on 14 June 1911 with 4840 tons of coal in her bunkers. She was commanded by Captain E J Smith.

Immigration rules and regulations

Migration to the New World during the seventeenth and eighteenth centuries was limited to, perhaps, less than half a million, and in the early years of the United States, fewer than 8000 people per year entered the country. Between 1836 and the time *Titanic* came to make her maiden voyage some 30 million Europeans had crossed the Atlantic. The USA passed its first immigration law in 1875.

With the advent of steamships able to carry an increasingly large number of passengers at lower fares towards the end of the nineteenth century, a surplus population in southern and eastern Europe meant that more and more, mainly young, people were migrating to the United States. They included Greeks, Hungarians, Poles and Italians, together with large numbers of Jews and Scandinavians.

While many of these emigrants would sail directly from their country of origin or from the nearest seaport, some would travel by land and sea to arrive in England before making their way to a British port of embarkation such as London or Liverpool. From the early years of the twentieth century, Southampton became a leading terminal for transatlantic passengers.

Nearly all migrants would travel by the cheapest means, and this invariably meant they would be travelling in steerage class. To meet the US entry requirements, certain restrictions were placed on those taking passage across the Atlantic in ships carrying first and second class passengers. Whilst on passage in multi-class ships, those travelling steerage had to be kept separate to ensure they enjoyed certain minimal living standards and did not spread disease to their more affluent fellow travellers. This involved having barriers in place to prevent the classes from mixing, and any ship found not to have them was liable to be held at the quarantine station at the entrance to New York Harbour. In extreme cases a ship could be held for 40 days. Most companies went to great lengths to ensure the rules were kept, to avoid such draconian action being taken,

Once a ship had arrived, health officers would personally inspect all incoming passengers – but in practice only the steerage class passengers were subjected to such scrutiny.

One early set of rules for entry was clear:

All passengers are liable to be rejected, who, upon examination, are found to be lunatic, idiot, deaf, dumb, blind, maimed, or infirm, or above the age of 60 years; or widow with a child or children; or any woman without a husband with a child or children; or any person unable to take care of himself (or herself) without becoming a public charge, or who from any attending circumstances are likely to become a public charge, or who from sickness or disease, existing at the time of departure, are likely soon to become a public charge. Sick persons or widows with children cannot be taken, nor lame persons, unless full security be given for the bonds to be entered into by the steamer to the United States Government, that the parties will not become chargeable to the State.

For New York arrivals the inspection was conducted at Ellis Island, just a short ferry ride across the water from Manhattan.

Maritime matters

North Atlantic routing

Until the end of the nineteenth century the route adopted by many ships heading either east or west involved skirting the capes of the south coast of Newfoundland. A longer but ultimately safer route took them much further offshore, and had the advantage of ensuring that they would remain clear of a frequently fog-shrouded coastline and the danger of meeting another ship proceeding in the opposite direction.

Given the likelihood of fog and the increased risk of collision with either another ship or drifting ice and icebergs, the great North Atlantic steamship companies came to an agreement in 1899 to establish lane routes for use by their ships at the different seasons of the year and without unduly lengthening the overall passage. The tracks were devised to separate outward- and homeward-bound mail steamers, and the resultant routes were marked on North Atlantic route charts. One of the perceived advantages of the system was that in the event of a breakdown a ship would be more likely to receive timely assistance from other ships following the same route.

The accepted mail steamer outward track between 15 January and 14 August followed the arc of a great circle between the Fastnet light and position 42° N, 47° W, and thence by rhumb line to just south of the Nantucket Shoals light vessel. It was referred to as the Outward Southern track. A more northerly version, followed between 15 August and 14 January, was the Outward Northern track. From the Nantucket light vessel ships inbound to New York would make for the Ambrose Channel and the entrance to New York Harbour.

Time

Three basic times featured in the *Titanic* incident: Greenwich Mean Time, New York Time, and ship's (or local apparent) time, which would be different for every ship.

Greenwich Mean Time (GMT) was established as the world's standard reference time base in 1884 at the International Meridian Conference, when it was decided that the Prime Meridian should pass through Greenwich, England. GMT was the time used by wireless operators as the standard time reference for all wireless transmissions. That said, the convention used by Marconi wireless operators in 1912 was that GMT would be used when east of 40° W and New York Time to the west of it, and others followed similar arrangements.

New York Time was five hours behind GMT and was used by wireless operators both on the western side of the Atlantic and in mainland North America.

Ship's time was that kept by an individual ship whilst on passage and would be determined by the longitude of her position. On a ship transiting east or west clocks would be adjusted once every 24 hours at midnight to a new time that would ensure that when the sun crossed the meridian at noon the next day, her clocks would read 12 o'clock precisely.

As *Titanic* progressed across the Atlantic her clock was retarded by several minutes each day at midnight, and at the time of the accident it was 2 hours 58 minutes behind GMT and 2 hours 2 minutes ahead of New York Time.

Navigation lights

Until the middle of the nineteenth century no convention existed for indicating the presence of a ship, or the direction she was travelling, during the hours of darkness. From 1848, British steamships were required to display a white masthead steaming light as well as red and green sidelights to indicate her basic direction of travel to an observer. These lights were shown over specific arcs and were fitted purely so that other vessels could see them. They served no function to illuminate the way but had to be of sufficient intensity to be visible to another ship in normal conditions for an acceptable distance.

The regulations that came into force on 1 September 1880 stated:

Seagoing steam-ships when under way shall carry:

(a) On, or in front of, the foremast head, at a height above the hull of not less than 20 feet, and if the breadth of the ship exceeds 20 feet then at a height above the hull not less than such breadth, a bright white light, so constructed as to show an uniform and unbroken light over an arc of the horizon of 20 points of the compass, so fixed as to throw the light 10 points on each side of the ship, viz, from right ahead to two points abaft the beam on either side, and of such a character as to be visible on a dark night with a clear atmosphere, a distance of at least five miles.

(b) On the starboard side a green light so constructed as to show an uniform and unbroken light over an area of the horizon of ten points of the compass, so fixed as to throw light from right ahead to two points abaft the beam on the starboard side, and of such a character as to be visible on a dark night, with a clear atmosphere, at a distance of at least two miles.

(c) On the port side a red light so constructed as to show an uniform and unbroken light over an area of the horizon of ten points of the compass, so fixed as to throw light from right ahead to two points abaft the beam on the port side, and of such a character as to be visible on a dark night, with a clear atmosphere, at a distance of at least two miles.

Following the first International Maritime Conference in 1889, a rule was introduced for steamships to carry a second masthead light. This became effective internationally in 1897. The carriage of a second fixed masthead steaming light did not, however, become mandatory for ships over 150 feet in length until 1948 when the requirement was included in the SOLAS update.

Titanic was fitted with a single masthead steaming light on her foremast. The *Californian* had two steaming lights, one on each of her forward masts and ahead of her sidelights.

Helm orders

In the days of sail, orders to the helmsman were given in terms of where the tiller should be put rather than the rudder. An order to put the helm to port meant that the tiller would be put in that direction. The effect on the rudder was that it would turn to starboard and so turn the ship's head to starboard. This custom extended well into the steamship era, and it took time for the more logical rudder order to become established. The new convention meant that when a ship was required to alter course to port the order would be given to turn the wheel to port.

The shipping world is instinctively conservative, but some European countries began to change to rudder orders at the beginning of the twentieth century. The British were more traditional, and it was not until 1933 that the change was made. Until that time British officers and helmsmen instinctively used the original sailing-ship helm orders. The United States Navy made the change in 1914 but its merchant ships did not follow suit until 1935.

The compass

Ships steered courses and took bearing by means of a compass influenced by the magnetic field of the earth and local anomalies. The magnetic compass aligns itself to the earth's magnetic poles, which are not co-located with the geographic poles and are constantly drifting. Depending on the ship's position in relation to the poles there will be a difference, sometimes substantial, between the direction of the true and magnetic poles. This error is measurable, predictable and marked on the charts used for navigation. It is known as variation.

The local anomalies are caused by the magnetism of the ship itself and anything with magnetic properties situated near the compass. Any errors resulting from these local influences can, to an extent, be removed by placing compensatory magnets in the immediate vicinity of the compass, but there is almost always a residual error that is dependent on the ship's head. This error is known as deviation.

Ocean-going ships at the beginning of the twentieth century carried at least two compasses and quite possibly more. Each would have had its individual errors. The main compass, known as the Standard Compass, was usually situated high up in the ship, usually on top of the wheelhouse. *Titanic's* standard compass was positioned on a dedicated raised platform made of brass on the amidships line between the second and third funnels.

The second compass was known as the Steering Compass, and, as the name implies, it was used by the helmsman to steer the ship. *Titanic* had two such compasses: one in the partially open fore part of the bridge and the second in a closed wheelhouse immediately abaft it. The forward compass would be used by the helmsman while leaving and entering harbour so he could, if necessary, see where the ship was going. A third steering compass was positioned aft on the docking bridge for use in an emergency.

Coal

The advent of the steamship gave rise to an increase in the need for a suitable fuel and a means of transporting it from its source to a point of embarkation. The fuel was coal and it was, in Britain, available in large quantities and at low cost. It was mined in the northeast of England, in the Clyde/Forth valley, in Lancashire and in south Wales. It was carried to the various ports by small colliers and, increasingly during the later years of the nineteenth century, by the railways. The best-quality coal for use in steamships was Welsh (Rhondda) steam coal as it produced a hotter flame and less smoke than that mined elsewhere. Coal as fuel for a steamship was always referred to as bunkers.

The three factors of greatest importance to the ship owner were availability, quality and cost. Ensuring that an adequate supply was embarked before sailing was a prerequisite for a successful voyage. The amount carried would depend on the anticipated daily consumption for the planned speed together with an adequate reserve in case of having to make a diversion to another coaling port, or a longer than expected voyage due to bad weather or some other unforeseen circumstance.

Distinguishing night signals of steamship lines

In 1912 many ships were still not equipped with wireless and had to rely on alternative means of communicating. These included flag signals, semaphore and mirrors reflecting sunlight by day, and both the Morse lamp and pyrotechnics by night.

The Merchant Shipping Act of 1894 permitted the use of pyrotechnics, including rockets and Roman candles, for identification purposes, but they had to be registered with the Board of Trade. The Act stated that requests to register such signals might be refused if, in the opinion of the Board, they could not 'easily be distinguished from signals of distress or signals for pilots'. In the event some 190 shipping companies sought to register their private signals. Only five such signals involved the use of rockets.

A typical example of the pyrotechnic signals used by just one company, the Aberdeen Line, was:

> Red pyrotechnic light burnt near the stern, followed by a Roman candle throwing up three groups of balls to a height not exceeding 50 feet, and each group consisting of a red, white and blue ball, the colours following in the order specified.

The signal could be used anywhere within British jurisdiction and on the high seas.

North Atlantic safety record

Natural hazards included hurricanes and storms, fog, uncharted rocks and ice. Manmade or man-induced hazards included poor navigation, leaks, fires, dismasting, steamships running out of coal and collisions with an unlit derelict or another ship. Bad health or disease could also play a major part in how a ship was handled, particularly on some of the longer voyages.

The foundering of the *Titanic* in 1912 was by far the most serious accident to occur on the North Atlantic, and it played a major part in bringing together the maritime nations of the world to agree a more effective international safety regime. Before this disaster there had been a number of other, less well publicised, marine casualties whose lessons should have been learnt.

In May 1833 the Scottish brig *Lady Of The Lake* was on passage from Belfast to Quebec, some 250 miles to the east of Cape Francis, Newfoundland, when she encountered some ice one morning. She tried to extricate herself by sailing out of it but stove in her bows in the process. The damage was substantial and she began to make water fast. Some of the crew managed to launch one boat successfully but the longboat was swamped with passengers trying to board it and many drowned. The brig sank with the loss of over 200 souls. The precise number is unknown but it is believed 15 survived, including the captain.

On 27 September 1854, in thick fog on the Grand Banks of Newfoundland, the 2856-ton American-flagged Collins Line paddle steamer *Arctic* collided with the 250-ton iron-built French-flagged auxiliary schooner *Vesta* some 50 miles south of Cape Race. The *Arctic* was on passage from Liverpool heading for New York with a crew of about 150 and some 230 passengers, while the *Vesta* had sailed from the island of St Pierre off the coast of Newfoundland the previous day and was making for Granville in France. She had a crew of 50 and about 150 passengers embarked.

Following the collision the wooden *Arctic* began to take on water and, because there were no watertight bulkheads, it began to spread throughout the ship. Although a lifeboat was launched the master decided to make for the shore but failed to see the *Vesta's* lifeboat, which had already been launched, and ran straight into it killing all but one of the occupants.

Whilst the *Arctic* carried the regulatory requirement of lifeboats for her size, the numbers actually embarked greatly exceeded this. The discipline of those on board was not good, and as each lifeboat was made ready some of the crew and a number of male passengers rushed the boats despite the captain's efforts to load them with women and children first. Not one woman managed to board a lifeboat. About four and a half hours after the collision the *Arctic* finally foundered. Some survivors were eventually rescued by other ships while others managed to make it to the shore. The precise number of souls who lost their lives has never been determined but is estimated at between 285 and 372. Not a single woman or child made it.

The other ship, the *Vesta*, fared better. Once the initial shock had worn off her master concentrated all his efforts into saving both his ship and did his best to contain the damage by shoring up the collision bulkhead with mattresses and bedding supported by baulks of timber. He also placed a tingle, a sail, over the damaged bows, Confident that his ship had a good chance of remaining afloat if the weather held, he headed for the nearest port, St John's, to make good the necessary repairs. He arrived two days before the first survivors of the *Arctic*, having saved both his ship and 184 lives.

A number of consequences arose as a result of this accident. Additional bulkheads were fitted in the other ships of the company and additional lifeboats were also installed, but the incident led, indirectly, to the demise of the Collins Line.

Among the shipping companies engaged in carrying passengers across the Atlantic in the years following the American Civil War was the Guion Line. One of its ships on the Liverpool–Queenstown–New York route was the single-screw 5417 grt liner *SS Arizona*. She entered service in 1879 and became a fast, but uncomfortable, ship with a high daily coal consumption. In November 1879 she was making an eastbound crossing from New York to Liverpool at just under 15 knots in reduced visibility when she failed to see an iceberg dead ahead of her. She steamed straight into it without reducing speed and badly damaged her bow. Although she listed to starboard after the impact and was evidently down by the bow, the damage was confined to the area forward of her collision bulkhead, which held. Having taken stock of the damage and waited for daylight the following morning in order to carry out an inspection of the bows, the decision was taken to make for St John's, Newfoundland. On arrival, 200 tons of ice was removed from the bow.

On 14 April 1897 the French brig *Vaillant* struck an iceberg south of Newfoundland with the loss of 78 lives. Four survived. She was one of the 14 vessels lost and 40 seriously damaged between the years of 1882 and 1890, but this figure excludes fishing vessels and whalers. A few years later the *Naronic*, en route from Liverpool to New York on 9 February 1893, struck an iceberg in a snowstorm on the Grand Banks and sank with all 74 hands. Later still, in July 1907, the German Norddeutscher Lloyd steamer *Kronprinz Wilhelm* struck an iceberg and damaged her bows but was able to make port safely under her own power.

On a voyage from New York to Le Havre in July 1898, the French passenger liner *La Bourgogne* of the Compagnie Générale Transatlantique collided with the British sailing ship *Cromartyshire* in thick fog some 60 miles south of Sable Island. She was carrying 725 passengers and crew including some 300 women. The collision occurred at 0500 and, despite extensive damage for'ard, the *Cromartyshire* remained afloat and survived. *La Bourgogne*, however, foundered within 40 minutes. In the minutes following the collision discipline on board broke down completely and members of the crew started to fight for places in the lifeboats. Refusing all orders from the officers, they totally ignored the needs of the passengers and physically attacked them. The 165 survivors were eventually rescued by the *Cromartyshire* and were found to be almost exclusively members of the crew together with some steerage-class passengers. Only one woman survived.

Until the loss of the *Titanic*, the worst accident in the Atlantic involving a commercial steamship was the sinking of the 3360 grt Danish passenger ship SS *Norge* on 28 June 1904. She was on passage from Copenhagen and Oslo to New York with a crew of 68 and about 727 passengers, mainly Scandinavian and Russian-Jewish emigrants, when she struck a reef close to Rockall. It rapidly became evident she was going to sink and attempts were made to launch the lifeboats, with priority being given to women and children. The *Norge* carried eight lifeboats and a single life raft with a total carrying capacity of 280 people. Six of the eight were more or less launched successfully. Twenty minutes after hitting the rock she sank with the loss of around 600 souls. There were more casualties when one of the lifeboats also sank. 160 passengers and crew spent up to eight days in the remaining five lifeboats and were eventually rescued by other ships and taken ashore. The subsequent inquiry into the loss found there were insufficient lifeboats to carry all on board and recommended that laws be introduced requiring ships to carry lifeboats to accommodate everyone embarked.

Passengers crossing the Atlantic were, meanwhile, warned that accidents at sea could happen. As Katherine Ledoux wrote in *Ocean Notes for Ladies* in 1877:

> Accidents and loss of life are possible at sea. I have always felt that a body washed ashore in good clothes would always receive more respect and kinder care than if dressed in those only fit for the rag bag.

The sinking of HM Troopship *Birkenhead*

Perhaps the one event that most clearly encapsulated the spirit of self-sacrifice, heroism and chivalry towards women, and which had a bearing on the *Titanic* story, was the sinking of the troopship *Birkenhead* after she struck rocks on the South African coast in 1852.

On 25 February that year the steam-propelled iron-built *Birkenhead* was en route to Port Elizabeth with troops embarked to participate in one of a number of wars between the Cape colonists and the Xhosa people of the Eastern Cape. After calling at Simonstown, she was on the last leg of her journey with 638 souls on board including 479 military personnel, seven women and 13 children.

She was expecting to make a landfall in the middle of the night in the vicinity of a headland known as Danger Point. It was dark, clear and calm with good visibility, and those on board were able to make out some lights ashore. A good lookout was being kept and a leadsman was closed up to take soundings as they approached the land.

A few minutes before 0200 on the morning of the 26th, and without any warning whatsoever, she hit an underwater obstruction with a resounding crash. Within seconds water began to pour into the ship, trapping many who were asleep in their hammocks below. What happened next has gone down in the annals of the British Army as one of the most outstanding displays of good discipline and chivalry ever recorded.

Although he was still uncertain as to what had happened, it became obvious to the commander that the ship was taking water fast and was already sinking. She had in fact struck a rock some 1.2 miles offshore. Both the ship's commander and the senior military officer on board began to issue precise orders to crew, troops and passengers. Realising that the number of boats carried was woefully inadequate to embark everyone on board, the order was given to collect the women and children from the darkness below, bring them onto the upper deck and then pass them into one of the cutters that had successfully been launched. Amid scenes of confusion and chaos, and with the ship rolling badly, it proved difficult to persuade the seven women to embark without their husbands. At the same time, not one soldier or seaman made any attempt to board this particular boat and the embarkation was successfully achieved.

As the ship began to sink bows-first and both masts and funnel fell, seamen continued to man the pumps while the soldiers mustered on the poop in perfect order. Aware that any rush to the boats now standing off the sinking ship would swamp them and lead to the certain death of the women and children, the officer commanding, Lieutenant Colonel Seton, instructed the troops to stand fast. To a man they did so, but very soon afterwards the hull split in two and began to go down, killing those manning the pumps below decks. Many of the soldiers were pitched into the sea, but not one of those who remained on the poop moved; over 200 men prepared to meet their deaths in the sea rather than jeopardise the lives of the women and children. The time between striking the rock and sinking beneath the waves was about 20 minutes.

Those who survived the sinking still had to fight for their lives. Some made it to the shore, others did not and were possibly taken by the sharks known to be in the area. The three boats picked up a handful of swimming survivors, but when the final count was taken it was discovered that 87 of the ship's company, nine officers and 349 other ranks had perished. All the women and children were saved.

The legacy of this incident was threefold. The legend of the 'Birkenhead drill' was born and forever became associated with steadfastness and sacrifice in the face of extreme danger; steps were taken to improve the watertight divisions in iron-built ships; and the understanding that women and children were to be rescued first in any shipwreck was confirmed in the psyche of the British people. All that was noble and praiseworthy in the Victorian era was demonstrated to wide popular acclaim and remained that way well into the twentieth century.

The conspicuous exception to the number of lessons that were learned was that nobody gave much thought to the need to provide a ship with sufficient boats to save lives should it sink.

Wireless telegraphy

There has always been a need for good communications at sea. Although the Romans and the Greeks were among the first to use a form of flag to communicate between ships, the first recorded use of flag signals by ships of the Royal Navy was around 1530. The system used evolved into a system of codes that eventually became somewhat cumbersome and unwieldy but, by the end of the eighteenth century, order was evident and a pattern of flag signals had been devised. The use of flags to communicate messages became widespread in the early years of the nineteenth century, and warships and merchant ships of many nations began to use them.

Although merchant ships would often remain at sea for weeks, if not months, between ports, they used flags or the speaking trumpet to 'speak' to other ships when in sight of one another. They would not only identify themselves to each other and ask for news but exchange their best estimates for longitude to either confirm or compare their respective estimates of position.

By far the most pressing requirement for an at-sea communications system was, however, a means whereby a ship in distress could alert others to her predicament and request assistance.

By the third decade of the nineteenth century the need for an effective, long-distance, instant and all-weather communications system capable of being used both ashore and at sea had become urgent. A number of experiments with electromagnetism had been undertaken in the 1820s and 1830s by Michael Faraday and William Sturgeon on the eastern side of the Atlantic, and by Joseph Henry in America. These opened up a range of possibilities. It was Henry who was able to demonstrate that it was possible to send an electric current along a length of wire to activate an electromagnet at the other end that was capable of striking a bell and making it ring.

The first large-scale use of electricity was for telegraphy, and two Englishmen, Charles Wheatstone and William Fothergill

Cooke, were the first to develop a workable electromagnetic telegraph for use with the railways in Britain. At the same time another American, Samuel Morse, invented a code of dots and dashes that could be used as a means of transmitting messages over long distances by wire.

A skilled operator could send and read these codes at up to 40 words a minute and sometimes even more. The electric telegraph system had arrived and, by 1840, telegraph networks were spreading across Britain, Europe and the United States. A telegraph cable was successfully laid across the English Channel in 1851, and six years later an attempt was made to do the same across the Atlantic. Unsuccessful at the first attempt, it was not until 1867 that a working cable link was established.

Helpful though the new telegraph system was, it still did not solve the problem of how to communicate with ships at sea. A 'wireless' system was required, and a number of people began to examine possibilities. Not everyone was enthused by the concept, and some of the telegraph companies opposed the development as a dangerous challenge to their monopoly.

Among those experimenting with electricity was the German physicist Heinrich Hertz. He was able to prove the existence of electromagnetic waves that could be transmitted at the speed of light. At the time called 'Hertzian waves', they are now known as radio waves. It was these experiments, conducted from 1888, that led to the development of the wireless telegraph.

Various scientists enjoyed a measure of success in their experiments with wireless transmission, but it fell to the young Italian inventor Guglielmo Marconi to build the first commercially viable apparatus that was capable of both transmitting and receiving radio signals over a modest distance. By 1895 he had improved his experimental equipment to the extent that he could transmit a signal outdoors over at least a mile. Due to the lack of any interest in his experimental work in his native Italy, he moved to England in 1896. Aged 21 and a fluent English speaker, he quickly came to the attention of the British Post

Office. His overriding objective was to try and increase the range at which wireless signals could be sent, and by 1897 he was able to demonstrate that he could transmit Morse-code messages over a distance of nearly 4 miles. In May that year he sent the first ever message across the sea from Lavernock Point in south Wales to the island of Flat Holm in the Bristol Channel. Soon afterwards he extended the range to 10 miles, and later in the year he founded the Wireless Telegraph & Signal Company, which, in 1900, became Marconi's Wireless Telegraph Company.

The first ship-to-shore communication occurred on Christmas Eve in 1898. Following the fitting of a wireless apparatus on board the East Goodwin lightship, moored off the coast of Kent, good two-way communication was established with the shore, a distance of 12 miles. Three months later this wireless link was used to summon the Ramsgate lifeboat after a German ship went aground on the Goodwin Sands in dense fog. At the end of April 1899 the lightship itself was hit by a steamer and, using the distress signal for the first time, called for assistance.

Further tests and high-profile demonstrations followed, and in 1899 the first cross-channel transmission took place between Wimereux in France and the South Foreland lighthouse to the east of Dover. In the same year the Royal Navy equipped three warships with sets built by Marconi. An experimental transmitting station was established at a hotel at Poole on the south coast of England, and distances of over 60 miles were achieved.

Although there was now no doubt that wireless messages could be transmitted and received successfully, many believed the range was confined to the straight line of sight. As the new century dawned, Marconi, anxious to develop his commercial success, realised that one way of confounding the sceptics would be to transmit a signal across the Atlantic, but he would have to build transmitters powerful enough to achieve this. Raising sufficient money for the venture was the first hurdle, but in 1901 he went ahead and constructed transmitters on both sides of the Atlantic. One was at Poldhu in the southwest corner of Cornwall, and the other at Cape Cod, Massachusetts, but strong winds at both sites damaged the extensive array of aerials. In the event concerns about the distance involved for making the first transatlantic test transmission prompted Marconi to build an experimental receiving station on that part of North America nearest to England, the British colony of Newfoundland. Landing at St John's in early December 1901, he quickly assembled a temporary receiving station on Signal Hill near the mouth of the harbour. The equipment used involved the receiver, an earth connection and a 510-foot (155-metre) aerial to be carried aloft by either hydrogen-filled balloons or a kite.

Despite some initial problems with high winds, the aerial was raised successfully and, on 12 December, the first ever wireless transmission from one side of the Atlantic to the other was received. It did not, however, satisfy the many sceptics who continued to believe it was impossible to send a wireless message over such a long distance by ignoring the curvature of the earth. At the same time, those with vested interests in the telegraph cable companies were far from amused and began to launch legal challenges to the experiments. Further proof of the viability of wireless telegraphy was sought, and a system was tested on board the SS *Philadelphia* as she sailed westwards across the Atlantic in early 1902. The tests were successful and, for the first time, it was discovered that signals transmitted by night travelled much further than those sent by day. Progress thereafter was rapid, and by the end of the year Marconi had established a permanent station on the east coast of Nova Scotia at Glace Bay. It was from here that the first west-to-east transatlantic message was transmitted to Poldhu in Cornwall in December 1902. A month later the first messages were being transmitted from Cape Cod in the United States. The ability to transmit telegraph messages without the need for wires was made possible by the use of spark-gap transmitters and very basic receivers.

By 1904 a number of ships employed on the North Atlantic

were equipped with wireless sets, with many being fitted with equipment built by Marconi. He was not, however, the only supplier, and a number of rival companies from countries such as Germany and France were also being set up and were competing for business. The early days of wireless at sea were not straightforward, and profits were hard to come by pending the development of a commercially viable system. At the same time the new profession of wireless operator was growing, and many of those who went to sea with the new equipment had previously worked as railway or postal telegraphers. Inevitably they brought with them some of the methods they had been using on landlines, including the use of the two-letter general call CQ. This was soon adopted internationally by both ships and shore stations as the general call for 'all ships'. In 1906 an International Radiotelegraphic Convention was held in Berlin at which a framework for international cooperation was drawn up, but competition between rival wireless telegraphy companies continued. Each had its own operators and its own codes and call signs. Ships fitted with Marconi equipment had call signs preceded by the letter M. *Titanic's*, for instance, was MGY.

There was, nonetheless, a requirement for some sort of system whereby operators speaking different languages could communicate. A method known as the Q code was devised in about 1909 by the British government whereby frequently used messages were abbreviated into three-letter signal groups preceded by the letter Q. For example, QRA meant 'What ship or coast station is that?' The system was soon adopted for international use and expanded.

By mid 1911 Marconi alone had installed over 300 wireless installations in ships, and the number was growing month by month. By April 1912 this had grown to over 400, representing about 40 per cent of the 1000 steamships so fitted. Although the use of wireless technology was spreading throughout the maritime community it was still a new and untested bit of equipment that had yet to make a full impact on the very conservative mariner of the day. Only a very small number of ships registered in the United States were equipped with wireless.

The new technology brought with it a need for men to operate it at sea, and laws were passed that required the new wireless operators to have a sound knowledge of their apparatus and to be aware of the international and national rules governing wireless telegraphy. The operators were also required to maintain and repair their equipment. Except in the largest ships it was very unusual for more than one operator to be embarked and, in the early years, wireless telegraphy was regarded as little more than a convenience. The operators were under the command of the master for the transmission and reception of messages relevant to the ship, but the operation was largely financed by the sending and receiving of telegrams. Passenger messages were seen as an important source of revenue, and handling them was a priority over weather reports and ship-to-ship transmissions. Received messages requiring the specific attention of the master would be prefixed with the letters MSG, for 'master's service gram'.

Because of the atmospheric conditions at night and the longer distances that could be achieved for both transmitting and receiving messages, the busiest time for wireless operators would be in the first few hours after sunset and before they went to bed.

The need to keep messages short was commonplace from the outset. Ships and wireless shore stations were allocated thee-letter call signs, and many commonly used expressions were abbreviated to just two or three letters. In the early days of wireless at sea many of the Marconi-trained operators knew each other, and they established their own jargon for use when communicating with each other. The two- and three-letter unofficial codes soon evolved into a wireless operator's shorthand, and letter combinations such as OM (old man) and SBI (stand by) began to emerge.

With headsets pressed against their ears, the wireless operators lived in a world of static, squeaks, dots and dashes. Messages would be received and sent but, as they worked at phenomenal speeds with this new technology, the operators would have little interest in the actual content of any message, and their handling of each message would be dictated by the prefix.

Distress signals: wireless

Ships in distress and requiring assistance had a requirement to alert others or stations to their predicament. This could be done either visually or by sound signals and, following the introduction of wireless telegraphy, by wireless.

There was no internationally agreed wireless signal when ships were first fitted with the apparatus. Until the first international congress on wireless telegraphy, held in 1903, the letter D had been used internationally as the signal for an urgent message after the letter S, and SSSDDD indicated a ship in distress. Pending international agreement on what should be used, Marconi devised the code CQD as a distress signal. He merely added the letter D for distress to the established CQ. CQD therefore became 'all ships distress', and this arrangement came into force for Marconi-fitted ships on 1 February 1904.

The first ship to use wireless following an accident was the White Star liner SS *Republic*, sailing from New York to the Mediterranean with 1500 passengers and crew embarked in January 1909. Soon after sailing and while some 50 miles to the south of Nantucket she was feeling her way slowly through thick fog when she was rammed by the Lloyd Italiano liner SS *Florida* and badly damaged. She was fitted with one of the early wireless systems, and her operator, Jack Binns, transmitted the three-letter signal CQD. It was the first time this signal had been used, and it resulted in another White Star liner, the *Baltic*, coming to her aid. All but a handful of those on board were saved and the success of wireless in calling for assistance made an impression on ship owners, who had not previously considered this new technology as a means for saving life. Following the accident and subsequent rescue, many ships were fitted with wireless. CQD, whilst effective in providing a distress signal, was technically a Marconi signal and not for general use.

At the Berlin Radiotelegraphic Convention of 1906 the decision was taken to adopt the letters SOS as the internationally recognised distress call, on account of its unmistakable character. The Germans had already adopted it the previous year. A feature of its use required stations hearing it to immediately cease handling traffic until the emergency was over. The use of SOS was ratified in 1908.

The first instances of SOS being used to indicate a ship in distress occurred in 1909. The Cunard steamship SS *Slavonia* was wrecked in the Azores on 10 June and SS *Arapahoe* radioed for help following the loss of a screw off Cape Hatteras in August.

Despite its international status, SOS was, for at least the next two to three years, less well known to operators than the Marconi CQD.

The people

Edwardians

The world in 1912 was very different to the one we know today. Every British adult involved in *Titanic*'s design, build, management and operation, as well as all those who sailed in her, had been brought up in the later years of the Victorian era.

The nation's wealth had grown with the output of the coal mines, factories and international trade. The last years of the nineteenth century had seen the introduction of the railway network, steam-powered ships, the first motor cars and electrical power generation. The British Empire was at its height and British merchant ships, protected by the Royal Navy, could be found on every sea and ocean. The nation was confident in itself and the Victorians had enjoyed growing prosperity, improvements to living standards and greater life expectancy. The middle classes had expanded and there had been a shift from a rural England to an urban one, with more and more food being imported at the expense of domestic production.

After a reign lasting almost 64 years, Queen Victoria died in 1901. She was succeeded by her son, Edward VII, who went about his duties in a very different way. More flamboyant and accessible, he ruled at a time of massive change and growing optimism. Peace seemed assured with the creation of the Triple Entente with France and Imperial Russia. Society was accepting, and adapting to, new technology. Fashion was changing fast, many of the foodstuff brand names we know today were created during the first decade of the twentieth century, and the 1908 Olympic Games were relocated from Rome to London.

And yet, for all this progress, the winds of change were not all favourable. England had been severely shaken by the bloodshed of the Boer War. Her industrial supremacy was being challenged by an increasingly confident Germany and a rapidly expanding United States. Simmering discontent among sections of society was manifesting itself, with the creation of trade unions representing the concerns and aspirations of the working classes while women, denied the vote or any form of representation, were becoming increasingly vocal. And in Ireland the demand for Home Rule was growing.

At the beginning of the Edwardian era some 70 per cent of the nation's capital was owned by 1 per cent of the population, and less than half a million people were earning more than £400 per year. Income tax at 1 shilling in the pound (5 per cent) began at £160.

Life in England was dominated by the inequalities of wealth distribution and an established, still unchallenged, class system. The landed aristocracy led a privileged and largely pampered life with the male head of house having almost total power over everything he surveyed. They ate better, were more mobile, lived longer, and owned and cultivated vast tracts of land. Many lived in large country houses as well as having property in London. The ritual of moving from country house to London property for the summer season involved the transfer of several tons of luggage. Huge numbers of domestic servants were employed. Some members of the aristocracy were very conscious that those less fortunate themselves needed help, and many ladies would indulge in what would today be described as charitable work. Philanthropy was very much part of some people's lives.

Generated by industrialisation, a feature of the late Victorian age was the growing urbanisation of the nation and the burgeoning middle class. By the Edwardian era the middle class was well established and embraced a wide range of occupations from the leaders of industry through the growing number of civil servants, professions, teachers, shopkeepers and clerks. Most lived in urban houses and could afford to live in varying degrees of comfort, enjoy better education and employ a small number of domestic servants. As with the aristocracy, hierarchy and deference dictated everyday life.

At the lower end of the social spectrum were the poor. More than 25 per cent of the population were living at or below subsistence level and about 10 per cent had no means of buying sufficient food to live on, let alone clothes to wear. In the slum conditions of some cities child mortality was high, with up to one-third of newborn children failing to survive their first year of life. The poorest families had to feed and clothe themselves on an income of less than a penny per person per day. The greatest fear among these lower classes was unemployment; those who did have jobs would do almost anything to keep them. Instinctively they were subservient and were totally accustomed to taking orders and being told what to do, to the extent that thinking for themselves was not a natural characteristic. It was against this background that rumblings of discontent began to grow, and the trade union movement began to campaign for better pay and treatment among the working classes. Strikes in sectors such as mining, the transport industries and the docks were beginning to occur, but it was not until the working classes had a voice in parliament that effective change began to be felt. The Labour Representative Committee, forerunner of the British Labour Party, was formed in 1900 and the first two socialist members of parliament were elected in October that year.

Underpinning the entire social structure of the nation were conventions and practices that had evolved over a number of years. Everyone knew their place and most would conform. In the large country or town houses, those undertaking the more menial tasks would be so segregated that they would rarely even be seen by the host family or their guests except on a Sunday, when the household would proceed to church and listen to interminable sermons. The upper classes knew how to behave and, in any event, set their own rules as they went along. The burgeoning middle classes did their best to emulate the customs and behaviour of their superiors and became slaves to 'getting it right'. A less than refined accent, awkward table manners or saying the 'wrong thing' was seized upon as being socially unacceptable to those who were acutely conscious of their standing in society and petrified of being ostracised by their peer group.

The lower classes meanwhile just suffered. They were used to being ordered around and had little to alleviate the many hardships of life. Among the few compensations they could call on was a very real community spirit among some of the most disadvantaged sections of society.

The Edwardian era was very much a man's world. It was a society where prejudice against women was widespread and where the concept of paterfamilias remained unchallenged. Men were invariably the breadwinners, enjoyed better education, had greater opportunities to do what they wanted, and ruled their families with varying degrees of affection. And the virtues most admired during this period were manliness, heroism, stoicism, self-sacrifice, bravery, duty and chivalry. The most despised was cowardice, and a man would go to almost any length to prevent being branded a coward.

Life for women was very different. A good marriage was the ultimate aspiration for any girl, and failure to achieve this was forever regarded as a misfortune. The role for most married women was to produce children and run the household. The fact that this 'weaker sex' could also be both clever and able was largely discounted, or even ignored, by most men. Women went to great lengths to retain their modesty and were denied the freedoms we take for granted today. They could not vote, could not choose when to have children, were severely restricted in the choice of a career and faced almost insuperable barriers in advancing their causes. The movement to grant suffrage for women grew throughout the Edwardian era.

Embedded in the minds of many Edwardians were stories of how the British had performed in times of crisis during both the Victorian era and the first years of the twentieth century. Although many of these stories revolved around failure to some degree, any such shortcomings were relegated to the sidelines if it could be shown that people had behaved with courage in adversity. The words hero, self-sacrifice, bravery and fortitude featured largely in the lexicon of the day.

Merchant seamen

The stratified society of the Edwardian era applied equally among seafarers.

Life on board a British ship reflected the social structure of the day. Officers and ratings would live and work separately. Officers would, by and large, live in the central part of the ship, be accommodated in individual or shared cabins and would eat together in the saloon. The ratings, both deck and engine room, would be accommodated in the ship's foc's'le with little more than a bunk each and communal tables for meals. The deck and engine room crews would live in separate messes but the conditions in each would be similar. It could be damp or stuffy, and filled with tobacco smoke. It was invariably uncomfortable, given the ship's motion, and privacy was unknown.

In the early years of the twentieth century the crew of a steamship would be divided into the deck, engineering, and the purser's or steward's departments. There was no easy mixing between the departments and tensions would often exist between the deck and engineering departments.

A rigid hierarchical structure existed on board and a man's status was determined by his age, position on board, seniority, professional qualifications and experience. Senior officers would be very conscious of their position and would find it difficult to fraternise with their subordinates. Any demotion, for whatever reason, could provoke resentment and friction.

The British masters and mates of the early twentieth century belonged to a very proud, very conservative and very skilled profession. They tended to come from middle-class families of modest wealth. Although they might live anywhere, the majority tended to come either from the major ports such as Glasgow, Liverpool, Cardiff, London and Newcastle, or from the coastal districts where the impact of the sea was most felt. Many set their sights on a sea-going career from an early age, and a high percentage came from families where seafaring was already a tradition.

Having decided to go to sea a young man would serve a four-year apprenticeship, known as 'doing his time', in either sail or steam before sitting for his first professional qualification, the Second Mate's Certificate of Competency. Once this had been achieved he would obtain work where he could and, if lucky, sail as a junior mate in the type of ship or trade of his choice. Work at sea, both on deck and aloft under sail, was hard and had to be carried out in every conceivable weather. Practical seamanship involved a deep knowledge of rope, canvas, rigging and masts, together with a profound understanding of the weather in all its moods. Their world focused on the amount of sail being carried, the magnetic compass with its various errors, the sextant and the chronometer, the lead line, a sharp lookout, and the natural world around them. Discipline could be very tough indeed and was often meted out with physical abuse.

Two further qualifications were needed to progress beyond

the most junior ranks, the Mate's Certificate and the Master's. The most dedicated and accomplished could, if they so wished, go one step further and sit for the highest professional qualification open to them, the Extra Master's. They would then slowly work their way up the seniority ladder until they achieved command.

The captain, as 'Master under God', was ultimately responsible for everything that happened on board, and exercised total authority over both crew and passengers. With voyages lasting for weeks, months and sometimes a year or two, many became very used to the unfettered powers they possessed and some would abuse it. The best could be very good indeed, were fine seamen and took their responsibilities seriously. The bad might take unnecessary risks, push their ships too hard and treat their mates, apprentices and crew with disdain. But good or bad, there was very little anybody could do about it and the only criteria by which they could be judged were how quickly and cheaply they delivered their cargoes to the port of discharge, and how popular they might be with their passengers.

A common feature in almost all ships was the total deference to seniority. Although a master, or a first mate, might be far from popular, they were obeyed instantly and few would dare challenge their orders or decisions. Each officer would, in turn, have his own area of responsibility and would be very reluctant to interfere with anyone else's. Fear of being rebuked or ridiculed was widespread among the less confident junior officers and crew, and many would avoid confrontation by keeping quiet. Many junior officers would leave important or contentious decisions to someone more senior.

No less important in steam-powered merchant ships were the engineer officers, who were drawn more from the industrial heartland of the nation. Many came from the north of England and Scotland, where they had served their apprenticeships in the shipbuilding and repair yards. They would start their careers as sixth, fifth or fourth engineers, obtain certificates of competency and work their way up to become the chief engineer and responsible for all the machinery on board.

The seamen, quartermasters, firemen, trimmers, greasers, cooks and stewards who made up the bulk of the crews tended to come from or near the great seaports. Known by many ashore as 'common sailors', they were often drawn from communities where poverty was commonplace, where good and nutritious food was hard to come by and where sanitary facilities were basic. Their income was far from reliable. They received a wage while signed on, but pay ceased at the end of a voyage. While some would be career seafarers, many would be casual labour seeking work. Some sectors of the maritime working class were attracted to the more regular schedules of passenger ships employed on the long-distance routes to North America, South America, South Africa, India, the Far East, Australia and New Zealand. Those so employed would often live in or near the great seaports of London, Liverpool and Southampton.

The deck crew were responsible for a range of tasks including keeping a lookout at sea, steering the ship, cleaning duties and maintaining both rigging and the ship's boats. They would tend the mooring lines when entering and leaving harbour and keep sentry duties in harbour. The engineering crew was responsible for the operation and maintenance of both mechanical and electrical machinery. Their world below decks was one of rotating pistons, escaping steam, coal and coal dust, ash and clinker, oil, constant noise and an all-enveloping heat of 38 °C or more. It was also where the most humble members of the crew worked: the trimmers, whose job it was to ensure that coal was evenly spread in the bunkers and was delivered to where the firemen needed it to stoke the boilers. Their work was the dirtiest, hottest, hardest and worst-paid job on board.

The third, and in a passenger ship the largest, department was the purser's or steward's. Responsible for food, catering and the care of both crew and passengers, many who worked here would be loyal servants of a shipping company, and it was the only department that offered seagoing employment for women. The trades involved included chefs, cabin and dining-room stewards, lift operators, bell boys and individuals devoted to the specialist needs of passengers. It was the only department that had any direct dealing with the travelling public. Steps were taken to ensure that, as far as possible, seamen and firemen would never mix with passengers. In a ship the size of *Titanic* they would have separate accommodation and separate access to it, so as to not interfere in any way with spaces allocated to any class of passenger.

In an entirely separate category, and treated very differently, were the wireless operators. They were neither ship's officers nor ratings but employed by the telegraph company that provided the wireless telegraphy equipment fitted in the ship. Although they would work in the close proximity with the watchkeeping deck officers, they rarely mixed socially and, in some ships, would eat separately. They might not even know the names of the deck officers who kept watches only metres away.

Crews would sign on the ship's articles just before sailing, and many would not expect to see their families again for many months and even years. The voyages, especially in tramp steamers on no fixed schedule, could last for months and even a year or two. Pay was never very good, and in the event of shipwreck it would be stopped the moment the ship went down.

Titanic's navigating officers

It was customary for all navigating officers in the larger White Star Line ships to hold either a Master's or Extra Master's Certificate of Competency and to have gained their experience in ships of other companies. All *Titanic*'s officers had done 'their time' in sail and some had served as a junior mate in one or more sailing ships before transferring to the slightly greater comfort of the steamship world. The skills and experience they brought with them to the exacting standards of a passenger-carrying mail ship on the North Atlantic run would have stood them in very good stead.

To give a flavour of the knowledge required of the most junior grade of officer, the second mate, the following is an extract from the syllabus needed to qualify in both navigation and seamanship.

Second Mate – Examination in Navigation

(a) To write a legible hand and spell correctly.

(b) To write a short definition of various astronomical and other terms and to draw a rough sketch or diagram to illustrate their meaning.

(c) To show a competent knowledge of the first five rules of arithmetic and the use of logarithms.

(d) To work a day's work complete, correcting the courses for leeway, deviation and variation.

(e) To find the latitude by the meridian altitude of the sun.

(f) To work any practical problem in parallel sailing.

(g) To find the true course and distance from one given position to another by Mercator's method: also the compass course, the variation and deviation being given.

(h) To find the time of high water at a given port.

(i) To find the true amplitude of the sun and the error of the compass therefrom: also the deviation and the variation being given.

(j) To find the longitude by chronometer from altitude of the sun by the usual methods, computing the daily rate of chronometer from errors observed when required; also to find the true azimuth of the sun, and the error of the compass; and the deviation and variation being given.

(k) To find the true azimuth of the sun by the 'Time Azimuth' tables; the error of the compass; also the deviation, the variation being given.

(l) To find on either a 'true' or 'magnetic' chart the course to steer and the distance from one given position to another; to find the ship's position on the chart from cross-bearings of two objects; from two bearings on the same object, the course and distance run between taking the bearings being given; also the distance of the ship from the object at the time of taking the second bearing.

The Candidate will be required to answer *viva voce* [i.e., oral] questions on the following subjects:

(m) The use and adjustment of the sextant, read off and on the arc, and the mode of finding the index error by both horizon and sun.

(n) The International Code of Signals.

(o) The construction, use, and principle of the barometer, thermometer and hydrometer.

Second Mate – Examination in Seamanship

The candidate must understand and give satisfactory answers on the following subjects:

(a) The standing and running rigging of ships.

(b) Bending, unbending, setting, reefing, taking in, and furling sail.

(c) Sending masts and yards up and down.

(e) Management of a steamship when under canvas.

(f) Management of a ship's boat in heavy weather.

(g) Dunnaging and stowage of cargo, &c.

(h) The Rules of the Road as regards both steamers and sailing vessels, their regulation lights and fog and sound signals.

(i) Signals of distress, and signals to be made by ships wanting a pilot, and the liabilities and penalties incurred by the misuse of these signals.

(j) The marking and use of the lead and log lines.

(k) The construction, use, and action of the sluices, and of the water-ballast tanks.

(l) Engine-room telegraph &c.

(m) Use and management of the rocket apparatus in the event of a vessel being stranded.

(n) Any other question of a like nature appertaining to the duties of a steamship which the Examiner may think necessary to ask.

The syllabus and prerequisites for both the mate's and master's certificate were broadly similar but demanded a much greater degree of knowledge. A mate, furthermore, had to be at least 19 years old and have served at sea for five years before he could sit for the exam, while a candidate for a master's certificate had to be aged over 21. He was also required to have either served for 'six years at sea, of which one year must have been in a capacity not lower than Only Mate, or six and a half years at sea of which one must have been in a capacity not lower than Second Mate of a foreign-going vessel.'

Those unfamiliar with the terminology in the syllabus will probably deduce that much attention was given to navigation out of sight of land and to handling traditionally rigged ships. Those sitting the examinations would rely very heavily on their practical experience when responding to questions put to them. In the light of what happened when *Titanic* foundered it will be noted that many features of her last voyage and in the period between colliding with the iceberg and the survivors being picked up by the *Carpathia* were covered in some form, but it will also be noted that other areas of professional skill were not covered at all. This does not imply that the officers concerned were ignorant of them, but it does suggest that some topics were not thought worthy of inclusion or relevant.

Marine accidents and their investigation

The mariner's traditional reaction to an accident at sea is 'There but for the grace of God go I,' followed rapidly by the unspoken, and more thoughtful, question, 'How on earth did that happen?'

For centuries the most common reaction was to accept shipwrecks as inevitable, the price to be paid for defying the elements. Very few concerted attempts were ever made to benefit from such losses, and it was not until the nineteenth century that any attempt was made to see what lessons could be learned.

The industrial revolution of the nineteenth century saw not only rapid growth in the shipping industry but a worrying increase in the number of shipwrecks. By 1836 the British parliament was sufficiently concerned to set up a select committee to inquire into their causes. Seven years later, it recommended that any investigation should not only warn masters and owners about any specific shortcoming but also 'stimulate and suggest the exercise of preventative measures for the avoidance of future casualties.'

The Merchant Shipping Act of 1894 included a provision for investigating serious accidents and directed that a wreck commissioner be appointed under the Act to investigate the circumstance of the casualty and to make a report to the Board of Trade.

The loss of the *Titanic* was investigated under the provisions of the 1894 Act, and within eight days of the accident the Lord Chancellor appointed a Wreck Commissioner, Lord Mersey, to conduct an inquiry. Three days later the Home Secretary nominated five assessors to assist him, and on 30 April the Board of Trade requested that a Formal Investigation of the circumstances attending the loss of the Steamship *Titanic* should be held. The court first sat on 2 May and began taking evidence from survivors and others on 3 May.

Twenty-six questions about the *Titanic* were submitted by the Board of Trade, and it was the task of the court to answer them. The key conclusion of its report, dated 30 July, was that the loss of the *Titanic* was due to collision with an iceberg, brought about by the excessive speed at which the ship was being navigated.

The British Formal Investigation was not the only one undertaken. Before the Cunard liner *Carpathia* had even arrived in New York with the survivors embarked, the US Senate directed the Committee on Commerce to carry out its own investigation into the loss, and under the chairmanship of Senator William Smith of Michigan, a subcommittee began its work on the day following the arrival of the *Carpathia*.

The Senate subcommittee was authorised to investigate the 'causes leading to the wreck of the White Star liner *Titanic* with its attendant loss of life; empowered to summon witnesses, send for persons and papers, to administer oaths, and to take such testimony as may be necessary to determine the responsibility'. The ultimate aim was to make recommendations for the introduction of 'such legislation as may be necessary to prevent, as far as possible, any repetition of such a disaster'.

The Senate committee produced its report on 28 May 1912 but came to no specific conclusion as to the cause, or causes, of the accident. In his speech to the Senate on 28 May, Senator Smith was, however, very critical of the British Board of Trade for its 'laxity of regulation and hasty inspection'. He went on to comment on the sack of action by SS *Californian*:

> Had assistance been promptly proffered, or had the wireless operator of the *Californian* remained a few minutes longer at his post on Sunday evening, that ship might have had the proud distinction of rescuing the lives of the passengers and crew of the *Titanic*.

Marine accident investigation today

For over a century the most significant British shipwrecks and disasters have indeed been formally investigated, but the system suffered from one serious weakness: the investigations were carried out by, or were commissioned by, precisely the same people who made up the rules.

It is only in recent years that the maritime profession has accepted the need for independent organisations to investigate accidents. It was not until 1989 that the United Kingdom formed an independent Marine Accident Investigation Branch (MAIB). This came about as a direct consequence of a recommendation arising from the inquiry into the 1987 capsize of the cross-channel ferry *Herald of Free Enterprise*. A handful of other nations have also set up similar organisations, but they are in a minority. Even today, despite there being an International Code for the investigation of accidents at sea, some of the main marine administrations resolutely refuse to set up independent investigation bodies. The reasons for this reticence are various, but they range from having too few resources to a reluctance to upset the ship owner, who has no wish to have any shortcomings exposed – and who may choose to register his ships under a flag where accident investigation is shrouded in varying degrees of opaqueness.

A century after the loss of the *Titanic* and the two investigations that followed, an internationally recognised code of practice has been drawn up by the International Maritime Organization (IMO), a United Nations agency based in London. Based on the best practices in marine casualty investigation after many years' experience, it contains much that featured in 1912 and upholds that the prime objective is to prevent marine casualties in the future. It specifically states that any such investigation does not seek to apportion blame or determine liability, and stipulates that it should be separate, and independent, from any other form of investigation.

The Code now in force requires that a marine safety investigation be conducted into any serious marine casualty, defined as one 'involving the total loss of the ship or a death or severe damage to the environment'.

Had the Code been in force in 1912, the loss of the *Titanic* would have constituted a very serious marine accident and, because it occurred on the high seas (in other words outside any nation state's territorial waters), it would have fallen to the

British authorities to investigate it. The actual body investigating the loss would, in turn, have been entirely independent of the regulatory regime – and this would have been one of the most significant differences between what occurred in 1912 and what would have happened today. In 1912, the Formal Investigation was ordered by the President of the Board of Trade but was totally independent of it. Any suggestion that it was a Board of Trade inquiry is erroneous, but a feature of the *Titanic* Formal Investigation was that the court was obliged to answer 26 specific questions put to it by the same Board. This had a very strong influence on the way the investigation was conducted and ensured that some crucial questions were inadequately addressed. Today's marine accident investigation organisation would have been totally free to form its own questions in order to identify the full range of causes. Had, say, the UK's Marine Accident Investigation Branch been charged with investigating the loss of the *Titanic*, it might have replaced the Board of Trade's list of 26 questions with just two of its own:

• Why did the *Titanic* hit an iceberg?

• Why did so many people lose their lives?

The questions might seem deceptively simple, but they were not asked by either investigation in 1912.

Numbers embarked

A curious factor about accident investigation is the difficulty, sometimes, of assessing how many people were actually embarked. This can occur in vessels carrying passengers of different nationalities. What should, in theory, be a straightforward process can turn out to be extraordinarily difficult.

The reasons are numerous but can vary from a failure to record exactly who was on board when a vessel sailed, to the way a list of survivors was compiled. If lists are drawn up by different authorities but reach different conclusions as to the identities and numbers of those involved, which one do you accept? A passenger might have his or her name on a manifesto but then fail to embark for some reason. There are others who feel the need to conceal their true identities and sail under false names. Unravelling their true identity should they fail to survive can prove troublesome, and doubts begin to emerge as to whether they were on board in the first place. Clerks can record people's names in different ways or spellings so that when it comes to compiling a list of victims in the aftermath of a tragedy the individual is recorded twice. The names of infants can be omitted altogether. The conventions of address can vary widely, especially among those who live in lands where family and given names follow different styles, yet the person recording them may attempt to follow the convention he is familiar with and make a mistake. A member of the crew can fail to join at the last moment, or desert, and the fact may not be properly recorded.

No matter what the reason, establishing who was on board a ship where there is great loss of life can tax the most assiduous researcher. The *Titanic* was no exception. Read any account of her loss and you rarely find agreement as to how many people sailed in her, were picked up or survived. Few people have conducted in-depth research from primary sources, and those who have done so readily recognise the complexities involved. This book is no better and, after much agonising, I have adopted the figures reached by those conducting the original inquiries, but accept that they are, almost certainly, wrong.

The human factor

It is often said that 80 per cent of marine accidents are caused by 'human error'. I would prefer to reword the statement to observe that the human 'factor' plays a large part in nearly everything that goes wrong at sea. Without attempting to put a percentage figure on it, I would go further and say that the industry's failure to really understand what is meant by the human factor lies at the heart of many of the accidents we still see today. In my opinion, our compulsion to blame people for 'mistakes' makes very little contribution to improving safety at sea.

The words 'human error' are much loved by those seeking to apportion blame, including the media, but are an oversimplification of something much more fundamental and usually only evident with hindsight. The reality is that slips, lapses, the taking of short cuts, misjudgements and bad decisions are a reality and we are all guilty of making them to a greater or lesser extent. More often than not no harm is done. Human behaviour is influenced by a range of circumstances including fatigue, diet, background lighting, humidity, the weather, sea state, prescribed medication and stress. Even the common cold can have a devastating effect on performance. Few things, however, determine human behaviour more than the custom and culture of the workplace. Individuals slip into questionable patterns of behaviour over time and then come to accept their actions as perfectly acceptable – until an accident or some other external scrutiny forcefully reminds them that what they are doing is wrong.

Whenever a mariner makes a mistake, there is always a reason for it. While it is very easy to conclude that the individual was lazy, incompetent or even negligent, such judgements are invariably too simplistic. The tendency to focus on those closest to the event means that the important underlying reasons are never properly explored. So often a bad regulation, sloppy or indifferent management ashore, poor ergonomics, or practices that have been allowed to fester over many years lie at the heart of so much that goes wrong at sea. They may only be contributory factors but, unless identified and reported, they lie dormant and are very likely to underpin the next accident.

Identifying relevant human factors can make fundamental differences to how seafarers are selected, trained, encouraged and motivated. The ergonomics of the workplace are highly relevant to how people perform at sea. If a seafarer responds erroneously to a badly designed display or control panel, the fault may well lie with the system, not the operator. If an example of bad practice is uncovered it may well be due to a lack of supervision, an absence of any training, bad management or a prescribed procedure that is so cumbersome that operators have been bypassing its provisions for years and getting away with it. The lack of standardised equipment on board a ship is often found to underlie 'mistakes'.

The seafarer is subject to a number of variables in his or her performance and requires four basic commodities to survive: food, water, heat and oxygen. Deficiencies in any one will adversely affect performance. He has the ability to absorb information from a number of sources. He can sense sound, smell, movement, touch, temperature and taste, and his eyes, given adequate light, will see things. But there are limits to his ability to process the data. The maximum number of inputs someone can absorb at once with training is, in an ideal setting, about seven. This diminishes significantly at times of stress or if many things are happening at once. In an emergency the average person is rarely able to absorb more than one or two inputs at the same time. Few systems on board a ship allow for this. Someone trained to work under stress is infinitely more capable of handling such situations.

Those working at sea have to work in a wide range of conditions and at any time of the day or night. The working environment embraces heat, light, humidity, noise and light levels. People's performance can be adversely affected when conducted outside normal tolerances. If this is not allowed for, they will not respond as well as they might. The level of activity also has an impact, and boredom can have just as much of an adverse effect as working in a stressful environment. Physiological and clinical factors such as poor health, drugs (both prescribed and illegal), injury, pain, mental health and fitness will all affect performance.

The cultural background of crew members can be a factor in marine accidents, as can deference and subservience. A domineering personality can deter effective team work.

Subordinates may well hold back from making a useful contribution for fear of being ridiculed, bullied or criticised. And yet so often these same people can see things that the other has not.

Fatigue at sea has always existed and comes in two forms, physical and mental. Physical fatigue stems from constant hard work such as handling sails aloft, heaving on ropes on deck, trimming coal or just keeping one's feet in a ship tossing about in heavy seas.

Mental fatigue on the other hand is caused by lack of sleep and disruptions to the circadian rhythm. Its effects are insidious and can be far, far worse than, say, the excessive consumption of alcohol, which can always be subjected to varying degrees of control. Whilst is possible to forego alcohol, even the most draconian prohibition cannot prevent fatigue once it takes hold. Performance falls off, concentration vanishes, coordination goes, memory fades and even the simplest task becomes more difficult. Someone who has been up all night repairing defective equipment will not, unless he has had an opportunity to catch up on sleep, perform so well the next day. Chronic fatigue is endemic in some ships.

Language can be an issue. English is the international language of the sea but many crews include individuals whose first language is not English. This is unlikely to be a problem until an emergency arises, when almost everyone will revert to their native tongue. The only foreigners among *Titanic*'s crew were the, mainly, contracted French staff working in the first-class A La Carte restaurant and Café Parisien. None survived.

By carefully analysing human behaviour it is usually possible to devise measures to prevent whatever went wrong from happening again. Solutions come in many forms, from redesigning equipment to changing the method of training. New regulations can, if carefully thought through, lead to long-lasting improvements, but too many catch-all rules become self-defeating when their very complexity forces mariners to take short cuts. Very often the solution to preventing mistakes by humans is to engineer the process out, to redesign the tools or equipment being used. Punishing someone for making a mistake does little to cure the problem.

So often in the past the need to pin the blame on one person completely overlooks the real reasons why things go wrong. Sometimes the real reason can remain unnoticed for many, many years.

Expressed in very simple terms, the loss of the *Titanic* was a textbook example of how accidents are caused – and, from start to finish, the human factor was a feature.

THE LOSS OF
RMS *TITANIC*

A REPORT

FOLLOWING A FRESH LOOK
AT THE EVIDENCE

30 July 2012

RMS *Titanic* - Departing Southampton 10 April 1912

Introduction

This report is divided into three sections. The first records the factual findings of the investigation and makes no attempt to analyse why actions were taken or decisions made.

It draws heavily on the transcripts of the testimonies given at both the US Senate Inquiry and the British Formal Investigation. Additional information has been obtained from other sources including the accounts written by survivors after the accident. I have also used some information that was not available to the original inquiry such as material linked to the discovery of the wreck in 1985 and the inspections made of it since. Knowledge of the wreck's precise position has been crucial in unravelling some of the issues in connection with the *Californian.*

No attempt has been made to replicate the technical detail that featured in the original Formal Investigation report published on 30 July 1912, and the content has been limited to the main features of the accident.

Part two analyses the evidence with a view to establishing why the accident happened, while the third section draws conclusions as to the many causes including the single initiating cause and the three key reasons why *Titanic* hit an iceberg, why she sank and why there was such grievous loss of life.

Although this 'report' has been presented in the style and format of one produced today, liberties have been taken with the language used. Whilst I have unashamedly used nautical terminology for large parts of the text, I have modified it where necessary to help the general reader. Accident reports do not contain an index, and none is provided. A glossary of terms has been added at the end of the book.

PART I

Factual information

Particulars of ship

Name:	*Titanic*
Official number:	131428
Owners:	Oceanic Steam Navigation Co. Ltd (The White Star Line)
Type of ship:	Triple-screw passenger steamer and emigrant ship
Flag:	British
Port of Registry:	Liverpool
Place of build:	Harland and Wolff, Belfast
Construction:	Steel
Date keel laid down:	31 March 1909
Date launched:	31 May 1911
Date accepted into service:	2 April 1912
Signal letters:	HVMP
Wireless call sign:	MGY
Gross tonnage (grt):	46,328.57 tons gross
Net registered tons:	21,831 net registered tons
Length overall:	852 ft 6 ins

Breadth:	92 ft 6 ins
Draught:	34 ft 7 ins
Propulsion:	Two sets of four-cylinder 15,000 hp reciprocating engines and a single 16,000 hp turbine fed by steam from 29 coal-fired boilers
Registered horse power:	50,000
Bunker capacity:	6611 tons of coal
Normal speed:	21 knots
Maximum speed:	23–24 knots
Crew:	885
Passenger capacity:	2603
Total capacity:	3547
Souls embarked:	2201 (885 crew and 1316 passengers) on departure Queenstown[1]
Type of accident:	Collision with an iceberg followed by foundering
Date and time of accident:	14 April 1912, 2340
Accident location:	Position as reported in 1912: 41° 46'N, 50° 14'W
Position of wreck found in 1985:	41° 43'N, 49° 56'W
Survivors:	711[1]
Fatalities:	1490[1]

---

1 The number of souls actually embarked on board the *Titanic* at the time of the accident has, for a number of reasons, never been accurately assessed. The numbers given in this report match those stated in the original Formal Investigation report published in 1912.

Time

The time used in this report is generally *Titanic* ship's time. The master clock for ship's time was kept in the chartroom and there were 48 other clocks keeping it throughout the ship.

Where appropriate, Greenwich Mean Time (GMT) or New York Time is given when referring to the transmission or reception times of wireless messages. GMT was kept by two chronometers in the chartroom, and the clocks in the Marconi room were set to GMT and New York Time.

The times used on board both the *Californian* and *Carpathia* are ship's time. In both cases the differences between their ships' times and that kept on board *Titanic* are relatively small. The differences are insignificant.

Narrative of events

The second ship in the White Star Line *Olympic* class was the 46,328 grt *Titanic*. She was laid down at Messrs Harland & Wolff's shipbuilding yard at Belfast on 31 March 1909 and launched at 1215 on Wednesday 31 May 1911. It had originally been intended that she should commence her maiden voyage from Southampton on 20 March 1912 but, following an accident involving her sister ship the *Olympic*, the date was postponed. Whilst outward bound from Southampton on 11 September 1911 she had collided with the Royal Navy cruiser HMS *Hawke* in the Solent and had to return to Belfast for repairs. She remained there for nearly six weeks during which time a number of the workers needed to make good the damage had to be transferred from the *Titanic*. This interfered with *Titanic*'s fitting out, delayed her departure from Belfast and led to the postponement of her maiden voyage from Southampton to 10 April. *Olympic* made one further return to Harland & Wolff for a few days in early March 1912 to replace a damaged propeller. Although this did not delay *Titanic* any further, it meant that there were more than the normal last-minute fitting-out tasks to be undertaken both in Belfast and later in Southampton. Her planned date of sailing from Belfast was 1 April.

The master initially appointed to command *Titanic* was Captain H J Haddock, who signed ship's articles on 25 March. For unknown reasons the White Star Line chose to relieve him almost immediately in order that he could succeed Captain E J Smith as captain of the *Olympic* for her sailing to New York on 3 April. Once he had been relieved, Captain Smith travelled to Belfast and assumed command of *Titanic* on the day she was due to start sea trials, 1 April. The ship's deck officers meanwhile had been joining *Titanic* during the last two weeks in March. On 29 March the passage crew for both trials and the passage to Southampton signed on. Prior to sailing from Belfast a form of emergency drill was undertaken, and this included laying out the fire-fighting hoses.

In the event, high winds delayed the departure for 24 hours and *Titanic* eventually left the builders' yard at 1000 on 2 April for one day's sea trials in Belfast Lough and the North Channel. They had been scheduled to commence at 1000, and by 2000 she departed Belfast Lough for Southampton. Her trials lasted less than ten hours.

The passage to Southampton was, apart from encountering fog in the Irish Sea in the early hours of 3 April, uneventful and made at speeds of between 18 and 20 knots. For a short spell a higher speed was reached. During the passage the Marconi operators continued to test their equipment and managed to work with stations as far away as Tenerife (2000 miles) and Port Said (over 3000 miles.)

Titanic's arrival time at Southampton was planned to coincide with high water, and she made her approach to her berth shortly before midnight. Tended by tugs, she was swung to lie bows south and port side to at Berth No. 44 shortly afterwards.

From the moment of her arrival at Southampton until her departure at midday on 10 April a range of activities took place including the completion of a heeling test to determine stability characteristics. The finishing touches to the fitting-out process were completed, she was stored with victuals, food and wine, naval stores were embarked and nearly 6000 tons of coal was loaded into her fuel bunkers. She took on fresh water. Her crew was assembled, although some did not join until the day of sailing. Cargo and mail were embarked, as was passengers' baggage.

On the day of sailing the crew were mustered before a doctor, and during the morning the Board of Trade's immigration officer, Captain Maurice Clarke, oversaw the crew muster and satisfied himself that two of the ship's lifeboats (Nos. 11 and 15) could be manned and lowered satisfactorily. During the forenoon she embarked her passengers and their baggage, and shortly before noon her senior officers reported their departments were ready for sea. The Report of Survey of an Emigrant Ship was produced and signed by the Board of Trade surveyor, Captain Clarke, and the Master's Report to the Company was also signed and handed to the White Star Line's marine superintendent.

The last member of the crew joined the ship about 10 minutes before the last lines were let go.

Titanic slipped and, tended by tugs, proceeded at 1200. Leaving her berth she had to make her way slowly south past a number of other occupied berths before turning slightly to port and the wider expanse of Southampton Water. As she gathered headway, the water displaced by her movement had to be replaced. The sudden surge created was felt by the White Star liner *Oceanic* and the Inman liner *New York* moored alongside. The water movement, both laterally and vertically, resulted in excessive strain coming on the *New York*'s mooring lines. They tensioned and then snapped with a loud report to leave the ship drifting into the path of the outbound *Titanic*. Way was immediately taken off using astern power, and a tug managed to get a line on board the *New York* to pull her clear. Once this had been done and she had been re-secured in another berth, *Titanic* was able to resume her passage to sea.

The incident delayed her departure by about an hour.

The pilot disembarked at the eastern end of the Isle of Wight in the vicinity of the Nab light vessel. *Titanic* then shaped a course for the entrance to the Port of Cherbourg in Northern France, some 67 miles distant. With the shafts turning at 60 rpm once full away, her average speed on this short leg was just below 19 knots. The conditions were good and the passage was uneventful. She anchored in Cherbourg's outer harbour at about 1830. Using two tenders to transfer passengers, mail and cargo, she remained at anchor for less than 2 hours. 22 passengers disembarked and 274 boarded. She weighed anchor at 2010 and proceeded out of harbour for the overnight passage down channel and thence to Queenstown in southern Ireland.

During the morning of 11 April an emergency drill was conducted. This did not include lifeboats but the alarm bells were sounded and the watertight doors closed. During the forenoon some simple manoeuvring trials were conducted involving putting the rudder hard one way and then hard the other to fully test the steering gear. The compasses were compared at the same time

The pilot for Cobh Harbour was picked up off the entrance by the Daunt Rock light vessel shortly before 1130 and, soon afterwards, *Titanic* let go her starboard anchor. As in Cherbourg, two tenders transported mail, baggage and passengers to the anchored ship. 120 passengers joined and 1385 bags of mail were embarked. Prior to getting under way the Report of Survey was signed by the local Emigration officer. Among other things this certified that *Titanic* was carrying the correct number of lifesaving appliances. Anchor was weighed at 1330 and *Titanic* headed for the open sea. The ocean passage began as she passed the Daunt Rock light vessel. The weather was fair and the sea slight as she turned to head west for her maiden crossing of the North Atlantic. The number of people as being on board on sailing was 2208.

Having taken her departure off the Fastnet light, *Titanic*

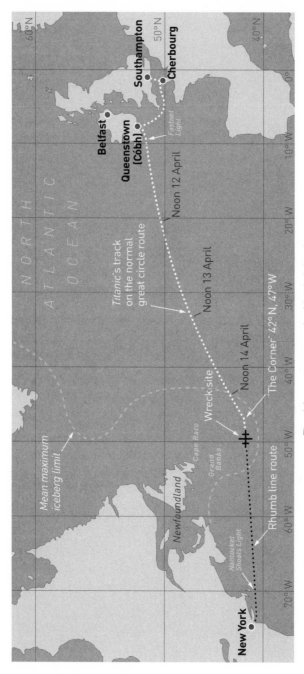

Titanic's route across the North Atlantic

followed a conventional great circle track across the Atlantic to a position some distance southeast of Newfoundland, 42° N, 47° W with her shafts turning at 70 rpm. Propeller revolutions were increased to 72 rpm on, probably, 12 April. The weather on passage was good, the ship performed well and speed was increased very gradually each day.

Between departure from Queenstown on 11 April and the evening of Sunday 14 April a number of wireless messages with ice warnings were received. Some, but not all, were noted.

Titanic was due to alter course to the west on reaching what was referred to as the 'Turning Point' at 1700 on 14 April. In the event this alteration was delayed by 50 minutes to a new course of S 86° W (true).

The second officer took over the bridge watch at 1800. The sun set at 1840 and, as darkness fell, the sea remained flat calm, there was no wind, the skies were clear and there was no moon. The air temperature was falling and the visibility was excellent. The second officer was briefly relieved at 1900 by the first officer for his evening meal and, with the onset of darkness, the lamp trimmer was ordered to shut the fo'c'sle hatch to prevent light emerging from it to ensure perfect darkness to aid the keeping of a good lookout on a dark night. The second officer returned to the bridge in time to take stellar observations at 1930 but handed over their calculations to the third officer to work out. These were completed by the fourth officer after he came on watch at 2000 and the resultant position was later plotted on a chart by the captain.

The two junior deck officers, the quartermasters and the lookouts all changed watch at 2000. It became steadily colder and, shortly afterwards, the carpenter was told to look to his fresh water because there was a likelihood of it freezing. Likewise the engineer responsible for deck equipment was called to open up the heating in the passage of the officers' accommodation, chartroom and wheelhouse.

The second officer was joined on the open bridge at about

Sunday 14 April:
Titanic's track and ice
warning locations

La Touraine reports
icefield, 12 April

Paris reports icefield and iceberg, 12 April

Noordam reports
ice, 14 April

Baltic reports
ice, 14 April

Athenai reports ice, 14 April

Amerika reports
2 icebergs, 14 April

Normal rhumb line,
course S 85° W,
from 'The Corner'
to Nantucket
Shoals Light

Passes 'The Corner'
(the normal turning point)
at 1700 on 14 April

Continues until 1750,
then steers S 86° W

Titanic, 22 knots

NORTH
ATLANTIC
OCEAN

1000

1200

1400

1600

1700

1750

1900

2100

2300

0000

45°N

44°N

43°N

42°N

41°N

45°W

50°W

2055 by the captain, and the two of them discussed the weather, the time they anticipated getting up to the ice, how they would recognise it when they reached it and the importance of slowing down if it became hazy.

The captain left the bridge at about 2120 with instructions to be called at once 'if it becomes at all doubtful'. Soon afterwards the second officer told the sixth officer to call the crow's nest and tell the lookouts to keep a good lookout for small ice and growlers. The message was acknowledged.

At 2200 the second officer was relieved by the first officer, Mr Murdoch, and the helmsmen changed over at the same time.

At a time that has not been determined with any accuracy the two lookouts saw what they described as low-lying haze ahead of them. It was not reported to the bridge but was seen to spread.

Shortly before 2340 both lookouts saw a black mass ahead. As soon as they were able to identify it as an iceberg they alerted the bridge. The officer of the watch reacted by ordering 'hard a starboard' and 'full astern'. He also shut the automatic water-tight doors.

The actions taken were too late and failed to prevent *Titanic* hitting the iceberg on the starboard bow below the waterline and at deck level.

Alerted to a problem, the captain came to the bridge, asked what had happened and called for a report on the extent of the damage. He was informed that water was beginning to flood the forward four watertight compartments. Together with the Harland and Wolff chief designer, Mr Thomas Andrews, he made a visit to the fore part of the ship to see the extent of the damage.

Although the initial impact was hardly felt, and was described as little more than a shudder, it soon became evident that the extent of the damage below the waterline forward was serious. Further assessment revealed that progressive flooding would eventually lead to the ship foundering.

The decision to seek assistance was taken and, 45 minutes after the collision, a distress message was transmitted by wireless. It was followed by many more. These were received ashore at Cape Race, Newfoundland, and by a number of ships within wireless range. None were very close.

Preparations to launch the lifeboats were made, but it became evident from the outset that there were insufficient to evacuate all on board. One by one the lifeboats were launched as *Titanic* began to sink slowly by the head. She listed initially to starboard, returned to an even keel and then listed progressively to port.

Despite a very slowly tilting deck, many passengers found it difficult to accept the ship was in any danger and chose to remain on board rather than take to an open boat on a very cold night. As a result many of the boats launched early in the evacuation process contained far fewer people than they were designed to carry. It also became evident that the officers were unaware of the loading capacity of the lifeboats and that many of the crew were unfamiliar with either launching or handling them. Women and children were, with different interpretations, allocated priority for boarding the lifeboats.

As *Titanic* began to settle, the lights of another steamer were observed ahead of her. Believing this to be a vessel sufficiently close to render urgently needed assistance, *Titanic* attempted to communicate with her by firing rockets. At the same time, attempts were made to contact her using the Morse signalling lamp. There was no apparent response and the other ship, initially thought to be approaching, slowly seemed to turn away.

Titanic meanwhile settled ever deeper in the water and the urgency to get people away increased. What had hitherto been a reasonably ordered process steadily deteriorated. Families became separated, and a sense of helplessness descended on those remaining on board when it became evident that there was no other means of getting away safely. Soon after 0200 *Titanic*'s bow-down angle began to increase and, within minutes, her stern started to lift out of the water. As the water surged along the decks, people were swept into the sea. The lights went out and, shortly before she finally sank, she broke into two halves.

Given the extreme cold, only a few of those who went into the water survived and, once the cries of the victims had subsided, silence prevailed. She foundered at 0220.

The 700 or so survivors in the lifeboats remained in the vicinity of where *Titanic* had gone down and were found by the Cunard liner *Carpathia* shortly before dawn. The *Carpathia* had been on passage from New York to the Mediterranean and was some 60 miles away when she intercepted *Titanic*'s distress message at 0035 (*Carpathia* time: 2245 New York time). She altered course immediately towards the position given and increased speed. In a well-conducted rescue operation she recovered all those embarked in the lifeboats. It was obvious from the outset, however, that a great many people had not survived, and it was assessed that about 1500 people had lost their lives when *Titanic* foundered.

The second ship to arrive at the scene on the morning of 15 April was the Leyland liner *Californian*, but she was too late to recover anyone. She had been making a westbound crossing of the Atlantic but, on sighting ice the previous evening, had stopped with steam up and waited until daylight before proceeding. Her sole wireless operator, having been on duty for most of the day, had turned in prior to *Titanic* transmitting her distress message.

Whilst lying stopped, *Californian* had swung very slowly in a clockwise direction. Soon after about 2230 her officer of the watch saw another ship approach from the east and pass some miles to the south of her, stop, turn away and fire white rockets. Attempts to communicate with this unknown ship were unsuccessful. *Californian*'s officer of the watch then saw this vessel slowly disappear and assumed she had got under way again to continue her westward passage. He reported these events to the master sleeping below. The next morning *Californian*'s wireless operator resumed his duties to discover that *Titanic* had sunk during the night. Once the position of the sinking had been established, *Californian* got under way towards the ice barrier and, making the best speed she could, made for the position given. Finding no sign of any wreckage or any other indications of a disaster, she headed eastwards through the ice barrier towards where the *Carpathia* was recovering the last of the survivors. The *Californian* continued searching for a few more hours but, finding nothing of significance, resumed her passage to Boston.

The *Carpathia*, meanwhile, with the survivors on board, returned to New York to disembark them and arrived alongside shortly after 2130 on 18 April.

Construction, equipment and certification

Titanic was a three-screw steam ship of 46,328 grt built by Harland and Wolff of Belfast for the White Star Line to carry passengers across the Atlantic. She was registered as a British vessel at the port of Liverpool and classed as an emigrant ship.

She was propelled by two sets of four-cylinder reciprocating engines each driving a three-bladed propeller either side of the centre line, and a low-pressure turbine driving a centre-line propeller with four blades. She was registered as having 50,000 shaft horse power. There were six boiler rooms.

Her outer hull was constructed on a flat keel plate 3 inches (7.5 cm) thick and double bottom 5 feet 3 inches (1.6 metres) deep. Projecting outwards from the centre steel girder were tank-top floor plates. Running parallel to the keel were four longitudinal girders on either side. Rising up from the double bottom were 300 frames between 2 and 3 feet (60–90 cm) apart, 66 feet (20 metres) high and terminating at B deck. They were covered with some 2000 plates of rolled steel measuring 6 feet (1.8 metres) from top to bottom and 30 feet (9 metres) wide. They were between 1 and 1½ inches (25–38 mm) thick and weighed between 2½ and 3 tons each. There was also a watertight inner bottom.

Titanic had nine steel decks internally. The uppermost deck was the boat deck with a length of about 500 feet (152 metres). The lowest was the orlop deck, which was divided into two sections, one forward of the boiler rooms and the other aft of the engine room. The boat deck and A deck contained extension joints which broke the strength continuity. Decks C, D, E and F were continuous from end to end. None of the decks was watertight except the weather deck and the aft part of the orlop deck. All decks had large openings or hatchways through which water could pass with ease.

There were 15 vertical watertight bulkheads dividing the ship into sixteen compartments. She was designed to survive a head-on collision, a side impact penetrating two adjacent watertight compartments or damage to the bottom of the hull. The two foremost and the aftermost watertight bulkheads had no openings in them at all. All the others did. Bulkhead C was penetrated by the fireman's passageway and was fitted with an automatically operated watertight door. Bulkheads D to O inclusive also had automatic vertical sliding doors at the engine and boiler-room floor level. Watertight passages through the bunkers provided a link between the boiler rooms. The bulkhead watertight doors were offset to the aft end of each passageway. There were no watertight doors at any watertight bulkhead on G deck. On both E and F deck nearly all bulkheads had horizontal watertight doors to allow communication between the various accommodation blocks. These doors were operated manually at the door or from the deck above.

The automatic watertight doors were operated in one of three ways: from the bridge by a lever that broke an electric circuit to allow the doors to shut through gravity, by a locally operated lever or, in the event of flooding, by a float that would lift and close the doors automatically. An escape ladder was provided in each of the engine or boiler-room compartments to enable anyone trapped inside to escape. Alarm bells would also ring once the automatic closure process had been initiated.

The two main through-passageways for crew and third-class passengers were situated on E deck. The forward end of these passageways was a cross-passageway linking one side of the ship with the other and leading to large gangway doors for use by third-class passengers and members of the crew. Leading aft from this cross-passageway on the port side was the main thoroughfare for use by both crew and third-class passengers. This was 8$^{1}/_{2}$ feet (2.6 metres) wide and was known as the 'working passage' or, more colloquially, as 'Scotland Road'. It provided access to crew accommodation, the engine rooms and boiler rooms.

Running parallel to this main thoroughfare was a much narrower passage on the starboard side for use by third-class passengers. It linked the forward third-class accommodation with the aft.

Boilers and propulsion

Steam for the two forms of propulsion was provided by the boilers in the six boiler rooms numbered 1 to 6 with No. 1, the smallest, being the furthest aft. Coal was stored in the bunkers situated on either side of the bulkheads that separated the individual boiler rooms.

Titanic was provided with 24 double-ended boilers and five single-ended boilers to produce steam at 215 psi. The single-ended boilers were normally used to provide steam when the ship was in harbour and for domestic purposes at sea. Uptakes from the boilers taking smoke and waste gases fed the three foremost funnels. Two boilers in each of boiler rooms No. 2 and No. 3 provided steam to the auxiliary equipment such as the auxiliary machinery and electric light plants. Two main steam pipes led from the boiler rooms to the engine room, with shut-off valves at three of the bulkheads. In addition a quick-acting emergency safety valve was fitted on each of the two main steam pipes, to be used in the event of a pipe rupturing and having to be shut down in an emergency.

The main propulsion was provided by two sets of reciprocating engines driving a single shaft each and a low-pressure turbine coupled directly to a single shaft positioned on the centre line and only capable of propelling ahead. The reciprocating engines were four-crank triple expansion type and capable of turning the shafts at over 80 rpm. The maximum number of revolutions was never, in the event, established. Each engine was reversed by a direct-acting steam and hydraulic engine with a steam-driven high-pressure pump fitted for operating either, or both, the reversing engines as a back-up.

The low-pressure exhaust steam turbine was situated in a separate compartment aft of the engine room. Because it could only propel ahead it was not used while the ship was being manoeuvred in harbour. When at full speed the $16^{1}/_{2}$-foot (5-metre) propeller could turn at 165 rpm.

Steam at 185 psi was also provided to the four 400 kW electrical generating engines in the turbine engine room at the aft end of the vessel. This compartment would have been the last to flood before the ship finally sank.

In addition two additional 30 kW engines were situated in a recess on D deck and could provide electricity in emergency.

Bunkers and ash

Titanic's bunker fuel was coal. The bunker capacity was 6611 tons but additional coal could be carried to a maximum of about 8000 tons. On the day she sailed she carried 5892 tons of coal – sufficient to carry her to New York, where she would embark further bunkers for the return voyage.

In the days leading up to the commencement of her maiden voyage a coal strike in England was having a major impact on shipping seeking bunkers before sailing. The shortages were such that several ships had to suspend sailing for want of coal. In Southampton alone a number of ships were temporarily laid up until such time as the situation had been resolved. In the event the strike was resolved by 6 April, but because of the need to meet the date of her scheduled departure it had been necessary to obtain bunkers from a range of unconventional sources including that already loaded into other ships lying alongside.

Coal was consumed at a rate of about 650 tons per day. It was loaded via 20 chutes on the side of the ship at F deck direct to the bunkers between the boiler rooms. Coal would be loaded before passengers embarked as the time required to clean the ship of coal dust could be extensive. Equal effort was required to trim the coal in the bunkers to ensure it was evenly spread and to prevent it shifting once at sea. The task fell to the trimmers, whose job was probably the dirtiest, most physically demanding and least pleasant of all on board.

Coal would be taken from the bunkers to the stokeholds by the trimmers, emptied onto the steel plates and fed to the furnaces by firemen whose work was both skilled and never-ending.

Burned fuel would accumulate as ash and had to be removed. Raked from the ash pits below the furnaces, it would be carried in a barrow to a device known as an ash ejector in each of the boiler rooms except No. 1. The ash would be dumped into a hopper where it would be carried by a water jet up an incline and then ejected well clear of the ship's side above the waterline.

Steering

Titanic had three steering positions, two on the bridge and one aft on the docking bridge. The forward steering position was on the open bridge abaft the bridge windows on the centre line and was used by quartermasters when entering and leaving harbour. The main steering position at sea was in the enclosed wheelhouse immediately behind the open bridge. The aft steering position was provided for use in an emergency.

There were two steam-driven triple-cylinder steering engines situated on C deck aft of the third-class general room and connected to the rudder stock. Both steering engines could operate independently, and under normal circumstances only one would be in use, with the other remaining on standby.

Bilge and ballast pumps

Titanic was fitted with five ballast and bilge pumps, each capable of discharging 250 tons of water per hour, and three bilge pumps of 150 tons per hour. One pump was sited in each of the large boiler rooms to work the ash ejectors and supply water to the boilers as required.

Gangway doors

Gangway doors were provided in the side of the ship to facilitate the embarkation and disembarkation of passengers and to give access to the accommodation of both passengers and crew. There was a baggage door on D deck in the forward third-class accommodation. There were two first-class entrances on each side of the ship on D deck. There was one door on each side of the ship in the cross-passage on E deck at the forward end of the working passage and, on the same deck, one door on the port side abreast the engine room and one door on each side of the ship to provide access to the second-class entrance.

All doors on E deck were secured by lever handles and were made watertight by rubber strips, while those on D deck had just the lever handles. They were kept firmly shut when at sea.

Charts

As part of her navigational outfit *Titanic* carried the relevant charts for Transatlantic crossings. These had been supplied by Philip, Son & Nephew Ltd of Liverpool prior to sailing.

The charts were kept and displayed in two chartrooms. The first was the navigation room used by the master, in the space between the wheelhouse and the captain's sitting room on the starboard side, while the second was the ship's chartroom used by the deck officers. It was abaft the wheelhouse on the port side.

An assumption is made that the chart outfit supplied to the *Titanic* included Chart No. 2058, the route chart of the North Atlantic. It showed the limits within which both field ice and icebergs might be encountered during the month of April.

It is not known which chart was in use by the officers of the watch at the time of the accident and what ice positions, if any, were plotted on it. There is evidence to indicate that charts were not normally displayed on the chart table whilst in open waters.

Wireless equipment

Titanic's wireless equipment was provided, serviced and operated by Marconi's Wireless Telegraph Company (the Marconi Company). The two operators embarked were Marconi Company employees.

The equipment consisted of both transmitting and receiving apparatus. The transmitting part consisted of five circuits that converted the ship's direct current into regulated oscillations that were transmitted via the ships 'T' type aerials. These were stretched between the two masts. The transmitting apparatus

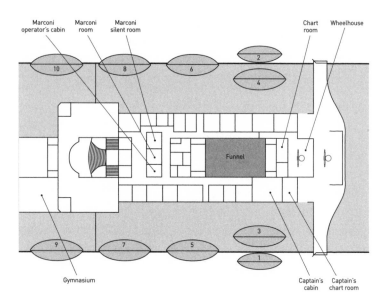

The forward end of the boat deck and bridge area

was housed in the 'silent room' situated to port of the centrally sited Marconi room and towards the aft part of the officers' accommodation on the bridge deck.

The nominal working range of transmissions was 250 nautical miles, but greater distances were achievable over night, to 2000 miles and even more.

The receiver was capable of detecting electromagnetic signals received through the aerial and converting them into audible signals. It was located on the operators' desk in the Marconi room.

The system had three sources of power: the ship's lighting power system, an emergency generator and batteries installed in the Marconi room.

Titanic was allocated the call sign MGY in January 1912.

Titanic carried two operators who, by mutual agreement, worked six-hour shifts changing over at 0200, 0800, 1400 and 2000.

Wireless defect

Titanic's wireless transmitter developed a defect at about 2200 on Friday 12 April. The two operators worked together to repair it over the next six hours, and once they had correctly identified the nature of the problem, after an initial misdiagnosis, they completed the repair between 0430 and 0500 on the Saturday morning.

For the 6–7 hours the system was not operating, *Titanic*'s operators were unable to receive incoming traffic from other ships. There is no evidence to show that anything significant was missed, but the possibility exists that it might have been.

Lifesaving equipment

In Section 428 of the Merchant Shipping Act of 1894 and under the heading of 'Duties of owners and masters as to carrying life-saving appliances,' it is stipulated that:

It shall be the duty of the owner and master of every British ship to see that his ship is provided, in accordance with the rules for life-saving appliances, with such of those appliances as, having regard to the nature of the service on which the ship is employed, and the avoidance of undue encumbrance of the ship's deck, are best adapted for securing the safety of her crew and passengers.

Lifeboats

Titanic carried a total of 20 lifeboats with a carrying capacity of 1178 persons.

- 14 wood lifeboats 30' 0" long by 9' 1" by 4' 0" deep with a capacity of 65 persons each

- 2 wood cutters 25' 2" long by 7' 2" by 3' 0" deep with a capacity of 40 persons each

- 4 Englehardt collapsible boats 27' 5" long by 8' 0" by 3' 0" deep with a capacity of 40 persons each

The lifeboats were stowed on hinged wood chocks on the boat deck and lowered to the waterline using Welin Quadrant davits capable of taking the full loaded weight. All lifeboats were fitted with Murray's disengaging gear, so both ends could be freed simultaneously once they were afloat.

Two Englehardt collapsible lifeboats were stowed on the boat deck abreast the cutters. Two more were stowed on top of the officers' accommodation immediately abaft the navigating bridge.

Covers were supplied for each boat, and both cutters and lifeboats were supplied with sails in painted bags. Every boat had oars, a mast, sails, a sea anchor, and the lifeboats had a special spirit boat compass together with a fitting for holding it. The compasses were carried in a boat locker on the boat deck. A provision tank and water beaker were supplied to each boat. When a boat was being prepared for use, the covers would be removed, the compass would be installed together with any provisions and a lamp with a supply of oil. A plug would be inserted into the drain hole prior to the boat being lowered into the water.

The lifeboats were lowered using manila rope falls of sufficient length for lowering the boats to the waterline.

Although there is no evidence to indicate that any of *Titanic*'s lifeboats had ever been subjected to a full load test, one had been carried out on board the *Olympic* in Belfast on 9 May 1911 and some three weeks before her sea trials eleven months earlier. On that occasion one lifeboat had been loaded with weights equivalent to 65 people and then safely lowered and hoisted several times without strain on the boat, davits or falls.

Boat drills

Board of Trade surveyors routinely witnessed a boat drill on board outbound White Star Line ships on the day of departure. This was done with *Titanic* at Southampton on Wednesday 10 April when two manned boats on the starboard side were lowered, sent away under oars and recovered. The inspection was stated to be satisfactory.

At the beginning of each voyage a list showing which lifeboat each member of the crew had been allocated was posted. It was up to individuals to inspect it.

White Star Line steamers calling at Queenstown usually took the opportunity while at anchor to conduct a further boat drill for the crew by sending two boats away and recovering them. This was not done by *Titanic* when she called on her maiden voyage.

It was further customary for a boat drill to be conducted on board White Star Line steamers on Sundays when at sea. No such drill took place at any time after *Titanic* sailed from Southampton, nor is there any explanation for this omission.

A boat drill involved mustering the men by their boats followed by a practical demonstration of competence. The boats would be manned by a nucleus crew of four or five, hoisted out and lowered to the water, where the falls would be disengaged.

The boat would then be pulled or sailed around the harbour or anchorage for a few minutes before returning to the ship. Such exercises were never carried out with a fully laden boat. The purpose of such drills was twofold. The pre-sailing boat drill was to satisfy the Board of Trade that the boats were in working order, while other drills were held for training and crew familiarisation.

All boat drills were required to be recorded in the ship's official log.

A problem known to the marine superintendents of the White Star Line was the failure of firemen to muster for lifeboat drills on the day of sailing. The firemen did not think it was part of their job, and the problem remained unresolved by the time *Titanic* sailed on her maiden voyage.

Prior to the events on the night of 14 April, many members of *Titanic*'s crew had failed to establish which lifeboat they had been assigned to.

Fire on board

At about the time *Titanic* sailed from Belfast a fire started in the coal bunker adjoining Nos. 5 and 6 boiler rooms. It is not clear when it was discovered and it was not, apparently, reported to Board of Trade surveyors during the time the ship was in Southampton. Attempts to put it out were under way when the ship left Southampton. It was extinguished by Saturday 13 April and left a slightly warped, but intact, bulkhead.

Sea trials

Titanic spent part of one day undergoing sea trials in Belfast Lough and the North Channel on Monday 2 April. They commenced at 1000 and consisted of adjusting the magnetic compasses, carrying out various handling manoeuvres and a speed trial.

From a speed of 20 knots her engines were put to full astern from full ahead to measure the stopping distance. It was found to be about 850 yards (780 metres). In a manoeuvring trial her wheel was put hard over to measure the advance and transfer measured in a turn. The maximum distance ahead in the turn was about 2100 feet (640 meters) and the diameter of the turning circle was in the order of 3850 feet (1175 metres). She heeled slightly whilst turning.

Titanic returned to the mouth of Belfast Lough at about 1900 and dropped both port and starboard anchors. The anchoring trial complete, she weighed successfully at about 2000 and prepared to depart for Southampton.

Prior to starting her southward passage she was granted her Passenger Certificate.

Readiness for sea

Before she arrived in Southampton from Belfast on 4 April the Report of Survey of an Emigrant Ship had been signed by the Board of Trade Marine Department's surveyor, Mr Carruthers, to the effect that:

- A passenger certificate was in force for the *Titanic*, valid for 12 months from 2 April 1912.

- He was satisfied that the hull and boilers were in good condition for the voyage.

- He had 'inspected the boats and their equipment and seen 16 swung out and lowered into the water.' He stated that the lifebelts were in order and conveniently placed. He went on to say that the distress signals and their magazines, and the other equipments, complied with the regulations and were to his satisfaction.

- He was satisfied that the steerage compartments complied with the regulation as regards light, air and ventilation, and measurements for the numbers for which they were fitted. He further confirmed that no cargo was stowed so as to affect the health or comfort of the steerage passengers.

Prior to sailing from Southampton for Cherbourg, Queenstown and New York, the local Board of Trade surveyor, Captain Clarke, added to the certificate by stating:

- That the amount of coal on board was certified to amount to 5892 tons, which was sufficient to take *Titanic* to her next coaling port.

- That he had been on board *Titanic* immediately before she sailed and had seen two boats swung out and lowered into the water. He added that, having seen the reports of inspection, and with what he had personally seen for himself, he was satisfied that the ship was in all respects fit for the intended voyage, and that the requirements under the Merchant Shipping Acts had been complied with.

At her last port of call, Queenstown, before setting across the Atlantic, the resident emigration officer, Mr E J Sharpe, added one further line to this same certificate to say:

- That he had satisfied himself that everything on board *Titanic* was in order and that he had issued the necessary certificate for clearance.

In addition to the Report of Survey a Board of Trade Certificate of Clearance had been issued by the emigration officer in Cherbourg on 10 April. It stated:

That all the requirements of the Merchant Shipping Acts relating to emigrant ships, so far as they can be complied with before the departure of the ship, have been complied with, and that the ship is in my opinion seaworthy, in safe trim, and in all respects fit for her intended voyage: that she does not carry a greater number of passengers than in the proportion of one statute adult to every five superficial feet of space clear for exercise on deck; and that her passengers and crew are in a fit state to proceed.

A similar certificate was signed in Queenstown.

Passengers

Titanic was registered as an emigrant ship but carried her passengers in three classes, first, second and third.

Following her departure from Southampton, *Titanic's* westbound sailing followed the established pattern for New-York-bound White Star liners by calling at Cherbourg and Queenstown to pick up additional passengers. Her passenger list reflected the international make-up of the transatlantic travelling public of the day, with a high percentage of wealthy Americans travelling in first class, a second class dominated by the British and a third class made up of citizens drawn from around the world including China, Japan, Syria and Turkey. Between them the Irish, British, Swedes, and Syrians accounted for nearly 60 per cent of those travelling in third class. In all, 27 different nationalities were embarked, and it is likely that as many as 400 people may not have been able to understand English.

Titanic was not fully booked on her maiden voyage.

Olympic class scheduling

In the fiercely competitive transatlantic passenger service, the White Star Line chose to provide comfort and luxury rather than speed. One of the Company's main rivals, the Cunard Line, placed more emphasis on speed.

The planned schedules for the *Olympic* class of ship meant they would depart from Southampton at noon on a Wednesday, and call at Cherbourg that evening before making an overnight passage to Queenstown. Scheduled departure from Queenstown would be early afternoon on the Thursday, to arrive off the Ambrose Channel light vessel at the approaches to New York in the early hours of the following Wednesday. After a period spent at the quarantine station off Staten Island, they would arrive in New York during the forenoon of the Wednesday. They would berth at Pier 59 in New York later that morning. The official starting point for the westbound voyage was the Daunt's Rock light vessel at the entrance of Queenstown harbour and the arrival point was the Ambrose Channel light vessel. The distance between the two was 2894 miles and the design service speed was 21 knots.

For the return voyage the *Olympic* class would depart New York at noon on a Saturday and call at both Plymouth and Cherbourg before arriving at Southampton the following Saturday.

It was not the White Star Line's practice to steam a vessel at its full speed for the first year in service.

Whilst in command of *Titanic*'s sister ship, *Olympic*, for her maiden voyage in June 1911, Captain Smith departed from Daunt's Rock off Queenstown at 1422 on Thursday 15 June 1911, and arrived off the Ambrose Channel light vessel at 0240 (local time) on Wednesday 21 June. After completing quarantine formalities at the anchorage off Staten Island during the early hours she continued up river and berthed at Pier 59 in New York at about 1000. Her average speed for the crossing was 21.44 knots.

Examination of the details of *Olympic*'s first westbound voyage reveals she covered 428 miles in the first 24 hours, 534 in the second, 542 in the third, 525 in the fourth and 548 in the third. The fastest speed achieved was 22.10 knots. On her second westbound voyage, the *Olympic* passed the Ambrose Channel light vessel at 2208 on the Tuesday evening but did not berth in New York until the following morning.

Titanic's schedule

The date and times of *Titanic*'s maiden voyage showed that she was scheduled to sail from Southampton at noon on Wednesday 10 April and arrive at New York on the morning of Wednesday 17 April. The planned time of arrival off the Ambrose Channel light vessel was to be 0500.

An article posted in the *New York Times* of 14 April stated that *Titanic* 'is due to arrive in New York on Wednesday afternoon at the end of her maiden westward passage of the Atlantic.'

At least six passengers sent Marconigrams from the *Titanic* on Sunday 14 April to alert friends or family to an arrival on Wednesday (17 April). Two other messages indicated arriving on Thursday, and a third on Friday.

The following notice appeared in the Ships' Arrival column of the *New York Times* on Monday 15 April:

> The last report received in New York from the *Titanic* was at 2:15 am yesterday. She was 1284 miles east of Sandy Hook, and in that message her commander said that he expected to reach New York in time to dock late tomorrow afternoon.

Sailing directions

As part of her navigational outfit *Titanic* carried the relevant Sailing Directions. As with the chart outfit, they had been supplied by Philip, Son & Nephew Ltd of Liverpool prior to sailing.

The outfit included the *United States Pilot (East Coast)*, and the *Nova Scotia (South-East) and Bay of Fundy Pilot.* Both volumes made reference to the presence of ice and the need for vigilance, caution and skill when crossing the dangerous ice-bearing regions of the Atlantic Ocean. *Titanic*'s planned track took her through such a region on her maiden voyage.

The *United States East Coast Pilot* made specific reference to the ocean passages of the large transatlantic mail and passenger steamers:

> To these vessels, one of the chief dangers in crossing the Atlantic lies in the probability of encountering masses of ice, both in the form of bergs and of extensive fields of solid compact ice, released at the breaking up of winter in the Arctic regions, and drifted down by the Labrador Current across their direct route. Ice is more likely to be encountered in this route between April and August, both months inclusive, than at any other times, although icebergs have been seen at all seasons northward of the parallel of 43° N, but not often so far after August.
>
> These icebergs are sometimes over 200 ft in height and of considerable extent. They have been seen as far south as lat. 39° N, to obtain

which position they must have crossed the Gulf Stream impelled by the cold Arctic current underpinning the warm waters of the Gulf Stream. That this should happen is not to be wondered at when it is considered that the specific gravity of fresh-water ice, of which these bergs are composed, is about seven-eighths that of sea water; so that, however vast the berg may appear to the eye of the observer, he can in reality see one-eighth of its bulk, the remaining seven-eighths being submerged and subject to the deep-water currents of the ocean. The track of an iceberg is indeed directed mainly by current, so small a portion of its surface being exposed to the action of the winds that its course is but slightly retarded or deflected by moderate breezes. On the Great Bank of Newfoundland bergs are often observed to be moving south or south-east; those that drift westward of Cape Race usually pass between Green and St. Pierre Banks.

The route chart of the North Atlantic, No. 2058, shows the limits within which both field ice and icebergs may be met with, and where it should be carefully looked out for at all times, but especially during the spring and summer seasons. From this chart it would appear that whilst the summer and eastern limits of field ice are about lat. 42° N, and long. 45° W, icebergs may be met much further from Newfoundland; in April, May and June they have been seen as far south as lat. 39° N, and as far east as long. 38° 30' W.

It is, in fact, impossible to give, within the outer limits named, any distinct idea of where ice may be expected, and no rule can be laid down to ensure safe navigation, as its position and the quantity met with differs so greatly in different seasons. Everything must depend upon the vigilance, caution and skill with which a vessel is navigated when crossing the dangerous ice-bearing regions of the Atlantic Ocean.

This advice was available to the deck officers on board *Titanic*.

The passage plan

White Star Line masters were advised to adhere to the tracks adopted by the great steamship companies in 1898. They were allowed to deviate from these routes in the interest of safety, and any such decision was backed by the company.

Titanic's maiden voyage to New York from Southampton via Cherbourg and Queenstown replicated the route taken by other

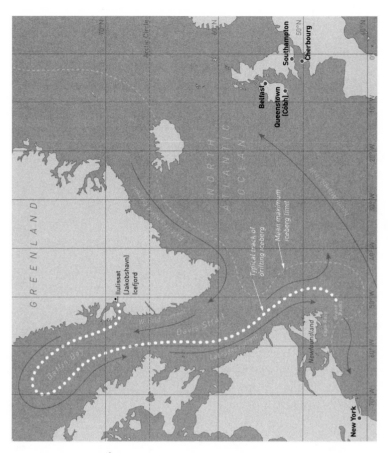

North Atlantic currents and ice limits

Southampton-based White Star Line ships and the times undertaken by her sister ship the *Olympic* on her maiden voyage a year earlier. This involved her departing Southampton at midday on 10 April with an estimated time of arrival in New York at 1600 on Wednesday 17 April.

On leaving the Queenstown anchorage and taking her departure from off the Fastnet light, *Titanic*'s plan was to cross the Atlantic on a conventional great circle track to a position known as the Turning Point at 42° N, 47° W, and thence by rhumb line to just south of the Nantucket light ship before heading for New York via the Ambrose Channel light vessel.

Ice warnings

Prior to departure from Southampton

Before *Titanic* sailed from Southampton some wireless messages giving the position of ice were received from an unknown source and the positions plotted on a chart.

The following announcement appeared in *The Shipping Gazette and Lloyd's List* on Wednesday 10 April. *Titanic* sailed at noon that day.

Ice in the North Atlantic
The Marine Superintendent of the Meteorological Office forwarded for publication the subjoined report in respect of ice in the North Atlantic. '*Mongolian* (Capt G Hamilton). March 10th in lat. 44°50'N, long. 48°41'W passed several pieces of field ice.'

The 1912 icefield

The mean maximum iceberg limit for the month of April was clearly marked on the North Atlantic routing chart. The Outward Southern track lay about 25 miles to the south of the area marked 'field ice between March and July' but from 100 to 300 miles to the north of a second, dotted, line marked 'icebergs have been seen within this line in April, May and June.'

Following a warmer winter than normal and some unusually high spring tides during January 1912, the ice being carried by the Labrador Current into the shipping lanes south and east of the Grand Banks was greater than normal. From early April a number of westbound ships were reporting an unusual quantity of heavy field ice together with numerous small and large icebergs. Several vessels sustained damage to their hulls. Many of these reports were made on arrival at their destinations, including Boston, New York and Philadelphia, but there is no indication as to whether, or how, these reports were collated and the information disseminated. Some of the information was available before *Titanic* sailed from Southampton but there is no specific evidence to indicate it was received on board.

On 7 April the British-registered steamship *Rosalind* encountered a strip of field ice about 3–4 miles wide in position 45° 10' N, 56° 40' W and extending north and south for as far as the eye could see.

On 10 April and in position 41° 50' N, 50° 25' W the German-registered steamship *Excelsior* passed a large icefield a few hundred feet wide and 15 miles long extending in a NNE direction.

On 11 April, the day *Titanic* called at Queenstown, the French passenger steamer *Niagara* on passage from Le Havre to New York collided with an iceberg in thick fog. Despite being holed below the waterline the flooding was contained by the pumps and she continued with her passage. The incident was reported to have occurred within 10 miles of where the *Titanic* collided with her iceberg. Having been alerted to the situation by wireless the Cunard liner SS *Carmania* went to her assistance and, in position 41° 58' N, 50° 20' W, reported passing 25 large icebergs. There is no evidence to show that *Titanic* was ever aware of this incident.

SS *Virginian*, on passage from Halifax to Liverpool, responded to *Titanic*'s SOS message in the early hours of 15 April and closed the given position to arrive by the late forenoon. Too late to be of any practical assistance, the *Virginian* reported the southern

The icefield photographed from *Carpathia* on 15 April

limit of the ice in position 41° 20' N, 49° 50' W before continuing her voyage to Liverpool.

Early in the voyage

At some stage early in the voyage, there is evidence to indicate that wireless messages giving the position of ice in the North Atlantic may have been received and, on instructions from the master, plotted on a chart by the fourth officer. There is no record of these messages or their contents, but it is known that other ships were sighting, and reporting, extensive quantities of ice during the first two weeks of April.

The eastbound Canadian Pacific liner *Empress of Britain* had passed *Titanic* on 12 April and had been in touch by wireless. It is known she had already encountered an immense quantity of ice and icebergs whilst on passage from Halifax, and had received a wireless message from the Allen liner *Virginia* warning her of ice. On Thursday 11 April the captain of the westbound Cunard steamship *Carmania* alerted the *Caronia* to the presence of ice as follows:

4 am. Lat. 41°45' N, long. 52° 12' W had light to mod SW to NW winds since leaving patches of fog from 48 to 51 W passed a large number of bergs growlers and field ice in lat. 41° 58' N, long. 50° 20' W.

There is no evidence to indicate that any of these reports were received in the *Titanic*, but it does show that ships were freely exchanging information about the presence of ice. It is also known that *Titanic*'s operators listened in and copied traffic being transmitted by other ships.

Friday 12 April

On the evening of 12 April, and some 30 hours after leaving Queenstown, *Titanic* received a wireless message from the eastbound French steamer *La Touraine*. It read as follows:

> My position 7 pm GMT lat. 49° 28' N, long. 26° 28' W dense fog since the night crossed thick icefield lat. 44.58, long. 50.40 *Paris* saw another icefield lat. 45.20, long. 45.09 saw a derelict lat. 40.56, long. 68.58 please give me your position.

The message did not give any times for the sighting of either the ice or the derelict. *Titanic*'s master acknowledged receipt of the message by thanking *La Touraine*'s captain for both the message and the information.

The ice positions given in this message were some 300 miles to the north of *Titanic*'s planned track.

Saturday 13 April

Sometime after dark on the evening of 13 April, the eastbound Furness Withy liner, 3884 grt *Rappahannock*, en route from Halifax (departed 9 April) for London (arrived Gravesend 19 April) and proceeding at 13 knots, spoke to *Titanic* by light and reported having passed through pack ice and that her rudder had been damaged. The message was apparently acknowledged but there is no evidence to indicate how this information was handled on board.

Sunday 14 April

During the day a number of ice warnings were received by the *Titanic*.

0900 *Caronia* to *Titanic*:
Westbound steamers report bergs growlers and field ice in 42°N from 49° to 51°W April 12.

1345 *Amerika* to *Titanic*:
Instructions *Amerika* via MGY Hydrographic Office Washington DC. *Amerika* passed two large icebergs in 41° 27' N, 50° 08' W on 14 April.

This ice position lay just over 30 miles to the south of *Titanic*'s planned track.

1342 *Baltic* to *Titanic*:
Have had mod var winds and clear fine weather since leaving. Greek steamer *Athenai* reports passing icebergs and large quantity of field ice today in lat. 41° 51' N, long. 49° 52' W last night we spoke German oil tank steamer *Deutschland* Stettin to Philadelphia. Not under control. Short of coal. Lat. 40° 02' N, long. 55° 11' W. Wishes to be reported to New York and other steamers.

This message was handed to Captain Smith, who subsequently showed it to Mr Ismay, the White Star Line chairman. Mr Ismay retained the message until about 1915 when the captain asked for it to be returned so he could take it to the bridge.

1445 *Noordam* to *Titanic* via *Caronia*:
Congratulations on new command had moderate westerly winds fair winds no fog much ice reported in lat. 42° 24' to 42° 45' N and long. 49° 50' to 50° 20' W.

1930 *Californian* to *Antillian* but intercepted by *Titanic*:
To captain *Antillian*, 6.30 pm. apparent ship's time: lat. 42° 03' N, long. 49° 09' W. Three large bergs five miles to southwards of us.

2140 *Mesaba* to *Titanic*:
In lat. 42° to 41° 25' N, long. 49 to 50° 30' W saw much heavy pack ice and great number large icebergs also field ice. Weather good, clear.

At about 2255 the *Californian* attempted to send the following to the *Titanic*: 'We are stopped and surrounded by ice.' But her transmission interfered with *Titanic* sending messages to Cape Race. *Californian's* wireless operator received a reply including the code letters DDD, meaning 'Keep out'. She did.

Weather

From departure Queenstown on 12 April to the afternoon of Sunday 14 April the weather conditions were good and the sea state slight with the wind generally from the southeast. The visibility remained excellent throughout.

On the evening of 14 April the wind had dropped completely, the sea was flat calm and the sky clear. There was no moon.

The temperature at 1730 was 43 °F (6°C), dropping to 33°F (1°C) by 1930. By 2200 it had fallen by 2 °F. With no wind the ship generated its own wind speed over the deck of about 22 knots (comparable to a strong breeze). The resultant wind-chill temperature was about 2 °F (−17°C).

The wind and sea began to pick up at around dawn on 15 April and, by the time the last survivors were being rescued from the lifeboats by the *Carpathia* at around 0800, it was blowing about force 3–4.

Visibility

A common feature of wireless messages between masters in the early days of wireless was a report on the actual weather. Many would make a specific reference to the visibility and the presence, or otherwise, of fog. Several of the wireless messages received by the *Titanic* contained such references, and from these Captain Smith would have deduced that the expected visibility would be good.

On the night of 14 April visibility was exceptionally good. In the clear atmosphere, lights of ships were being seen at ranges far in excess of normal. Many stars, including those of low magnitude, were unusually bright.

Given the low sea temperature (32°F, 0°C) prevailing as

Titanic entered the area affected by the cold Labrador Current, unusual optical effects occur. The following are extracts from a recent edition of the Admiralty publication *The Mariner's Handbook*:

> The propagation of electromagnetic waves, including light and radar waves, is influenced by the lapse rate of temperature and humidity (and therefore density) with height.
>
> When conditions are normal in the near-surface layers of the atmosphere there is a modest decrease of temperature with height and uniform humidity, and no significant refraction of electromagnetic waves occurs. Variation in these conditions can cause appreciable vertical refraction of light rays.
>
> Extraordinary radio propagation and optical effects can result, including ... the phenomenon known as mirage.
>
> **Caution.** Whenever abnormal refraction is observed or suspected ... visually ... the mariner should exercise caution.
>
> Super-refraction or downward bending is caused when humidity decreases with height or when the temperature lapse rate is less than normal. When temperature increases with height (i.e. when an inversion is present), the downward bending of rays and signals is particularly enhanced.
>
> Super-refraction increases the optical horizon, so that it is possible to see objects which are actually beyond the geometrical horizon. It can be expected:
>
> - in high latitudes whenever the sea surface temperature is exceptionally low;
>
> - in light winds and calms.

Speed

The International Regulations for Preventing Collisions at Sea refer to ship's speed in the context of being moderate in times of reduced visibility: 'Every vessel shall in a fog, mist, falling snow, or heavy rain storm go at a moderate speed, having careful regard to the existing circumstances and conditions.' No such restrictions applied on this occasion.

Titanic's maximum speed was never determined, but with all 29 boilers on line it was expected to exceed 23 knots with the shafts turning at over 80 rpm.

On each successive day of her maiden voyage across the Atlantic speed was increased slightly. Between departure Queenstown and noon on 12 April *Titanic* had covered 386 miles. In the next 24 hours she travelled 519 miles, and by noon on 14 April her daily run had increased to 546 miles.

There is evidence to indicate that on 15 April some form of full-speed trial was to be attempted. To do so for any length of time would have depleted the coal bunkers. She had enough.

In specific instructions to all White Star Line masters, the company made it clear in writing that they were to 'dismiss any idea of competitive passages with other vessels' and to 'concentrate your attention upon a cautious, prudent and ever watchful system of navigation, which shall lose time or suffer any other temporary inconvenience rather than incur the slightest risk which can be avoided.'

There is evidence to suggest that the captain was aware his ship was running ahead of schedule and was in a position to arrive in New York a day earlier than scheduled. There is no evidence to indicate that this possibility had been made public on board. He still had two days to run in a region notorious for fog.

At the time *Titanic* collided with the iceberg, 24 of the 29 boilers were lit and producing steam, the shafts were turning at 75 rpm and the estimated speed was about 22 knots. Except at the very last moment before she struck the iceberg, there was no reduction in speed, nor is there any evidence to indicate that the engine room had been alerted to a possible reduction during the night.

Lookout

The International Regulations for Preventing Collisions at Sea contain a clause that states:

> Nothing in these rules shall exonerate any vessel or the owner or master or crew thereof from the consequences of any neglect to carry lights or signals, or of any neglect to keep a proper lookout, or of the neglect of any precaution which may be required by the ordinary practice of seamen or by the special circumstances of the case.

Titanic's lookouts were drawn from the seven deck officers and six seamen carried for that specific purpose. At any time three officers would be available on the bridge, keeping four-hour watches but, more often than not, only one would be keeping a lookout. It would, usually, be the senior officer on watch. The crow's nest would be manned by two of the dedicated lookouts, keeping two-hour watches.

The dedicated crow's-nest lookouts were experienced sailors, and received 5 shillings extra pay per day in recognition of their special responsibilities. Additional lookouts could be closed up in fog or at other times of reduced visibility. No additional lookouts were deployed on the night of 14 April.

The master, although not expected to keep a lookout, was able to provide an extra pair of eyes should he think it necessary. In thick weather or at any time when the master judged his presence would be advantageous or appropriate he would remain on the bridge. Most seafarers would agree that masters had the knack of seeing things long before anyone else.

When appropriate in reduced visibility, or in vessels not equipped with crow's nests, it was customary for additional lookouts to be posted on the fo'c'sle. It is not known whether Captain Smith ever required this to be done during his time in the *Olympic* but, without the provision of some form of shelter the position would have been very exposed and not conducive to an efficient lookout. There is no evidence to indicate it was ever considered.

There were three quartermasters on watch at any one time.

Quartermasters had a number of duties but were primarily responsible for steering the ship using the wheel in the wheel-house. They had no role in keeping a lookout and in any event had a very limited field of view from where they stood. A stand-by quartermaster was available on the bridge to carry out any tasks ordered by the officer of the watch, to ring the ship's bell at 30-minute intervals, tend the binnacle lamps and take both air and sea temperatures at the appropriate times. He was neither required nor expected to keep a lookout. The third kept watch aft in the vicinity of the docking bridge. His task was to read the log, react in the event of a man overboard and, during daylight, tend the ensign. He had no lookout responsibilities except to report ships approaching from astern. Given *Titanic*'s speed this would have been a rare event.

The crow's nest was 95 feet (29 metres) above the waterline and access to it was by means of a ladder inside the foremast. The line-of-sight distance to the horizon was 11.2 miles but, visibility permitting, larger objects and lights could be seen at longer ranges. Apart from a small canvas dodger on the after part to prevent any light infringement from abaft the crows nest, it was exposed to the elements. In the flat calm conditions that pre-vailed on the night of 14 April, the relative wind speed felt by the lookouts would have equated the ship's speed of 22.5 knots and from dead ahead.

The height of eye on the bridge was about 75 feet (23 metres), giving a line of sight distance to the natural horizon of 9.9 miles but larger objects or a light being displayed at a higher level could be seen at greater distances. Mariners had access to tables giving the ranges at which a terrestrial object, such as a light, could be seen under conditions of normal refraction and unim-peded visibility. Given perfect visibility, a bright light displayed by another ship at, for instance, a height of 50 feet (15 metres) would be observable at a range of 18.1 miles by an observer on *Titanic*'s bridge.

The importance of retaining night vision was recognised

by all navigating officers, and they would be at pains to avoid exposure to white light when keeping watch during the night. It takes between 25 and 30 minutes to ensure the eyes are fully adapted to the dark but most acclimatisation is achieved within the first 5–10 minutes. As darkness fell on the Sunday evening, *Titanic*'s first officer had taken the precaution of ordering a foc's'le door to be shut to prevent light spoiling the night vision of those keeping watch on the bridge.

The bridge watchkeeping practice in *Titanic* was for at least one of the officers, usually the most senior, to be on the outer bridge and keeping a lookout at all times. The other two would only join him if told to do so and were employed on other tasks such as doing rounds, comparing and checking the compasses, working out celestial observations or working in the charthouse. At night the officer keeping the lookout would remain on the bridge and would not enter either the wheelhouse or chartroom, in order to maintain his night vision. In the lead-up to the collision on 14 April, the first officer was keeping the lookout, the fourth officer was working on unspecified tasks in the chartroom until about 2200, and the sixth officer was in the chartroom. Only one of the three bridge watchkeeping officers was therefore maintaining a lookout in the 30 minutes or so prior to the accident.

At about 2125 the two lookouts on watch were told by the officer of the watch to keep a good lookout for ice, particularly small ice and growlers. This instruction was passed on to their reliefs when the watched changed at 2200. Neither of the two lookouts who came on watch then had access to a watch or clock so their ability to recall time was limited and estimates must be approximate. Their sole reference was the striking of the ship's bell rung at half-hourly intervals.

There is no evidence to indicate that any vessel or object was sighted by either the lookouts or the watchkeeping officer before the iceberg was detected right ahead shortly before 2340 on 14 April.

Binoculars

Binoculars were used by *Titanic*'s officers, and on the initial voyage from Belfast to Southampton they were issued to the lookouts stationed in the crow's nest. On arrival at Southampton the lookouts' binoculars were returned to the ship's second officer, Mr Baird, and locked in a cupboard. Soon afterwards Mr Baird left the ship and was replaced in the rank by Mr Lightoller. It is possible the departing second officer took the key with him, because it could not be found. When the lookouts asked if the binoculars could be reissued for the voyage, the request was refused.

At no stage of the voyage did any lookout have access to, or use, binoculars.

Ice sighting

At some indeterminate time after they came on watch the two lookouts observed haze ahead. Their primary concern was that it would interfere with their ability to see through it. It cannot be ascertained at what time they first became aware of this 'haze' but it became thicker as the watch progressed and was at its most dense at about the time the iceberg was sighted.

Very shortly before 2340 the lookouts in the crow's nest detected what they described as a 'black mass' ahead and identified it as an iceberg. They alerted the bridge watchkeepers by striking the lookout's bell three times to signify having seen something dead ahead and followed this up with a telephone call to the bridge. They reported seeing an iceberg dead ahead.

There is no evidence to indicate the time interval between seeing the 'black mass' and identifying it as an iceberg. There is also no specific evidence to indicate how many seconds or minutes elapsed between the report being received by the sixth officer on the bridge and the initial wheel order 'hard a starboard' being given. There is no credible evidence to suggest that the officer of the watch saw haze, a black mass or an iceberg in the moments before being alerted by the warnings of the lookouts.

Actions on sighting the iceberg

The telephone call from the lookouts was answered on the bridge by the sixth officer. It is not known how long the telephone rang before it was answered but, once the message had been received and relayed to the officer of the watch, the order 'hard a starboard' was given, the telegraphs were put to 'full speed astern', and the automatically controlled watertight doors were shut from the bridge. The time is assessed as being 2340.

The helmsman responded by turning the wheel to port and, soon after the ship began to swing, the wheel was reversed and the engines stopped. It is not known precisely when the telegraphs were put to stop but there is no evidence to indicate that the initial 'full astern' order ever resulted in the propellers turning astern. It is equally possible that the engines were never ordered astern in the first place and were put to stop.

The captain arrived on the bridge after these initial orders were given and asked what had happened. He was told and briefed on the actions taken. The ship, in the meantime, was slowing and swinging to starboard as the captain and his first officer went out onto the starboard bridge wing to see if

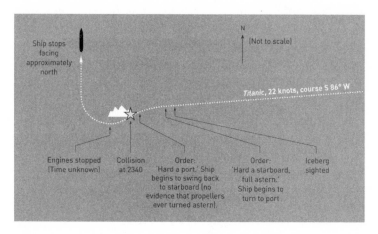

Actions on sighting the iceberg

they could see the iceberg they had just collided with. They could not.

There is some indication that the telegraphs were put to 'ahead' for a few minutes immediately afterwards and before a final 'stop' was rung on.

Damage assessment

Aware that ice had fallen onto the foredeck, those on the bridge knew that *Titanic* had hit the iceberg above the waterline on the starboard side. They realised straight away that the ship might have been damaged below the waterline. Soon afterwards the captain sought information on the extent of any damage and ordered the fourth officer to go below and report back on what he found. The first inspection revealed nothing visible, but soon afterwards the carpenter reported to the bridge that the ship was making water up forward, and this was confirmed by the fourth officer a few minutes later.

The initial reports reaching the captain suggested that at least three watertight compartments had been breached and that the hull had been penetrated about 10 feet (3 metres) above the keel. He made a personal inspection of the fore part of the ship in the company of Mr Thomas Andrews and also consulted with his chief engineer. By midnight the flooding had extended to G deck forward. He knew the damage was serious and, shortly after midnight, warned the Marconi operators to get ready to send a distress message.

By 0020 the water had reached E deck. All the damage was confined to the fore part of the ship and there was no indication of any damage abaft No. 4 boiler room. The four aftermost boilers continued to produce steam and the main electrical generators continued to work.

Ship's officers

The master: Captain E J Smith

The master of the *Titanic* on her maiden voyage was 62-year-old Captain E J Smith. He had first gone to sea as an apprentice in sail with A Gibson & Company of Liverpool aged 13. His first trip as a 'boy' in the American-built *Senator Weber* took him to Hong Kong via the Cape of Good Hope and back via San Francisco and Cape Horn. He joined the White Star Line in 1880 as the fourth officer of the *Celtic* and subsequently served in a number of the company's ships sailing to both Australia and North America. He was appointed in temporary command of the *Republic* in 1887 and obtained his Extra Master's Certificate of Competency the following year. He went on to command 17 White Star vessels including the *Runic, Germanic,* and *Majestic,* where he remained for nine years. He was appointed as master of both the *Baltic* and *Adriatic* on their maiden voyages and commodore of the line in 1904. When the first of a new class of 40,000-ton passenger ships entered service in 1911 he assumed command of the *Olympic* on her maiden voyage and remained with her until the end of March 1912.

He was highly regarded by the White Star Line and enjoyed a reputation as a competent sailor. He was liked by passengers and respected by his crews.

His record was not entirely blemish-free. He had been in command of the *Republic* when she ran aground off Sandy Hook in 1889. He had also been captain of the *Adriatic* when she, too, went aground in the Ambrose Channel in 1909. While berthing the *Olympic* in New York in 1911 he had been involved in an incident involving a tug, and in September 1911 he was involved in a collision with the cruiser HMS *Hawke* while under way in the Solent.

Immediately before assuming command of the *Titanic,* Captain Smith had been master of the *Olympic,* having completed a round trip to New York during March. On that return leg, the *Olympic* departed from New York on 23 March and arrived in Southampton a week later. He left the *Olympic* on 30 March to assume command of the *Titanic* on 1 April. He replaced Captain H J Haddock, who had previously been assigned as her first master.

Although his actual date for retirement remains unknown, he would not have expected to remain at sea much beyond 1912. He was to spend only 14 days on board the *Titanic* before he lost his life in the early hours of 15 April 1912.

Chief officer: Henry Wilde

Titanic's chief officer was 39-year-old Henry Tingle Wilde. He served his apprenticeship in sail with Messrs James Chambers & Company, Liverpool, and after gaining his Second Mate's Certificate of Competency he joined the Maranhan Steamship Company as a second officer. On obtaining his Master's Certificate, he joined the White Star Line as a junior officer.

Wilde served on a number of White Star Line ships on both the Australian and New York runs and had been with the company 14 years by the time he joined the *Titanic*. He held a Master's Certificate and was a lieutenant in the Royal Naval Reserve. His wife died in December 1910, as did two infant sons. Soon afterwards, in 1911, he was appointed chief officer of the *Olympic* under Captain Smith. He remained with the ship until he was relieved shortly before the ship sailed for New York on 3 April 1912 and signed on as *Titanic*'s chief officer on 9 April. He actually joined the ship at Southampton a few hours before she sailed on her maiden voyage.

Mr Wilde was the senior bridge watchkeeper and kept watches four hours on and eight hours off, keeping the 0200 to 0600 and 1400 to 1800 watch. His last watch before the events of 14/15 April was from 1400 to 1800, and he was off watch at the moment of impact.

It is not known how he was alerted to the collision, but

shortly afterwards he was seen in the fore part of the ship seeking information as to the extent of the damage. During the evacuation he was seen helping to load the boats on the boat deck.

He did not survive.

First officer: William Murdoch

The first officer was a 39-year-old Scot, William Murdoch, who came from a seafaring family. On leaving school he served his apprenticeship in sail and went on to serve in a number of sailing ships in various capacities up to and including chief officer. He gained his Master's Certificate in 1896 and joined the White Star Line in 1900. He served in a number of the company's vessels as both a junior and a senior officer. While serving in the *Medic* in 1900, one of his fellow officers was Charles Lightoller. He was appointed to the new *Olympic* in 1911 and then to *Titanic* as chief officer in Belfast at the end of March 1912. Shortly before sailing he was replaced as chief officer by Mr Wilde and reverted to being the ship's first officer.

He was one of *Titanic*'s three senior watchkeeping officers and was the officer of the watch at the time the ship collided with the iceberg. He subsequently supervised the loading of lifeboats on the starboard side of *Titanic*'s boat deck.

He did not survive.

Second officer: Charles Lightoller

Titanic's second officer was 38-year-old Charles Lightoller. He first went to sea as an apprentice in sail aged 13. His first few years at sea were characterised by his involvement in a number of situations that included a shipwreck, a fire at sea and a cyclone. He also had first-hand experience of sighting ice. Having obtained his Mate's Certificate of Competency in 1895 he transferred to steamships and served on the African Royal Mail Service. He left the sea temporarily in 1898 but returned a year later and obtained his Master's Certificate.

He joined the White Star Line in 1900 and sailed as fourth officer of the *Medic*, employed on the Australia run. In a later appointment in the same ship the master was Captain E J Smith. Lightoller spent some years on the Atlantic and again found himself in a ship, the *Majestic*, where Captain Smith was in command. Further appointments followed in more senior positions, including the *Oceanic*, where he became the first officer. He was appointed to the *Titanic* as first officer in March 1912 and joined her in Belfast. Shortly before the ship sailed from Southampton a change in the senior officer appointments on board resulted in Lightoller reverting to second officer.

He was the senior officer of the watch from 1800 to 2200 on the evening of 14 April and was off duty in his cabin when the collision with the iceberg occurred. During the evacuation process he supervised the loading of lifeboats and was the officer who sought approval to start filling the lifeboats with women and children.

When the *Titanic* sank he was initially thrown into the water but managed to board an upturned collapsible lifeboat. He was the most senior of *Titanic*'s officer to survive.

Third officer: Herbert Pitman

Titanic's third officer was 34-year-old Herbert Pitman. He first went to sea aged 18 in 1895 as an apprentice with James Nourse Ltd and stayed with them as a junior officer for five years. He then served with the Blue Anchor and Shire Lines, gained his master's certificate in 1906 and joined the White Star Line. He served as a junior officer on the *Dolphin* and *Majestic* and as fourth officer on the *Oceanic*.

He joined the *Titanic* as third officer on 29 March 1912 in Belfast. One of the junior bridge watchkeepers on board, he was off duty and half asleep in his cabin when the collision with the iceberg occurred.

He left the sinking ship in charge of lifeboat No. 5 and survived the accident.

Fourth officer: Joseph Boxhall

Titanic's fourth officer was 28-year-old Joseph Boxhall. He went to sea aged 15 and served his time as an apprentice in sail with the William Thomas Line of Liverpool. Having obtained his Second Mate's Certificate he served with the Wilson Line of Hull and gained his Extra Master's in 1907. He joined the White Star Line in the same year and served as a junior officer on board both the *Oceanic* and *Arabic* before joining the *Titanic* in Belfast on 27 April 1911. He had never previously sailed with Captain Smith but had served with Charles Lightoller.

On the evening of the accident he was on watch, but not on the bridge, when the collision occurred. He was walking towards the bridge from aft on the starboard side of the boat deck when he heard the lookout's three strikes of the bell and joined both the first officer and the captain on the bridge following the collision.

During the evacuation process he helped load some lifeboats but was primarily responsible for working out the ship's position for the Marconi operators to include in their distress messages, for firing distress rockets and for calling up the unknown ship in sight a few miles off *Titanic*'s port bow.

Shortly before embarking in lifeboat No. 2 he placed a box of flares in it. He left the sinking ship in charge of lifeboat No. 2 and survived.

Fifth officer: Herbert Lowe

Titanic's fifth officer was 29-year-old Harold Lowe. Born in Caernarfonshire, he left home at the age of 14 to sail as a ship's boy, serving on the West African coast before switching to coastal schooners. He worked to gain his Second Mate's Certificate and gained this in 1906. Two years later he passed for mate and by the time he joined the White Star Line in 1911 he had gained his Master's Certificate. He served as third officer in the *Belgic* and *Tropic* before being transferred to the *Titanic* as fifth officer in 1912. He joined on 27 March in Belfast. He was making his first crossing of the Atlantic when the accident occurred and had not previously met Captain Smith.

He was one of the four junior watchkeepers on board *Titanic* and was off watch in his cabin when the accident happened. For half an hour afterwards he remained sound asleep but, on hearing voices and sounds on deck, he got up and helped fill the lifeboats on the starboard side. He eventually left the sinking ship in charge of lifeboat No. 14 and used it to rescue some of the survivors from the water.

He survived the accident.

Sixth officer: James Moody

Titanic's sixth officer was 24-year-old James Moody. Born in Yorkshire, he went to sea at the age of 14 as an apprentice in sail. He gained his master's certificate in April 1911 and joined the White Star Line shortly afterwards. He had served in the *Oceanic* together with Charles Lightoller and was appointed to the *Titanic* as the sixth officer at the end of March 1912, joining the ship in Belfast. He had not previously sailed with Captain Smith.

He kept watch with the fourth officer and was on duty when the accident happened. In the minutes before the collision occurred he was working in the chartroom and was the officer who took the call from the lookouts in the crow's nest that an iceberg had been sighted dead ahead.

He was last seen on *Titanic*'s boat deck attempting to launch one of the collapsible lifeboats.

He did not survive.

Damage and flooding

From the outset it was evident that *Titanic* had been damaged, but it took several minutes to establish how badly. Following the accident she began to list to starboard and it became evdent that the hull had been breached over several watertight compartments.

Once the initial damage assessment had been made Mr Andrews almost certainly made a more detailed inspection of the damaged part of the ship and realised that five compartments were flooding. He returned to the bridge and informed the captain that the situation was serious and, in his view, the ship would founder within an hour to an hour and a half. This assessment was made shortly before 0025.

The only part of the ship to be flooded in the first two hours was the forepart, forward of No. 4 boiler room. Thereafter the water began to make its way aft along the passages, to start filling both No. 4 boiler room and the spaces on either side. The rate of flooding increased significantly from about 0150 when the list to port began to increase.

From shortly after 0200 the pitch angle steadily increased as the bow submerged.

Mustering of crew and passengers

Following the collision, firemen in Nos. 5 and 6 boiler rooms, and off-duty members of the crew together with some of the male third-class passengers accommodated forward were under no illusions that the ship had been damaged. They were among the earliest to become aware of the extent of the flooding, and many started to make their way to the upper decks. Some took their possessions with them.

The hands were nevertheless called and a message passed to inform the passengers to put on their lifebelts. There was no general alarm system, and the information was passed by word of mouth. Some form of alarm bell was, however, rung in the forward crew and third-class passenger accommodation.

No concerted attempt was made to 'shake' (waken) all the off-watch deck officers once the extent of the danger had become evident. Some were aware that something had happened and got up to find out but one, the fifth officer, slept through the early stages. Some 25–30 minutes after the collision, stewards were alerted to the need to wake passengers and tell them to don life preservers and put on warm clothes. At some stage the captain, accompanied by one of the senior officers, personally entered the accommodation spaces, spoke to some of the passengers and told them to put on lifebelts. The time has not been ascertained but was probably soon after 0030.

Clearing away, launching and deployment of the lifeboats

Some time between five and ten minutes after midnight, the captain ordered the lifeboats to be cleared away and made ready.

The process of uncovering the lifeboats on the boat deck was undertaken in the limited light available. It was not made easier by the lifting of the steam safety valves on the funnels. The resultant noise, which lasted for about 45 minutes, was deafening and made conversation and communication on the upper decks difficult. Although several passengers had by now appeared, a combination of the bitter cold, the noise of escaping steam, the warmth and heat of the accommodation inside, and the absence of any indication that a serious situation existed persuaded most of them to return inside. The most frequently asked question by passengers was whether there was a serious problem. They were generally reassured there was not. The boats were ordered to be swung out at around 0020.

In the early stages of loading the lifeboats there was no panic. Those members of the crew involved in loading and lowering the lifeboats did so both efficiently and professionally.

At about 0035 the first lifeboats were ready for launching and the second officer sought the captain's permission to begin embarking the women and children. Despite the noise generated by the escaping steam, approval was given together with an instruction to lower them. The first lifeboat to be filled and lowered was No. 7 at about 0045, but because of the paucity of women and children on the upper deck, and the lack of any conviction that the *Titanic* was in any danger, it was eventually lowered and sent away with just 28 people embarked. In only half-filling it the second officer had it in mind to embark additional people from one of the gangway doors on D deck, and detailed off the bosun to take some hands to go and open one.

During the next 90 minutes officers and crew worked hard to load, fill and lower the lifeboats. There was little effective organisation to ensure passengers were mustered and told what to do, the officers were not aware of the full loading capacities of the boats. Priority for embarkation was determined in different ways. There was confusion as to where passengers should board the boats. Both the boat deck and A Deck were being used.

Lighting on the boat deck in the vicinity of the lifeboats was limited and provided by bulkhead lights shaded so as to not shine forward. Lighting on A deck was good throughout.

Too few members of the crew were capable of taking charge of the lifeboats or even handling them, and several demonstrated a lack of knowledge in disengaging the falls, or rowing.

Several factors combined to deter passengers from boarding the lifeboats. Many did not believe the ship was in any danger, others thought help was on its way, and some ladies refused to leave their husbands.

Owing to the ease with which first and second class passengers were able to reach the boat deck, they were the first to be loaded. There was no discrimination, as such, against third class passengers but, because they had no ready access to the embarkation points, or didn't know where to go, far fewer of them made it to the boats in time.

From shortly before 0200, when it became evident that rescue was unlikely, that the ship was sinking and that nearly all the lifeboats had gone, order began to break down, and the officers resorted to using firearms.

As *Titanic* began to settle ever deeper forward, a list to port developed and steadily increased. It consequently became increasingly difficult to launch the boats on the starboard side. As they were lowered their rubbing strakes began to catch on the riveted hull plating of the ship's side. The list in the final moments was in the order of 6–8 degrees.

The last boats to leave the ship were much fuller that those sent away earlier. The crew had great difficulty preparing the two collapsible boats stowed above the officers' accommodation, and from 0200 many third-class passengers arrived on the boat deck. Water began to creep up the decks and by 0205 the bows had submerged. By 0210 the stern began to rise out of the water and by 0217 the sea was lapping at the boat deck. The two Marconi operators were released from their post and made for the remaining boats. The last two, collapsibles A and B, floated off the deck with B upside down at about that time. Shortly afterwards the forward funnel collapsed, killing some swimmers in the sea beneath it. The lights finally went out as the stern rose higher out of the water. The hull then split in two, leaving the stern half to resume a more horizontal position before it, too, rose to a near-vertical position before it began its final plunge. *Titanic* finally foundered at 0220, leaving hundreds of people struggling in the sea.

Women and children

From the outset, priority for loading the lifeboats was for women and children. The rationale for this was described as being 'the natural order'. In the early stages of the embarkation officers had great difficulty in finding sufficient women and children to put in the boats.

The officers responsible for loading the lifeboats interpreted this requirement in different ways. Mr Murdoch on the starboard side of the boat deck implemented a 'women and children first' process, whereas Mr Lightoller on the port side insisted on a 'women and children only' policy. This insistence by the second officer led to delays while efforts were made to bring them forward. Further delays arose as attempts were made to eject some men who had managed to board without permission. Most men accepted the ruling, but emotions ran high as women bade farewell to their husbands.

There is no evidence to indicate that any distinction was made for the class of travel, but the final headcount revealed that far fewer female third-class passengers were saved than in either first or second class.

Wireless distress messages

Once the captain realised *Titanic* had been seriously damaged he alerted the Marconi operators to prepare a distress call. Both operators remained on duty to meet any new requirement and, furnished with a position provided by the fourth officer, sent the first message using the Marconi distress code CQD at 0027. It was picked up instantly by the Newfoundland shore station at Cape Race, SS *Mount Temple* and SS *Provence*. Only Cape Race had sufficient operators to maintain a 24-hour watch.

The fourth officer provided a corrected position within ten minutes, and this was included in all subsequent transmissions.

Until they were released by the captain a few minutes before she sank, the two wireless operators continuously transmitted a distress message. They used the Marconi distress code CQD initially but switched to the international code SOS at about 0050. Although they were in touch with a number of other ships few were close and the distress call was continually sent in the hope that it would be picked up by a ship much closer,

In the event good two-way communications was established with the Cunard steamship *Carpathia*, who had indicated she was proceeding to assist her and had been identified as the vessel most likely to arrive first.

Titanic's final transmission was made at about 0217. She sank moments later.

Visual distress signals

In 1912 the regulations for the use of distress signals, and applicable to all vessels on the high seas, were contained in Article 31 of the International Regulations for Preventing Collisions at Sea and published on 27 November 1896. Article 31 stated that when:

A vessel is in distress and requires assistance from other vessels or from the shore, the following shall be the signals to be used or displayed by her, either together or separately: viz.:

In the daytime

(1) A gun or other explosive signal fired at intervals of about a minute

(2) The International Code signal of distress indicated by N.C.

(3) The distant signal consisting of a square flag, having either below or above it a ball or anything resembling a ball

(4) A continuous sounding with any fog-signal apparatus

At night

(1) A gun or other explosive signal fired at intervals of about a minute

(2) Flames on the vessels (as from a burning tar-barrel, oil barrel, &c

(3) Rockets or shells, throwing stars of any colour or description, fired one at a time, at short intervals

(4) A continuous sounding with any fog-signal apparatus

Titanic carried the full outfit of distress signals required by the Board of Trade. These consisted of 36 socket signals, 12 ordinary rockets, 2 Manwell Holmes deck flares, 12 blue lights and 6 life-buoy lights.

Of these she used a number of socket signals, with their characteristic sound signal component. At least eight, and almost certainly more, were fired at unknown intervals. The first one was fired shortly after 0045.

By all accounts the rockets functioned correctly, and there

were no reports of any misfire or failure. Mr Boxhall, who was in charge of firing the rockets, was also preoccupied helping to launch the lifeboats and to call up the ship in sight to the north, using the Morse lamp. He was not, therefore, best placed to give his undivided attention to the rockets, or to judge the intervals at which they were being fired.

Deck officers sitting for their certificates of competency were required to be familiar with distress signals, but it was not laid down that they should acquire practical experience in using them. Mr Boxhall had never seen one used until that night.

No attempt was made to produce flames, and no fog-signal apparatus was used. Escaping steam from the safety valves made a very loud noise but was not a recognised distress signal. There are no reports of anyone hearing this noise other than those on board *Titanic*.

A Morse lamp was used to attract attention but without apparent response from the one vessel that appeared to be in sight as *Titanic* foundered.

Sinking to rescue: the lifeboats

All 14 standard lifeboats, the two emergency cutters and the four collapsible lifeboats survived the sinking. One collapsible, B, capsized and the occupants clung to the upturned hull. Most had space for additional people on board. Only four had officers in charge and only one had a means of showing flares to attract attention. Some had lights to indicate their presence.

Once in the water, the boats were not, in general, widely dispersed and several remained close to where *Titanic* sank. The calls and cries of the people in the water could be clearly heard, and the occupants of several lifeboats discussed returning to rescue them, but conflicting views emerged. Prevalent was the fear that, by doing so, their own safety would be jeopardised. Only a few of the crew had any knowledge how to handle the lifeboats, let alone be in charge of so many people of very different backgrounds. The situation was quite beyond anyone's experience. It was pitch dark and extremely cold. Only the fifth officer made the decision to make space available by transferring the occupants of No. 14 lifeboat to some others and then went in search of survivors. He found just three amongst the many dead bodies.

As the first light of dawn began to break and the wind started to pick up, a sail was hoisted in lifeboat No. 14 and the fifth officer went to join the other lifeboats and soon found the three he had linked together two hours earlier. He took collapsible D in tow and managed to organise the rescue of the occupants from the capsized collapsible B. He was just in time. A little later he took on board the occupants of collapsible A, but left the bodies of three people who had died during the night.

The fourth officer, meanwhile, in boat No. 2 was focused on keeping a lookout for any ship heading in their direction, and while it was still dark he fired green flares to attract attention. At the same time the *Carpathia* was steaming towards the position given in the original distress signal and also firing flares from 0245. Her lights and flares were spotted by some of the occupants, as were the flares being shown by boat No. 2.

When *Carpathia* finally slowed right down and stopped at 0400, lifeboat No. 2 was dead ahead. It came alongside at 0410 and the *Carpathia* received its first report as to what had happened.

All the survivors were successfully recovered by 0830.

Ships in the vicinity

SS *Californian*

No ship was very close to the *Titanic* when she foundered, but at least one was within sight and it could have been the Leyland liner SS *Californian*. Her role is examined more closely.

Any reference to time in connection with the *Californian* is liable to error. There was no clock on her bridge and there will have been a few minutes' time difference between *Californian*'s local time and that being kept on board *Titanic*. As times recalled in evidence were only approximate, no significance is attached to apparent discrepancies.

The *Californian* was a 6223 grt cargo vessel belonging to the Leyland Line, which was, in turn, owned by the International Mercantile Marine Company. She had departed London for Boston on 5 April with a cargo of cotton and, although she had accommodation for 47 passengers, none were being carried on this voyage. Her captain was 35-year-old Captain Stanley Lord, who held an Extra Master's Certificate.

Her passage across the Atlantic at 11 knots was uneventful, and the first incident of any note was during the early evening of Sunday 14 April when she sighted three icebergs some five miles to the south of her. Captain Lord reported the position of these icebergs to another Leyland liner, the *Antillian*, by wireless at 1930. The transmission was intercepted by the *Titanic*.

At the same time the chief officer took an observation of the Pole Star and calculated the ship's latitude to be 42° 5½' N. *Californian*'s course was S 89° W.

As night enveloped the *Californian* the sea was flat calm, the visibility was excellent and the temperature was falling. Aware that they were approaching an area where ice had been reported, the captain increased the lookout by placing an extra man on the foc's'le head. In view of the potential risk to the ship he chose to remain on the bridge himself. Shortly before about 2220 (*Californian* time) a whitening of the horizon ahead of the ship was seen and the captain, interpreting it as ice, took the way off the ship and altered course round to starboard. By the time the ship was stopped she was heading in, roughly, a northeasterly direction surrounded by light field ice. There was nothing else in sight.

Deciding that further progress west was unwise during the hours of darkness, Captain Lord decided to remain where he was overnight and continue at first light the next morning. The chief

SS *Californian* photographed from RMS *Carpathia*, forenoon 15 April

engineer was told to maintain steam, in case it should necessary to move the ship because of the ice.

At some time between 2230 and 2250 the single white light of another vessel was observed to the southeast and seen to be moving slowly to the right. The captain asked his wireless operator what other ships were around and was told only the *Titanic*. Captain Lord then told his operator to contact her and inform her that *Californian* was stopped and surrounded by ice. An attempt was made to send the message about 2255 but, because *Titanic*'s Marconi operator was preoccupied with working Cape Race, it was not taken down and Californian was told to 'keep out'.

Attempts were made to identify the other vessel, but it seems the only certainties are that the initial sighting was of a single white light, followed by a green side light as the range closed. Very shortly after this some accommodation lights also became visible. It is known that the bearing movement of this unknown ship was slowly right. There was a report to suggest that a red sidelight was visible indicating that the *Californian* was on the other vessel's port bow, but this does not tie in with the reported

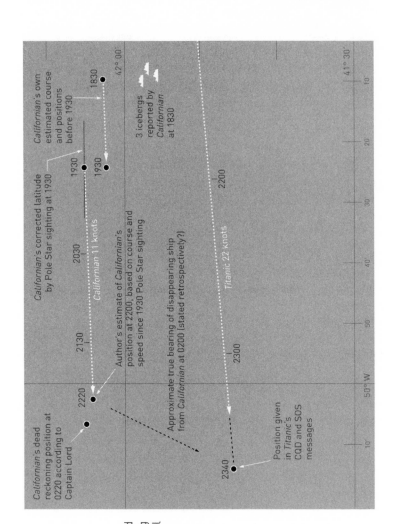

Movements of *Titanic* and *Californian* on the evening of 14 April

Californian's own estimated course and positions before 1930

Californian's corrected latitude by Pole Star sighting at 1930

1830

1930

1930

2030

3 icebergs reported by *Californian* at 1830

Californian 11 knots

2130

Author's estimate of *Californian's* position at 2200, based on course and speed since 1930 Pole Star sighting

Approximate true bearing of disappearing ship from *Californian* at 0200 (stated retrospectively?)

2200

Californian's dead reckoning position at 0220 according to Captain Lord

2220

Titanic 22 knots

2300

2340

Position given in *Titanic's* CQD and SOS messages

50° W

42° 00'

41° 30'

bearing movement. This other vessel was passing to the south on *Californian*'s starboard side, and, on the instructions of the captain, the officer of the watch began to call her up using the Morse lamp situated above the bridge. There was no reply. Throughout the time this other vessel remained in sight *Californian* was very slowly swinging to starboard.

There was no common view as to the other vessel's type or identity, but she was thought by some who saw her to be a passenger vessel, while the captain, the most experienced mariner on board, judged her to be a cargo vessel of a size similar to the *Californian*. Her range was variously assessed to be between 5 and 10 miles and her lights were said to be flickering. Meanwhile *Californian*'s wireless operator continued to listen to *Titanic* working Cape Race until he decided to turn in shortly after 2330.

At a time estimated to be between 2330 and about 2340 the other vessel appeared to stop at a range thought to be between 5 and 7 miles and turn out her lights. In the view of *Californian*'s officer of the watch this was entirely consistent with a practice undertaken in passenger ships operating in other parts of the world, where a lights-out routine encouraged passengers to turn in.

Californian's bridge watchkeepers changed at midnight. At about 0110 the new officer of the watch observed what he took to be a white flash on the horizon and coming from the direction of the ship he held in sight. Through his binoculars, he saw further flashes, but this time identified them as white rockets being fired at intervals of 4–5 minutes. The captain was informed and asked if they were company signals. The second officer did not know and was told to call her up to establish her name. The captain was under the impression this other vessel was relatively close by.

The other ship continued to be observed and the light, taken to be her stern light, seemed to grow more distant and finally disappeared over the horizon at about 0220. The assumption was made that she had got under way and continued her voyage. Her last known bearing was SW ½°W.

The watch changed again at 0400 and the chief officer took over. He was briefed about what had been seen overnight and was informed that white rockets had been seen coming from the direction of this unknown ship. Half an hour later the captain was called just as it was starting to get light. At the same time a ship was seen to be lying stopped to the south and on the same bearing as the vessel that had been observed earlier but further away. This new ship was estimated to be at a range of about 8 miles, and the chief officer suggested to his captain that they might head south and look at this other steamer on the grounds that she might have lost a rudder or something.

Captain Lord was unconvinced that anything was wrong with her and had already realised that this new ship, whoever she was, could not be the same steamer as that observed during the night. She had two steaming lights whereas the earlier vessel had only one. At the chief officer's suggestion, however, the captain agreed that the wireless officer should be called to establish what ship it was. In the meantime preparations were made to start making way, and at 0515 she began to move again. Within 15 minutes news began to be received that a ship had sunk. Captain Lord stopped the engines once again until he had further details and within ten minutes had discovered the *Titanic* had indeed gone down in a position some 19½ miles away to the southwest and on the other side of the field of ice to the west of them. Once this new information had been absorbed the *Californian* was pointed in the direction of *Titanic*'s last known position before heading west at slow speed to penetrate the ice barrier.

The last known position of *Titanic* indicated she was further to the west than any of the activity observed in the early hours of the morning.

Californian passed through the icefield and found herself in open water again by 0630, whereupon she turned south, increased speed to about 13 knots and ran down its western edge. By 0730 she had reached the position given in the distress message but only saw another vessel, the *Mount Temple*, and a steamer with a pink funnel, the *Almerian*, heading north. There was no sign of either the *Titanic* or any survivors.

A further message was received to say that the Cunard liner *Carpathia* was picking up survivors. The *Carpathia* was in sight to the east and on the other side of the icefield, so *Californian* altered course to the east, made her way through the ice for the second time that morning and joined the *Carpathia* at about 0830. She was too late to be of much assistance but, having communicated with the *Carpathia* by semaphore, assumed the search whilst *Carpathia* recovered some of the lifeboats. The *Californian* continued to conduct a search until about 1120, when it was concluded that they were unlikely to find anything further. She turned westwards, passed through the icefield for the third time that morning and proceeded to Boston.

Shortly after leaving the area, observations were taken and established *Californian*'s noon position as 41° 33' N, 50° 09' W. From this it was calculated that the position of the wreckage had been 41° 33' N, 50° 01' W, or some 32 miles south-southeast from where she estimated she had remained stopped overnight.

At some indeterminate moment thereafter her rough logbook was destroyed.

SS *Carpathia*

The 13,555 grt Cunard passenger liner SS *Carpathia*, under the command of Captain Arthur Rostron, was on passage from New York to Fiume on the Adriatic coast of Austria-Hungary on the night of 14 April 1912. Her first port of call was Gibraltar.

Before turning in for the night soon after midnight in the early hours of Monday 15 April, her wireless operator remembered that Cape Race had said earlier that it had several private messages waiting for the *Titanic*, which he knew was westbound

RMS *Carpathia* at the quayside in New York

in the same general area. Wishing to be helpful, he called the *Titanic* to establish contact, but received instead a distress call saying that she had hit an iceberg and asking *Carpathia* to come at once. Ship's time was 0035.

The wireless operator immediately reported the message to the bridge and, together with the officer of the watch informed the captain what had happened. Having received an assurance that the message was authentic, the captain ordered his ship to be brought round to the northwest, to make for the position contained in *Titanic*'s CQD message, some 58 miles away. Every effort was then made to increase speed by as much as possible and every non-essential steam-heated equipment on board was shut down.

Over the next three and a half hours, and as the *Carpathia* slowly increased speed from her normal 14 knots and the lookout was doubled, extensive preparations were made to receive survivors. Under the direction of the captain they included:

- Allocating the doctors on board to various parts of the ship

- Making arrangements to receive survivors and establishing their full names

- Having food and drink ready for survivors

- Ensuring all survivors were cared for and their immediate needs met

- Reassuring *Carpathia*'s passengers

- Insisting on quietness and order

- Opening gangway doors and rigging suitable means for embarking passengers of all ages, and crew

- Rigging electric cluster lights by gangways and over the side

- Rigging heaving lines over the side

- Preparing cargo derricks for embarking lifeboats

- Preparing to fire company signals from 0245 to reassure occupants of any lifeboats that help was at hand

As *Carpathia* approached the known icefield, extra lookouts were posted to detect any ice, and course had to be altered on a number occasions to avoid icebergs. Speed increased to an estimated 17 knots. Company signals were fired at 15-minute intervals from 0245 after a flare from an as yet unidentified source was observed ahead. It was thought initially to be from the *Titanic* herself but it became apparent that it was from a lifeboat. *Carpathia* stopped her engines at 0400 and had the first lifeboat from the *Titanic*, No. 2, alongside at 0410. She estimated she had reached the position given in *Titanic*'s distress message.

Over the next four hours over 700 survivors from the *Titanic* were successfully embarked. Many, but not all, were wearing warm clothing. They were cold, some were seasick or weeping and many were in an obvious state of shock. Dawn began to break soon after 0420, and for the first time those on board the *Carpathia* were able to see the extent of the icefield around them. At least 20 large icebergs were sighted nearby as well as an extensive icefield to the west. By 0500 it was light enough to see two other steamships to the north at a range judged to be between 7 and 8 miles distant.

The *Californian* was first identified at about 0800, having approached from the west. The two ships communicated with each other by semaphore, whereupon the *Californian* continued to search while the *Carpathia* embarked a number of *Titanic's* lifeboats before turning her head, getting under way and heading for New York with the survivors embarked at 0900. A headcount of the survivors on board indicated *Carpathia* had rescued an estimated 703 souls, comprising 493 passengers and 210 crew. The passengers included 126 men, 315 women and 52 children. Twenty-one members of the crew were women. Only six of the survivors were officers. These numbers would be revised in due course.

Carpathia encountered substantial fog on her passage to New York, where she arrived on the evening of Thursday 18 April. After offloading *Titanic's* lifeboats adjacent to West 20th Street, she berthed at Pier 54 at about 2135.

SS *Mount Temple*

On 14 April 1912 the 8790 grt Canadian Pacific Railway steamer *Mount Temple* was on passage carrying immigrants from both London and Antwerp to Saint John, New Brunswick on the western side of the Bay of Fundy, Canada. Her average speed was in the order of 9 knots. Having crossed the Atlantic on a great circle track she had been alerted to the presence of ice as she approached the Grand Banks and adjusted her course accordingly. She chose to steer about 10 miles to the south of it and cross longitude 50° in latitude 41° 15' N. The precise latitude of rounding the ice is not clear, but having done so during the early evening of 14 April she adjusted her course to the northwest to make for a position south of Cape Sable and the Bay of Fundy.

At 0030, ship's time, her sole Marconi operator intercepted the distress signal from the *Titanic*. The position given lay to the north of east at a range of about 40 miles, and course was adjusted to make for it. Making about 11 knots, *Mount Temple* began to encounter ice soon after 0300 but arrived at the position given in the distress signal at about 0430, having stopped briefly or slowed down an hour earlier. She saw nothing but found herself on the western edge of a large icefield and went no further.

While steaming east, her Marconi operator had listened to *Titanic* transmitting her distress signals and the replies of a number of other ships but made no further contact himself. There are indications that some people on board *Mount Temple* saw rockets and even lights from a ship well to the east in the early hours of 15 April.

An observation of the sun was taken to obtain a longitude soon after sunrise, and this put the *Mount Temple* within 4 miles of the position given in *Titanic's* SOS message. The longitude was 50° 09' W. At 0600 *Mount Temple* saw the *Carpathia* to the east and on the far side of the icefield, which he judged to be between 5 and 6 miles wide. At 0730 the *Californian* joined her from the north only to alter course to push through the ice on an easterly heading. *Mount Temple* remained where she was, to be joined by SS *Birma* at about 0800.

Having seen nothing, and having been assured that the *Carpathia* had rescued survivors from 20 boats, *Mount Temple* resumed her voyage to Saint John at about 0900.

Other ships

- SS *Provence*. Eastbound French Line liner on passage New York to Le Havre. Picked up *Titanic's* distress signal at 0025 and helped relay it to other vessels.

- SS *Virginian*. Allen liner on passage from Halifax to Liverpool. Received *Titanic*'s CQD at 0040 on 15 April and estimated she was some 178 miles away. *Virginian* altered course towards *Titanic*. She was probably the only ship to intercept *Titanic*'s final wireless message, sent moments before she sank. It was also the *Virginian* that confirmed to *Californian* that *Titanic* had sunk, shortly after 0600 on the morning of 15 April. Following the sinking *Virginian* continued her voyage heading east and encountered the ice barrier at about 1100 on the morning of 15 April. She altered course to the south to navigate around it and did so in position 41° 20' N, 49° 50' W. The *Virginian* was later, and erroneously, reported to be towing a damaged *Titanic* to Halifax.

- SS *Birma* of the Russian East Asia Line was bound east. Having received *Titanic*'s distress call from a range of about 70 miles, she proceeded to the position given and saw nothing. She then headed south to find clear water to the south of the ice-field before heading north. She played no further part in the incident.

- SS *Frankfurt*. North German Lloyd liner bound east from Galveston to Bremerhaven. She was the first ship to be in contact with *Titanic* after the initial CQD had been transmitted, but was not apparently aware that a distress call had gone out. Some confusion followed but *Frankfurt* eventually understood the position and altered course towards to provide what assistance she could. She arrived at the western edge of the ice barrier shortly before 1100 on the 15th, as *Californian* was leaving the area to resume her voyage. She played no further part in the incident but was the first vessel that passed on information about the sinking of the *Titanic* to the *Californian*.

- SS *Olympic*. *Titanic*'s sister ship, eastbound from New York to Plymouth, Cherbourg and Southampton. She was called by *Titanic* at about 0045 and was sent the SOS distress message. She altered course to provide assistance. Her distance from *Titanic* was assessed as being 512 miles. *Olympic* was one of the very few ships to carry two wireless operators and was among those to inform *Titanic* that she was steering towards her to provide assistance.

- SS *Almerian* was a 3030 grt Leyland liner with two masts. Eastbound from Mobile, Alabama, for Liverpool, she did not have wireless but, in the early hours of 15 April, she found herself steaming north on the western side of a large icefield and to the south of another vessel of the same line, the *Californian*. She took no part in the response to *Titanic*'s sinking but continued north, seeking a way through the icefield, and knew nothing of the disaster until she arrived in Liverpool on 25 April.

- SS *Baltic*. Eastbound White Star liner on passage from New York to Liverpool. Picked up *Titanic*'s faint distress message at 0055 from a position 243 miles to the southeast. Course was altered towards *Titanic*'s position and she later offered to embark some of the passengers already on board the *Carpathia*.

Wireless traffic post sinking

Following the sinking of *Titanic* a number of ships tried to establish what had happened, what the current situation was, or offer assistance. At times it became very difficult for some of them to communicate due to constant transmissions by one or two vessels. By dominating the airways they made it very difficult for others to transmit.

The rules for transmitting messages in a distress situation are clear:

> Failing any mention of a particular station in the signal of distress, any station which receives the call is bound to answer it. In doing this ships must beware of interfering with each other, and not more than one ship should answer if it is found that confusion results. A ship which knows from the strength of the signals of distress that she is near the ship requiring assistance should take precedence in answering and taking the necessary steps with regard to the distress signal.

Discovery of the wreck

The wreck of the *Titanic* was discovered by a French-American team led by Robert Ballard and Jean-Louis Michel on board the French research ship *Le Suroit* in the early hours of 1 September 1985 using the submersible *Alvin*. It was lying, in two main pieces, at a depth of 12,415 feet (3784 metres) in position 41° 44' N, 49° 57' W. The distance between the two sections is 1970 feet (600 metres).

This position is 13.5 miles to the east-southeast of the position given in *Titanic*'s CQD wireless message.

Images of the wreck show substantial damage. Most of this would have occurred:

- as *Titanic* broke up on leaving the surface

- on her descent to the seabed

- through implosion very shortly after leaving the surface

- as she impacted with the seabed

The section of the bow damaged by the collision with the iceberg was embedded in the seabed and was not visible.

A study was made to identify what windows, portholes and watertight doors might have been open before the ship foundered. Although a number of windows were seen to be open, particularly those of the officers' cabins overlooking the boat deck, it is judged that these must have been opened somehow during the descent to, or when hitting, the seabed.

The best analysis suggests that a number of portholes were open while *Titanic* was still on the surface, as was the forward gangway door on the port side of D deck.

No assessment is made of any internal watertight doors that may have been left open.

PART 2

Analysis

The purpose of the analysis is to determine the circumstances and contributory causes of the accident as a basis for making recommendations to prevent similar accidents in the future.

The captain

The captain joined the *Titanic* in Belfast on 1 April, having just completed a round voyage to New York in command of the *Olympic*. The *Titanic* sailed on sea trials the next morning.

Captain Smith was a highly regarded and extremely experienced seaman. He had been with the White Star Line for 32 years and had held command of a number of passenger ships on the North Atlantic since 1887. Prior to joining the *Titanic* he had been in command of her sister ship *Olympic* since her maiden voyage in June 2011.

Despite his distinguished career he had experienced a number of mishaps as a captain, including two whilst in command of the *Olympic*. The first involved an incident with a tug whilst berthing at New York at the end of her maiden voyage in June 1911, and the second was a collision with the cruiser HMS *Hawke* in the Solent whilst leaving Southampton Water in September the same year.

Many ship masters suffer misfortunes from time to time and most learn from them, but a ship owner must form a judgement as to whether they were merely 'accidents' or something more fundamental involving faulty judgement or misplaced confidence. There is no evidence whatsoever to suggest the White

Star Line was in any way concerned about Captain Smith's professional competence and, in appointing him to command *Titanic*, everything indicates they had complete faith in his abilities. It would also appear that he had the complete confidence of Mr Ismay.

Being popular with regular passengers is a great asset on the transatlantic run, and being held in high esteem by officers and crews lends itself to having a happy ship, but these are not the only criteria necessary to being a successful passenger-ship master. Good judgement, consistency, reliability and painstaking professionalism are key elements to being a successful and safe liner captain.

Whilst it was customary for a master to join a new ship shortly before sailing on sea trails, the less than 24 hours that Captain Smith had to prepare his ship, himself and his untried crew was ambitious. He had already taken *Olympic* out of build a year earlier so was familiar with the requirements and the class of ship. This was an undoubted advantage, but the minimal interval between joining the *Titanic* and sailing was unfair on both himself and his ship. He had no time to familiarise himself with his new command, identify any differences between the two ships, meet officers he had not previously sailed with and generally satisfy himself that *Titanic* was fit for purpose. He can have had almost no influence on the conduct and acceptability of the sea trials, and to expect an officer, even one of Captain Smith's abilities, to shed the habits of running a fully operational ship and take on the very different role of bringing a new one into service was asking much. Whilst he could reasonably expect that everything was in order, and that his complement of officers met the highest professional standards, no captain of a new ship will ever accept everything entirely on trust and would wish to make a number of personal checks to satisfy himself that all was in order.

Notwithstanding the short interval between joining and sailing, Captain Smith was, by all accounts, satisfied with the way *Titanic* performed on sea trials, and I have no reason to think he was anything other than totally confident in his ability to take such a new ship out of build and run her successfully.

Despite his competence and ability, Captain Smith was not, in my opinion, given sufficient time to settle into his new ship and become familiar with it before being required to sail.

Also in my opinion, the White Star Line's decision to appoint Captain Smith in command of the *Titanic* just after he had completed a round voyage to New York in the *Olympic* and immediately before sailing for cursory sea trials was a factor in the way the ship was run from the outset. He had no opportunity to get to know his ship, his new officers and key personnel.

It is reasonable to assume that there was much for him to attend to during the few days *Titanic* remained alongside in Southampton after arriving from Belfast. On the morning of sailing, and almost certainly at the captain's behest, Mr Henry Wilde joined to replace Mr William Murdoch as the chief officer. This necessitated a shuffle among the officers, with Mr Murdoch having to strep down a rank to become to become the first officer. Mr Lightoller, who had been the first officer, became second officer, and the previous second officer left the ship. To replace such a senior officer just before the ship sailed was unusual but not unique. There is no evidence to suggest that the changes created any resentment, but it is possible. The new chief officer had previously served under Captain Smith in *Olympic* but had been landed shortly before the ship sailed for New York to await a new appointment. It must be assumed that Mr Wilde enjoyed the full confidence of the captain, but by any criteria such a change-round of senior officers with only hours to go before sailing on a maiden voyage must have been unsettling to the other officers.

Once at sea Captain Smith would have been comfortable with his new command. It was almost identical to the one he had just relinquished. By all accounts the ship was running satisfactorily and, apart from conducting some manoeuvring trials early on, he was treating the voyage like any other. Whilst he appeared to carry out all his normal duties efficiently, there is no evidence that he ever talked to, or briefed, his officers on how he wanted things to be done. Many of the practices undertaken on board *Titanic* may well have reflected the custom of the day, but they fell short of the standards for which he was renowned. His command style was, in my opinion, built on familiarity with the crossing and not on working up his team to the standards the White Star Line could reasonably expect. To give just two examples, there is no evidence to indicate that ice warnings were handled efficiently, and for unknown reasons no lifeboat drill was held, as was the custom on board White Star Lines, on a Sunday at sea. 14 April was a Sunday.

The navigating officers

Prior to the maiden voyage none of her seven navigating officers had been on board *Titanic* for more than a few days. All bar the chief officer joined the ship in Belfast before she sailed on sea trials but none had any real opportunity to settle in properly. They were all professionals doing familiar work and probably needed little guidance as to what was required, but even the most competent and experienced officer requires time to adjust to a new ship. There is no hard and fast rule, but a conscientious officer would probably accept that it probably takes about two weeks to know one's way around a large passenger ship with confidence.

The new chief officer joined the ship at 0600 on the morning *Titanic* was due to sail from Southampton.

By the time she departed at noon on 10 April, none of her crew, including the deck officers, had had any real opportunity to work as a team, and this would have implications on how everyone related to each other during the course of the voyage. Everyone had a job and was expected to get on with it.

The three senior officers had all served in sail, were confident in their ability to carry out their responsibilities in a professional manner, and relied on the junior officers to do as they were told and carry out the more routine tasks.

All the navigating officers were well qualified, and some had extensive experience on the North Atlantic. Seniority and hierarchy on board reflected society ashore and were features in the merchant ships of the day. Junior officers were reluctant to voice their own opinions or offer advice to those more senior to them, and there is ample evidence to indicate the practice of following custom. If something was the 'custom' then it tended to take precedence. There is no evidence to indicate that a decision taken by the master or someone more senior was ever either questioned or challenged even if evidently wrong. Such interventions were neither invited nor countenanced. The superior's word was law.

It is assessed, nonetheless, that all bar one of *Titanic*'s officers were sufficiently competent, experienced and professional to be fully aware that ice posed a potential risk to any ship at sea in the vicinity of the Grand Banks in April. They will also have been aware that the routing of ships had, since 1899, been dictated by an agreement between the great North Atlantic companies whereby the tracks for both 'outward' (westbound) and 'homeward' (eastbound) steamers had been separated to reduce any possibility of collision as well as to keep them well clear of the anticipated region of fog and ice at two clearly defined periods in the calendar year. Between 15 January and 14 August, when the threat of ice was greatest, they would have known that these tracks took ships some miles further south than was the case in the period 15 August and 14 January.

The one officer who may not, perhaps surprisingly, have been aware of the presence of ice in the region of the Grand Banks during April was the fifth officer, who was making his first transatlantic voyage. In itself this may not have been a significant factor, but it indicates a possible lack of shared information between the deck officers.

The officers did not fraternise with the passengers, and there is every indication that they applied themselves to the job in hand to the best of their ability from the moment the ship sailed from Southampton.

The passage plan

Titanic's passage plan across the North Atlantic followed the normal Outward Southern track for a westbound steamer in April. Having called at Queenstown and taken her departure off the Fastnet light, her intention was to follow a conventional great circle route across the North Atlantic to position 42° N, 47° W, known colloquially as the 'Turning Point' or 'Corner' and some miles to the east of where ice and fog is most likely to be encountered on a normal voyage. She would then alter course to the west to complete her voyage by steering a straight course to a position just south of the Nantucket Shoals light vessel and thence to New York. She was scheduled to arrive at her destination on the morning of Wednesday 17 April.

Until 14 April the passage was entirely normal. Although the Outward Southern track had been devised and promulgated to ensure ships would remain clear of ice and fog, as well as to keep westbound and eastbound shipping separated, it was not unknown for ships to proceed further south in years when more ice than normal was encountered. This had occurred in 1903, 1904 and 1905, and westbound steamers had proceeded some 60 miles further south to cross longitude 47° W at latitude 41° N.

An aspect of the planned passage that would not have gone unnoticed by the captain was that *Titanic* would be passing through the area most likely to be affected by ice during the hours of darkness. This would not be unusual but would require additional care. Seeing unlit objects at night is not easy.

Ice warnings

The presence of ice in the North Atlantic in the vicinity of the Grand Banks in spring was well publicised in both sailing directions and on charts. All *Titanic*'s officers were certificated master mariners or extra masters, and with one exception would all have been familiar with both the warnings and the extent to which ice could be encountered.

1912 was unusual, but not uniquely so, in having a greater presence of ice than normal. Following a warm winter, a large quantity of ice was being carried south by the Labrador Current. Ships were encountering it on the Outward Southern Track from the first week in April. Messages describing its extent were circulating before *Titanic* sailed from Southampton. On the morning of her departure, the daily shipping newspaper *Lloyd's List* featured a small article about ice in the North Atlantic, but it is not known if this information or any other ice-related warnings were received on board. They may have been.

At an undetermined time after sailing, a number of messages containing ice information were received and handed to the fourth officer to plot. The one message he remembered in detail was from the eastbound French steamer *La Touraine* on 12 April. He recalled that the ice in the report was 'considerably' further to the north of *Titanic*'s intended track and, as such, posed no threat. Taken at face value, this judgement was correct. The position very much conformed to what an officer would have expected at this time of the year, and the fourth officer informed the captain accordingly. It was the first of a number of wireless reports received by the *Titanic* indicating the presence of ice.

On the following evening, 13 April, the eastbound Furness Withy steamer *Rappahannock* signalled by light that she had encountered ice but omitted, apparently, to provide any information as to the location.

On 14 April a number of messages from other ships and containing ice reports were received in various forms. The following table presents the information received on board *Titanic* from 12 April and describes how it was handled.

Ice reports received by *Titanic*

Time of receipt and origin	Relevant content of message	Action and reaction in *Titanic*
12 April, pm SS *La Touraine*, eastbound	*La Touraine* had ˈcrossed a thick icefield in position 44° 58ˈ, 50° 40ˈ, saw another icefield and two icebergs in lat. 45° 20ˈ, 45° 09ˈ ˈ, and had ˈseen a derelict in 40° 56ˈ, 63° 38ˈ ˈ Message prefixed MSG	Seen by the captain and the fourth officer, who plotted the position on a chart. It showed the ice some 180 miles to the north of *Titanic*'s planned track and was assessed not to be of any concern. The presence, and position, of a derelict would have been noted.
13 April, 2230 SS *Rappahannock*, eastbound Halifax to London	Message passed by light, reported having passed through pack ice and that her rudder had been damaged No position or time was included	Receipt by light implies it was received by an officer on watch, but there is no record as to how the information was handled on the bridge.
14 April, 0900 (shipˈs time) SS *Caronia*, eastbound New York to Liverpool	ˈWestbound steamers report bergs growlers and field-ice in 42° N from 49° to 51° W April 12ˈ Message prefixed MSG	Seen by Captain Smith and plotted by the fourth officer. When plotted, the ice referred to in this report lies about 10 miles to the north of *Titanic*'s intended track. (*Continues*)

Time of receipt and origin	Relevant content of message	Action and reaction in *Titanic*
(**14 April, 0900** SS *Caronia*)	(Westbound steamers report bergs growlers and field-ice in 42° N from 49° to 51° W April 12 Message prefixed MSG)	(*Continued*) The report referred to the presence of ice two days earlier. In assessing the potential risk to the ship no allowance appears to have been made for its set due to the current. The second officer was shown this message at about 1245 and made a mental calculation that the ship would not reach the position contained in the message until after he came on watch at 1800. The information contained in this message was passed on to the first officer when he took over the watch at 1300. The message implied that although westbound steamers had encountered ice, they had not been prevented from proceeding through it.
1342 (ship's time) SS *Baltic*, eastbound New York to Liverpool	'Have made mod var winds and clear fine weather since leaving. Greek steamer *Athenai* reports passing icebergs and large quantity of field ice today in lat. 41° 51' N, long. 49° 25' W. Last night spoke German oil tank steamer *Deutschland* Stettin to Philadelphia. Not under control. Short of coal. Lat. 40° 42' N, long. 55° 11' W' Message prefixed MSG	Received by wireless operator Philips and delivered to Captain Smith, who acknowledged it before showing it to Mr Bruce Ismay, who retained it. It was recovered by the captain at 1915 and taken to the bridge, where it was posted in the chartroom. The plotted position of this ice straddles *Titanic*'s planned track. It does not appear to have been plotted.

Time of receipt and origin	Relevant content of message	Action and reaction in *Titanic*
1345 (ship's time) SS *Amerika* to US Hydrographic Office, Washington DC, intercepted by *Titanic*	*'Amerika* passed two large icebergs in 41° 27' N, 50° 08' W on April 14' Message prefix XMSG	There is no record of this message being shown to the captain but the fourth officer recalled having plotted the position and remembered it as being to the north of the planned track. When re-plotted it lay some 20 miles to the south of the intended track.
1445 SS *Noordam*, eastbound New York to Rotterdam	'Had moderate wly winds fair weather no fog. Much ice reported in lat. 42° 24' to 24° 45' and long. 49° 50' to 50° 20' ' This message was received twice by *Titanic* via SS *Caronia*, with the second one, received 15 minutes later, having the latitude corrected to read 42° 24' to 42° 45' Both messages prefixed with MSG	Received on board by Philips and acknowledged by Captain Smith. There is no record of this message being specifically seen or plotted by any officer. The reported ice was some 40–50 miles north of *Titanic*'s planned track.
1750	*Titanic* alters course to S 86°W	
1930 SS. *Californian*, westbound London to Boston (stopped and surrounded by ice) to SS *Antillian*, intercepted by *Titanic*	'...6 30 pm. Apparent ship's time: lat. 42° 03' N, long. 49° 9' W. Three large bergs five miles to southward of us.' Message prefixed with MSG	Received by wireless operator Bride and taken to bridge but it is not known to which officer it was given. There is no record of the positions being plotted, but it put the *Californian* 12 miles north of the track actually undertaken by *Titanic*.

Time of receipt and origin	Relevant content of message	Action and reaction in *Titanic*
2140 SS *Mesaba*, westbound London to New York	'In lat. 42°, to 41° 25′N, long. 49° to 50° 30′ W saw much heavy pack ice and great number large icebergs also field of ice. Weather good, clear.' Message prefixed with 'ice report' but not MSG.	Received on board *Titanic* by Philips, but there is no indication as to how it was handled or to whom, if anyone, it was shown. The lack of the prefix MSG may have been significant. Had the ice positions contained in this report been plotted it would have shown the ice straddling the track along which *Titanic* was steaming.
2307 SS *Californian*	'We are stopped and surrounded by ice.' There was no prefix to the message.	Received by Philips as he was in the process of receiving a message from Cape Race. *Californian*'s transmission drowned out the incoming Cape Race, prompting Philips to respond 'Keep out. I am busy, I am working Cape Race.' *Californian* did not attempt to repeat her message.

Analysis reveals that in the 24 hours preceding the collision with the iceberg *Titanic* received a number of wireless messages containing ice warnings and that some, but not all, had been shown to the master or a navigating officer. There may have been others for which no record exists.

Handling ice warnings

To ensure wireless messages containing the ice warnings were heeded, an effective system for handling them had to be in place. There was no such system.

The wireless operators' commercial *raison d'être* was handling passenger traffic, and with a number of wealthy passengers embarked their workload was heavy. Because of the limitations in transmission imposed by the restricted range of communications by day, the workload at night was greater, and even more so when the ship was within range of a shore station such as Cape Race on the southeastern tip of Newfoundland.

Notwithstanding the time spent handling passenger traffic, the operators realised the significance of handling any messages prefixed with the letter MSG (master's service gram). Of the incoming ice warning messages received during 14 April five were prefixed with MSG and one with the words 'ice report'. The report from the *Californian* saying she was stopped and surrounded by ice had no prefix. Messages prefixed with MSG were drawn to the attention of someone on the bridge but those without it were not.

The failure of some operators in ships transmitting service messages to apply the correct prefix was a contributory factor in all that went wrong on 14 April.

At the same time there is little to show that the Marconi operators had a close working relationship with the deck officers. They were not White Star officers and were, as employees of the Marconi Company, treated very differently. Technically signed on as part of the victualling department, they messed separately with the postal clerks on C deck. Although the Marconi room was adjacent to the officers' accommodation, they had no direct means of communicating with the bridge and there was no telephone link. This meant that to deliver a message the Marconi operator had to leave his office and walk to the forward end of the bridge accommodation and give a message to someone he did not really know and at a time when he might have been fully occupied. The system was not conducive to efficiency. The lack of a telephone meant they could not even ring the bridge to see if a junior officer was free to collect a message.

The operators had no reason to understand the significance of any message passed to them and positions would have

The ice positions in reports that were never passed to *Titanic*'s bridge on 14 April

Titanic, 22 knots

1000
1200
1400
1600
1700
1750
1900
2100
2200
0000

Californian reports 'stopped and surrounded by ice'

Mesaba reports ice

45°N
44°N
43°N
42°N
41°N

45°W
50°W

meant nothing. They had no awareness of the deck officer's responsibilities and any feeling that they were being socially excluded may have had some justification. This lack of awareness was reciprocated. The deck officers made no effort to integrate them in their work and had little appreciation of their value. Wireless was still an innovation and most seaman officers were far more familiar, and comfortable, with the traditional means of communicating at sea using visual means.

This instinctive barrier between deck officers and Marconi operators was a factor in the reducing the level of cooperation between the two departments.

It is also not clear what system was in force for ensuring that all officers saw ice warning messages once they had been received on the bridge. Some were 'posted' in the chartroom, at least one or two were plotted on a chart and one note merely had the single word 'ice' written on it. What seems to have been lacking was any methodology for handling any such messages. No specific directive was given to having them plotted on the chart so that the officers were aware of them, and no serious consideration was given to assessing the risk of danger or reducing it.

When reference is made to plotting the position of ice it is not readily apparent which chart is being referred to, as *Titanic* had two chartrooms and two sets of some charts. The captain had his own navigation room adjacent to both his day cabin and the wheelhouse, while the officers used the ship's chartroom and, probably, two sets of charts. It is known that the captain used his personal chart to plot some navigational information but it is not known if this was duplicated on the chart used by his officers. Although there is evidence to indicate that at least one ice report was plotted, there is no indication to show which chart was used.

Had all the ice reports been plotted it would have been evident that there was an accumulation of ice in the vicinity of *Titanic*'s proposed track, but there is nothing to indicate they were unaware of this anyway. They expected to see ice.

There is some evidence to indicate that the officers made relatively little use of charts when out of sight of land. Sun and stellar observations, together with amplitudes and azimuths, required access to nautical tables to produce positions and true bearings of heavenly bodies, while courses to steer and distances to go could be accurately calculated and did not necessarily need to be plotted on a chart. It was customary for noon positions stellar observations to be plotted on at least one chart, but not necessarily the one in the chartroom. Deck officers would habitually do some of the more straightforward calculations in their heads, and there is evidence to suggest that this was the practice on board *Titanic*. This apparent shunning of chart work may have been a factor in deterring officers from plotting ice warnings on a chart.

There is also evidence to indicate a lack of communication between officers. While three of the officers made mental calculations as to when the ship would be 'up to the ice' on the evening of 14 April, the fifth officer was unaware that ice was a potential hazard in the vicinity of the Newfoundland Grand Banks. This suggests he was not briefed by anyone on what might be expected while passing through the area of risk during the night of 14/15 April. The fact that this one officer was unaware the ship was approaching an area where ice was known to exist indicates a lack of any team approach to safe navigation and a failure by officers to share basic information. It was a factor in the chain of events.

The failure to collate ice reports and to plot them on a chart, and to ensure that all the watchkeeping officers had access to the information, was a contributory cause of the accident. That said, it is assessed that the captain, and at least some of the deck officers, were well aware that ice lay ahead of them on the night of 14/15 April. Furthermore, they knew when the ice was likely to be encountered.

Navigation plan: 14 April

Until 1700 on 14 April the passage had been entirely normal. The weather had been good, the engines had performed well, the distances covered each day had been promising and there were sufficient bunkers to ensure no shortage prior to arrival in New York.

Captain Smith was very familiar with the track planned and had already made a return crossing of the Atlantic that spring while in command of the *Olympic*. As a master with extensive experience of the North Atlantic he would have been well acquainted with the movement and presence of ice and would have known that April and May were the months when ice was most likely. He would have known that his planned track fell within the limit marked on the chart with the warning, 'Icebergs have been seen within this line in April, May and June.' He would also have known that the individual ice reports were part of a much wider picture. The ice reports received would have been both expected and predictable.

They would, however, have also told him something else: that the ships making the reports were able to pass through the affected area without untoward difficulty.

In selecting the route to take the master had two basic choices. He could either maintain, more or less, the planned Outward Southern track and steam into an area where ice had been reported, or proceed further south before altering course to the west. There is no evidence to indicate he knew where the southern limit of the reported ice lay, but the further south he went the greater the chance he had of leaving it clear to the north. The first option would be totally dependent on seeing ice in sufficient time to take avoiding action and, if necessary, reduce speed or even stop. The second option would involve an extension to the length of the voyage. *Titanic* had time in hand to accommodate both options.

In the event the captain chose, with a minor adjustment, to maintain the original planned track and rely on seeing the ice in time to take avoiding action. It is not known how he reached this decision, but the weather was good, other ships had passed this way previously, the visibility was perfect and he was more than familiar with the track being taken. He had already undertaken it once within the previous month.

The estimated time of arrival at the 'turning point' (42° N, 47° W) for the alteration of course to S 85° W was 1700 but, for unknown reasons, the change of course was delayed. It is not known whose decision this was, but it most likely fell to the master, who was probably on the bridge at the time. The course alteration at the 'turning point' was always a feature of a transatlantic passage, and there is no reason to think this voyage was any different. In the event course was altered to a new course of S 86° W at 1750 to take her, initially, 7 miles south of the planned track. The new course would very slowly converge with the one previously planned and so reduce the full impact of the initial diversion to stay further south. It is assessed that the most logical reason for this small deviation was to take the ship clear of at least some of the ice known to be in the vicinity of latitude 42° N. It is not known if any consideration was given to delaying the course alteration even further, but a number of options were available, including asking other ships by wireless where clear water existed and manoeuvring accordingly, delaying the alteration to the west until daylight, or proceeding much further south until well clear of any possible ice.

Had the captain decided to stay on the original southwesterly course until such time that it intercepted the 50th meridian *Titanic* would have found herself some 75 miles further south. This would have added some 25 miles to the overall passage, or just over an hour's steaming. There was ample time in hand to accommodate this extra deviation but, if the captain ever considered it as an option, he discarded it.

Wireless defect

Titanic's wireless suffered a defect at about 2200 on Saturday 13 April. The two operators worked continuously for about six hours to repair it but at the expense of their time off duty and sleep. This meant that when *Titanic* was within range of Cape Race the next evening, there was a backlog of traffic to clear by two tired operators. The pressures they faced would have had an impact on their performance. It is known that the senior operator was tired during the following day and, although it cannot be proved beyond doubt, it is likely that both operators were affected by a degree of fatigue. Fatigue is one of the least understood factors in seafaring and can have a devastating effect on performance. Most mariners would refuse to accept they might be affected by it, as they are familiar with being tired and take immense pride in being able to handle it.

The performance of even the most competent and conscientious individuals can, however, be adversely affected by even limited fatigue and may lead them to overlook things that would normally come naturally. During the evening of 14 April both Marconi operators were guilty of making very small but nonetheless significant slips while coping with a heavy workload. Nobody knows, for instance, what happened to the ice warning received from the *Mesaba* at 2140, while the later attempt by the *Californian* to inform *Titanic* that she was stopped and surrounded by ice was rebuffed.

In spite of the difficulties the two Marconi had to endure during 14 April, it is greatly to their credit that they both overcame any tiredness later that night and responded so well to subsequent events.

There was a second consequence of the wireless defect. It occurred during the night when transmission and reception conditions were at their best. Although there is no evidence as such, this may have meant that the operators were unable to clear all their outgoing traffic that night and had to carry it over to Sunday evening, when it would have added to their already heavy workload as they closed Cape Race. At the same time the down time over several hours may have meant they missed further ice warnings from other ships. It is known, for instance, that the eastbound Leyland Line steamer *Corinthian* relayed an ice warning from her sister ship the *Corsican* to the westbound *Mount Temple* during the night of 13/14 April, giving an indication as to how far south the ice had spread. Although she was within reception range of these transmissions no record exists of *Titanic* either being sent this message or intercepting it. There may have been others.

It should not be overlooked that had the repair work not been undertaken, *Titanic* would have been denied the one piece of technology that eventually led to a distress message being transmitted and over 700 souls being saved.

Weather

Throughout her voyage across the Atlantic, *Titanic* experienced fine weather. As night fell on the evening of 14 April, the conditions were unusually benign. There was no moon, no fog, and it became progressively colder under a starlit sky. It was flat calm and there was no wind. Such conditions, while known in Arctic waters, are relatively unusual in the Atlantic, and the evidence indicates that at least some of *Titanic*'s officers were witnessing something out of the ordinary. They would, however, have anticipated the rapid reduction of temperature as *Titanic* moved from the relatively warm water of the Gulf Stream into the far colder water of the Labrador Current. Such a drop in both air and sea temperature on the approach to the Grand Banks does not, in itself, predict the presence of ice but it does alert the bridge watchkeepers to the possibility that they were entering an area where ice could be expected.

As expected, both air and sea temperature fell over several hours throughout the late afternoon and evening of 14 April.

The weather remained calm throughout the night but both wind and sea began to get up as dawn broke on the morning of 15 April when the *Carpathia* was rescuing survivors.

Visibility

One thing that ships' masters intensely dislike is poor visibility, in particular fog. Conversely, excellent visibility in a region where fog was commonplace would have been very welcome. The visibility on Sunday 14 April was excellent. It was also very cold, and cold dry air has the characteristic of being extremely clear. This in turn provides the conditions that produce exceptionally good visibility. It is assessed that these are the conditions that prevailed that night.

The various messages from other ships and received by *Titanic* so far during the voyage contained much useful information. Not only did some contain ice warnings but most contained a reference to visibility. With one exception they indicated clear weather. They would also have indicated, by implication, that the ships making the reports were, again with one exception, maintaining their passages without being impeded by any ice. Such information would have been noted by *Titanic*'s master.

The exceptionally good visibility would have a bearing on the ability to see the two types of object most likely to be encountered: a ship with lights and something without such as an iceberg, ice or even a derelict.

A feature of exceptional visibility at night in such cold conditions is that lights can be seen at distances far in excess of the normal. The only limitation to seeing a ship's light against a very dark background is the curvature of the earth. The range of detection can be extended further if factors such as refraction or superior mirage exist, but there is no specific evidence to suggest that either was present that night. These conditions have therefore been discounted for the purposes of this analysis.

There is also a human element involved. Unless they have extensive experience of working in Arctic waters at night, few mariners have practical experience of seeing normal ships' lights at very long distances and they tend, very naturally, to assume that what they can see matches their normal expectations. As a result, they grossly underestimate the range at which the light can be seen. It is assessed that this is precisely what happened.

Unlit objects present a different challenge. There was no moon on 14 April but the stars were seen to shine with great intensity. The only external illumination was that provided by star light. There are two aspects: direct illumination and reflected light. Both the captain and his second officer discussed the effect of seeing an iceberg in the prevailing conditions and regretted the lack of any wind to cause a sea to break visibly on its base. They did, however, talk about seeing reflected light on any icebergs and appeared confident that the white outline would give sufficient warning. Several ship masters said in evidence that they would normally expect to see icebergs at night in good visibility at ranges of up to 10 miles.

It is not known if the discussion between the captain and Mr Lightoller went on to embrace the effects of starlight being reflected from an icefield, but the captain made it very clear that in the event of encountering haze they would have to slow down.

It is assumed that when course was eventually altered to the west, at 1750, the captain had concluded that despite the ice warnings received, the visibility was so exceptional that any ice encountered would not only be seen, but seen in good time. He maintained his speed.

Speed

During the *Olympic*'s maiden voyage in 1911 with Captain Smith in command, speed was slowly increased on successive days. The maximum speed of nearly 22¾ knots was achieved on the final day before slowing for the final 300+ miles. Although it is not known what he had in mind for the last two days of

Titanic's maiden voyage, it is quite possible that Captain Smith had a similar plan in mind.

After leaving Southampton, *Titanic*'s revolutions were, like the *Olympic*'s, increased slowly each day, and by the evening of 14 April they had reached 75 rpm. The engines had run well and the last of the double-ended boilers had been fired. Everything indicated an intention to increase speed further on the 15th, and it is probable the five single-ended boilers would have been lit at some stage before the end of the voyage. It is almost certain that some form of full power trial was to be attempted prior to completing the voyage.

It is not known which of the ship's officers knew of this intention, but it is probable that both the senior engineer officers and the navigating officers were aware of it, as well as Mr Bruce Ismay.

The *Olympic*'s fastest westbound passage occurred on her fourth voyage when she took the shorter Outward Northern track. With a passage time of 5 days 7 hours and 29 minutes, she achieved this with an average speed of 21.8 knots. There is no credible evidence to suggest that either the master or Mr Ismay had any intention of trying to beat this on the longer southerly route, or were attempting any other 'record' for *Titanic*. By virtue of her design, and the White Star Line's emphasis on comfort for passengers rather than speed, there was never any prospect of *Titanic* breaking a speed record. She could, however, still beat the *Olympic*'s maiden-voyage passage time. It might have enhanced the marketing strategy for the new *Olympic* class in general and *Titanic* in particular, but there is, again, no evidence to support this ambition.

It is not known what the actual intentions were but, by the evening of 14 April *Titanic* was already ahead of where *Olympic* had been at the same time on her first voyage. It was therefore entirely feasible for *Titanic* to have arrived in New York during the late afternoon or early evening of Tuesday the 17th, and on the balance of probability this is what Captain Smith may have had in mind. While the weather and visibility were excellent on the night of 14 April, he could not necessarily expect it to remain so for the rest of the voyage. The presence of fog during the last two days was always a possibility and he may well have decided to delay making any decision regarding his arrival time until he was much closer to his destination. To this end no official announcement of an earlier ETA (estimated time of arrival) had been made on board and, so far as can be established, nobody other than, possibly, Mr Ismay was aware that such an option existed. The captain had, however, alerted New York to a possible early arrival.

There is no evidence to indicate that the captain was under any pressure to maintain high speed regardless of the circumstance. The one person on board who probably knew as much about the potential hazards of ice and fog on the North Atlantic was Mr Ismay. Having chaired the conference in London in 1898 when the routing arrangements for steamships were agreed, it is judged unlikely that he would have pressurised one of his captains to take unnecessary risks.

As darkness fell on the evening of the 14th, and with *Titanic* heading towards an area where ice was known to exist, there is no evidence to suggest that any consideration was given to reducing speed. There is, furthermore, no evidence to indicate that the engine room had been alerted to the possibility of having to reduce speed if the circumstances changed. She was propelling at 75 rpm, and although this was not, technically, the maximum she could reach it was probably not far short.

In choosing what speed to use, *Titanic*'s captain chose what almost every other master would have done in the circumstances: press on regardless and rely totally on a good lookout to avoid any encounter with ice. Given the clarity of the visibility, his familiarity with the route and the brilliance of the star light, Captain Smith clearly accepted the risks involved. Everything depended on ice being sighted in sufficient time to take avoiding action.

Lookout

On the night of 14 April five members of the crew were available to maintain a lookout: three officers on the bridge and two seaman lookouts in the crow's nest.

The number could have been supplemented by the master himself remaining on the bridge and additional seamen lookouts stationed on the bridge wing and in the bows. Although the master had been present on the bridge for half an hour between 2055 and 2125 he had retired to his cabin by 2130. This was a perfectly legitimate decision, but it is interesting to note that the masters in at least two other ships in the vicinity that night, the *Carpathia* and the *Californian*, had both elected to remain on the bridge as they approached the area where ice was predicted.

Of the three officers available to maintain a lookout on the bridge, with its almost unobstructed view, only one was doing so: the first officer. The captain gave no orders requiring all three officers to keep a lookout as they approached the known area of ice. Insisting on having them all keeping a lookout did not appear to be the custom; junior officers were required to do other things. In the minutes before the iceberg was sighted the two junior officers on watch were engaged elsewhere. The sixth officer had either been in the chartroom or the wheelhouse and the fourth officer was not on the bridge.

At face value the two lookouts in the crow's nest some 95 feet (29 metres) above the waterline were well placed to see anything ahead. The visibility was excellent, there was nothing to obstruct their view forward and, given their height of eye, they could see things further than those keeping a lookout on the bridge.

In reality their task was not quite as simple as it might seem. Given the calmness of the night, the ship would have created a relative wind of about 22 knots from dead ahead. This equates to a strong breeze or a force 6. With an air temperature of 31 °F (−0.5 °C) and no effective form of windbreak, keeping a proper lookout was far from straightforward. The temptation to seek some protection from the cold would have been immense, but there is no evidence to indicate that the lookouts did anything other than perform their duty. The combination of the cold and wind speed would produce an intense wind-chill temperature of 2 °F (−17 °C). With such cold air in their eyes, their ability to keep a proper lookout would have been compromised.

No additional lookouts were posted on either the fo'c'sle or the bridge wings. The posting of a lookout in the bows was an option open to all ships, and one often adopted in poor visibility. A lookout at the lower height of eye in the bows would have been better placed to see any unlit objects against a marginally lighter sky. In both the *Carpathia* and the *Californian* extra lookouts were posted forward to improve their chances of sighting ice and icebergs as early as possible.

Lookouts in vessels that operate in routinely waters where ice is likely to be encountered usually maintain a lookout from as high a position as possible. This is not so much to keep a watch for ice as to identify the best way through it. Such vessels invariably navigate through ice in the long hours of daylight associated with high latitudes and rarely have a need to do so in the dark. Ships crossing the North Atlantic, and in particular during April and May in the vicinity of the Grand Banks, are among the few that are likely to encounter ice at night. In such circumstances maintaining a lookout from as high a position as possible improves the chances of seeing an icefield early. The first indication of seeing ice is often the glow of reflected moon or starlight from the ice. It has an uncanny resemblance to haze.

As *Titanic* steamed westward on the Sunday evening, the second officer, and almost certainly the first officer to whom he turned over, were totally confident in their ability to see ice in good time. They knew they were approaching it and the visibility remained excellent. The captain had satisfied himself the conditions were good, and had made the judgement that there was no need to either increase the lookout capability or slow down. He had retired to his cabin having commented that if it should become the slightest degree hazy they would have to slow down. He had also given instructions that he was to be called if they were in any doubt. That confidence was misplaced. Given the expectation of ice ahead they should have utilised the full complement of potential lookouts.

It is assessed that given the known proximity of ice on the evening of 14 April, the full lookout capability on board *Titanic* was not fully utilised but those on watch in both the crow's nest and on the bridge were fully aware that ice lay ahead. At least two officers had calculated the time they would reach it. One estimate of the time it would be encountered was 2300. They were very nearly right.

Binoculars

During *Titanic*'s delivery voyage from Belfast to Southampton between 2 and 4 April, the crow's-nest lookouts had been provided with binoculars. When the ship sailed from Southampton on her maiden voyage they were not reissued. It appears they had been locked away whilst in port and the key holder had left the ship. Nobody knew where the keys were and no binoculars were issued for the transatlantic crossing. No matter whether binoculars were issued or not, there appeared to be no policy for their use by lookouts.

The relevance of binoculars for use by lookouts is examined. Their purpose is to view a distant object and magnify it to both aid identification and improve detail. Different types of binoculars are used for different functions, and four characteristics determine their effectiveness: magnification, field of view, angle of view and objective lens diameter, which determines the amount of light gathered. The weight of the binoculars can also be a factor, as heavy ones become very tiring to hold to the eyes for long. Marine binoculars tend to be a compromise of the types available, with a magnification of 7 and an objective lens diameter of 2 inches (50 mm). It is not known what type was used by either *Titanic*'s ships officers or the lookouts.

It is unusual for merchant-ship lookouts to make an initial detection of an object using binoculars. Nearly all sightings are made with the naked eye, often to one side of the direct line of sight, and reported to the officer of the watch, who may well use binoculars to identify it. Once the report has been made, the lookout resumes his search for the next object. It is not his task to identify it. The officer of the watch may do so if he thinks it is necessary but will often do little more than take a bearing of it. Binoculars are therefore not essential for use by lookouts and may, in certain situations, be counterproductive. Officers of the watch, on the other hand, can, and do, make extensive use of them.

The lookouts in the crow's nest of *Titanic* on the night of 14 April did not have binoculars, nor did they need them. Their overriding task was to report having seen something and leave the identification of it to the officer of the watch. They made no report about seeing any haze, nor did they know that sighting it was so important. It is not known if the first officer was carrying, and using, a pair of binoculars that evening.

The 'failure' to issue the lookouts with binoculars for the crossing of the Atlantic was not a factor in the lookout's ability to see any ice on the night of 14 April. The naked eye was by far the best means of seeing objects early, but the very cold wind would have detracted from its overall effectiveness.

Haze

When the captain visited the bridge shortly before 2100 to discuss the conditions with his second officer he recognised the need to slow down should it become in the slightest degree hazy. It is possible the second officer interpreted this as an obstacle to sighting ice.

Shortly after the captain left the bridge the second officer instructed one of the junior officers, Mr Moody, to contact the lookouts in the crow's nest and tell them to keep a sharp lookout for small ice and growlers. The message had to be sent twice but there was no mention of the need to report any lightening of the horizon, a low-lying glow or haze. The message was acknowledged.

Between sunset on the evening of the 14th and 2340 when the iceberg was sighted, nobody on board *Titanic* saw anything untoward other than the haze. No ships were sighted, no lights were seen and there was no sign of any other ice. The horizon remained clear throughout.

The second officer turned over the watch to the first officer, Mr Murdoch, at 2200, and although they did not, apparently, specifically discuss icebergs they did reflect on how clear it was and how far they could see.

The lookouts in the crow's nest changed over at the same time, and the briefing about the need to keep a careful watch for both small ice and growlers was passed on.

At some stage after taking over, the lookouts became aware of something ahead they described as haze and, to all intents and purposes, this is precisely what they thought it was: an obstacle to seeing things clearly. As they watched the arc over which it could be seen grew but they saw no need to report it and, so far as can be judged, it was never seen by anyone on the bridge.

Bright starlight reflected from floating ice on a dark night with perfect visibility has an appearance akin to a shimmering glow or haze. The sighting of 'haze' is entirely consistent with seeing light reflected off an icefield at a range of, quite possibly, several miles. The haze is the reflected light illuminating the cold moist air lying in the first few metres immediately above the surface of the ice and where it has been cooled to below its dew point.

It is not possible to gauge the range at which this haze, and therefore the ice, was first detected, but the evidence indicates it was an appreciable time, equating to at least 3–4 miles and possibly as much as 10 or even more. Had the earlier brief by the

View from *Titanic*'s crow's nest – artist's impression of the haze

officers of the watch on the bridge included the importance of reporting the sighting of any haze there is no reason to think that such a report would not have been made. Sailors of the day were good at doing what they were told but reluctant to take the initiative on the grounds that it was not their place. While it is impossible to state what might have happened had such a report been made, there is no question that the captain had already articulated the need to slow down should it be sighted. In the event the lookouts did not report it and *Titanic* did not slow down. In exploring the reasons as to why the lookouts did not tell the bridge, there is no evidence to indicate that they had ever seen ice at night before, or been trained to recognise it in the first place. Because the phenomenon was so unusual on the normal transatlantic shipping routes it is equally feasible that the officers were equally ignorant of what ice might look like in such situations.

In my opinion the 'haze' seen ahead of *Titanic* was the ice senior officers had fully expected to see. Their estimate of the time it would be reached was good, though it was a bit later than expected. It was seen in ample time to take avoiding action, including slowing down.

The failure to ensure the lookouts were properly briefed,

and their ignorance of how important it was for them to report the 'haze', were significant factors in why *Titanic* collided with an iceberg.

The iceberg: sighting

Shortly before 2340, the lookouts saw what they initially described as a 'black mass' right ahead but which rapidly materialised into an iceberg. This description suggests it was almost certainly seen as a silhouette against the marginally brighter background created by the reflected light on the icefield beyond. The range at which this black mass was sighted is not known, nor is the time it took to report it. While the initial sighting and its positive identification may have been simultaneous there is at least a possibility that it took the lookouts a few moments to recognise what they were looking at, and the balance of probability suggests there was some delay. They alerted the bridge to the presence of something ahead by striking the crow's nest bell three times, and then amplified this by reporting an iceberg dead ahead over the telephone. The call was taken by the sixth officer, who relayed the message to the first officer. There is no evidence to indicate that any officer saw the iceberg at any stage until it was close ahead, but the possibility remains.

View from *Titanic*'s crow's nest – artist's impression of the 'black mass'

The iceberg: avoiding action

The conflicting and incomplete evidence surrounding the events immediately before and after the collision makes analysis difficult.

The interval between the crow's-nest bell being struck three times and the telephoned report being made to the bridge was short. It is not known, for instance, how many seconds elapsed between the message being received on the bridge and Mr Murdoch ordering 'hard a starboard'. The possibility exists that he would have wished to see the iceberg himself before giving any orders. Despite having been told it was right ahead he had no idea of its range and, for all he knew, it could have been 2–3 miles away, or even slightly biased to one side. Most officers would have wished to see the object ahead for themselves before taking any action, and there is some evidence to suggest that several seconds may have elapsed between receiving the report and taking avoiding action.

The action taken by Mr Murdoch had three constituent parts: the order 'hard a starboard', the placing of the engine room telegraph to full astern and the closing of the automatic watertight doors.

The order 'hard a starboard' conformed to the convention and practice of the day to turn the ship's head to port. The ship responded to the rudder being put hard over and began to alter course to port. Once the ship's head had swung off by several degrees the wheel was reversed to swing the stern away from the iceberg. Had this not been done *Titanic* would have continued the turn to port and the iceberg would have scraped all the way down the starboard side. In all probability the wheel was reversed to 'hard a port' very early in the avoiding process and soon after the swing to port had begun. It is likely the wheel was kept hard over to ensure the stern swung clear of the ice. All the evidence indicates that the ship was swinging to starboard by the time the captain arrived on the bridge and confirmed the report that the officer of the watch had tried to 'port round' the iceberg. It is not known what subsequent wheel order was given or what course, if any, was ordered.

Although the engine-room telegraphs were put to full astern there is very little evidence to indicate the order was ever applied. The application of stern power, and the resultant vibration from propellers turning astern, is among the most distinctive sensations to be felt in any ship. The overwhelming evidence from survivors is of stillness after the collision, and many described becoming aware that the engines had stopped. It is judged that, very soon after the order 'full astern' was rung through on the telegraphs, 'stop' was ordered and the ship slowed until all the way was off her.

There is some evidence to indicate that following the initial actions the telegraphs were again put to ahead. If so, few people were aware of it and any headway would have been limited to a few minutes before the telegraphs were finally put to 'stop'.

No further engine movements were ordered. With the build-up of steam in the boilers, the safety valves lifted to generate a deafening noise on the upper deck that lasted for about 45 minutes.

Once way had finally fallen off, the *Titanic* must have been facing a specific direction. Although there is an element of uncertainty about this the best assessment is that it was somewhere about north. Although she may have swung either way slightly, it is probable she remained pointing in that general direction until she sank.

The third action to be taken by the officer of the watch on receipt of the ice report was to shut the watertight doors. While the 12 automatic watertight doors in the engine and boiler room spaces were successfully shut, it is not known what steps were taken to ensure the manual watertight doors elsewhere in the ship were closed at the same time.

Damage assessment

The impact with the iceberg was felt by individuals depending on where they were. Those in the most forward boiler room, No. 6, knew instantly that the hull had been breached. Elsewhere in the ship people merely felt a slight jar or a judder, and others knew nothing about it at all.

Some ice was knocked off the iceberg onto the forward well deck to indicate having hit a near vertical wall of ice. The iceberg itself was judged to be little more than about 100 feet (30 metres) high.

Following the initial reports and the personal inspections made by the captain in company with Mr Andrews, the latter made a more detailed inspection, returning rapidly to the bridge to report his assessment that the ship would sink within an hour to an hour and a half. It is probable that between about 0020 and 0025 he became fully aware that the ship was badly damaged and was going to sink

It would have become evident at that stage that the hull had been breached along the starboard side from No. 1 cargo hold in the bows to No. 5 boiler room, with further leaking into No. 6 boiler room. There is no evidence, however, to indicate that the captain gave any thought to trying to contain the extensive flooding forward. A known technique, applied with varying degrees of success in other vessels in similar circumstances, involved placing a patch or tingle on the outside of the hull in the general area of the damage to restrict the rate of flooding. Typically a tingle might be a tarpaulin such as that used to cover a hatch. Such a task would have been manpower-intensive and taken time. Manpower and time, however, were not readily available.

Whether he gave any thought to containment is not known, but the captain would have been aware of two inescapable truths within 45 minutes of the accident: *Titanic* was going to sink, and there were insufficient lifeboats embarked to carry everyone.

Whatever action he took would be constrained by time, but whether this factor featured in his thinking is far from clear.

The issue of lifeboats is examined in greater detail.

Lifeboats

Lifeboats in merchant ships have one specific purpose: to save life in the event of a major catastrophe. They are unlikely to be used in minor incidents but become essential when the ship is likely to founder or when it becomes impossible to remain on board for any reason. Possible scenarios include a ship on fire or engulfed in smoke. They must be capable of being launched quickly, without power, and capable of withstanding reasonable sea states and wind conditions. They must be ready at all times and in all conditions regardless of the time of day. To achieve these exacting requirements they need to be tested and inspected regularly. They also need to be manned by crew members who are competent in handling them.

Titanic met the Board of Trade regulations for the carriage of lifeboats on a British steamship. The lifeboats carried had only recently been installed and tested, and could carry 1178 souls. *Titanic* was capable of carrying 2440 passengers and about 900 crew, to give a total of 3330. This meant the shortfall in lifeboat carrying capacity was about 2152 souls had she been fully laden. This was regarded as acceptable.

When *Titanic* sailed from Queenstown, the record showed that she had 2208 passengers and crew embarked, meaning there was a shortfall of 1130 had every lifeboat place been filled. In the event only 711 survived, meaning that a further 419 could, and should, have been accommodated but weren't. The reasons for both discrepancies are examined.

Lifeboats: capacity

The regulations determining the number of lifeboats to be carried on board the *Titanic* were drawn up by the Board of

Trade on the basis of advice provided by a Departmental Committee and the Merchant Shipping Advisory Committee.

The rules and regulations covering the provision of life-saving appliances on merchant ships had been made under the Merchant Shipping Acts 1894–1906. The number of boats to be carried on board merchant ships was determined by the gross tonnage of the vessel concerned and not the number of people to be carried. In a table in the 1894 Act showing the minimum number of boats the minimum number of boats of any vessel of over 10,000 grt was 16.

The matter had been looked at by some experienced and able officials but they had seen no reason to increase the number of boats carried in larger vessels carrying a greater number of people. The arguments deployed in favour of maintaining the status quo were:

(1) Sea travel had an excellent safety record and was regarded as the safest mode of travel available.

(2) The Department had neither right nor duty to impose regulations on such a mode of travel as long as the record was a clean one.

(3) The measures being taken by ship owners to install watertight compartments, which increased the absolute strength, should not be interfered with.

(4) The belief that 16 boats was the maximum that could be safely housed without unduly encumbering a vessel's decks.

(5) The defined North Atlantic routes lessened the risk of collision or encounters with ice and fog.

(6) The widespread fitting of wireless telegraphy to ships meant they had the ability to summon help in sufficient time for another ship to render assistance.

(7) The role of the lifeboat was to ferry passengers and crew from the vessel in distress to a rescue ship, and 16 such lifeboats was considered sufficient.

(8) The additional crew needed to operate such a large number of boats meant they would have nothing to do in normal circumstances.

(9) Ship owners were fitting lifeboats in excess of the requirement laid down in the regulations, and any state department should hold its hand before it stepped in to introduce a new scale for larger vessels.

(10) That a ship such as *Titanic* had been made so safe that it would never be necessary to put so many people into lifeboats.

Ship owners were known to fit additional boats on their vessels, and the matter of additional boats had been raised during the building of the *Titanic* and, indeed, at a meeting of the subcommittee to the Advisory Committee. The subcommittee made no recommendation to change the number of boats to be carried but it was decided that the *Titanic* would be provided with four additional collapsible boats above the scale for the size of ship. This meant that *Titanic* carried more boats than she was required to do by law.

There is evidence to indicate that had the Board of Trade required additional lifeboats to be fitted the White Star Line would have done so. In anticipation of some future regulation being introduced that required additional lifeboats to be fitted, the company had checked its plans and designs to ensure it could be done. No such requirement was called for before *Titanic* sailed on her maiden voyage.

The US government's regulations for the carriage of lifeboats stipulated that a passenger ship should carry sufficient number to accommodate two-thirds of the maximum number carried on board. It is not known how rigorously these regulations were enforced.

The loss of life resulting from the sinking of the *Titanic* demonstrated the total inadequacies of both the Board of Trade regulations and the arguments put forward to support the original decision to base the number of lifeboats being carried on tonnage and not the numbers of people embarked.

The decision by the Board of Trade to limit the number of lifeboats to 16 on board vessels in excess of 10,000 tons, and not to base the lifeboat carrying capacity on the number of people being carried, was the root cause of so many losing their lives when *Titanic* foundered in the early hours of 15 April 1912.

Lifeboats: preparation, loading and lowering

The decision to start clearing away the lifeboats was taken by the captain shortly after midnight. Thereafter the action taken to implement the order was slow for a number of reasons. The crew capable of preparing the lifeboats were slow to materialise, nobody had briefed those in charge on the need to expedite the process, and the complexities involved were not conducive to fast work. The noise from the escaping steam cannot have helped. Providing trained members of the crew were involved in preparing a lifeboat, it would take them 20–25 minutes to do so.

Preparation involved removing the canvas covers, clearing the falls, unlashing oars and masts, placing lamps, compasses and food in the boats and inserting plugs in the drain holes. The process of swinging them out was eased by the use of the Welin Quadrant davits with which *Titanic* was fitted. In the event, however, it took longer than expected because of the limited amount of available manpower, the general unfamiliarity with the task, the noise generated by escaping steam and the reduced lighting on the upper deck. Some items of equipment such as lamps were not readily accessible.

The availability of manpower was further reduced by the

decision of the second officer to detail the bosun and six hands to open one of the gangway doors to facilitate the embarkation of passengers. They were ordered to do so at about 0045 but were never seen again. Their absence adversely affected the speed with which lifeboats were prepared on the port side of the boat deck.

It is assessed that the first lifeboat to be launched was No. 7 on the starboard side, with three members of the crew and 25 passengers embarked, at about 0045. In view of the perceived lack of any urgency, passengers were, at this early stage of the evacuation, being invited to board the lifeboats rather than directed. Many of the women declined.

Thereafter lifeboats were launched at about ten-minute intervals until about 0120 when the launch rate was increased to five-minute intervals. The precise timings have not been established, but it is evident that there were fewer delays on the starboard side than on the port, and that the starboard boats contained more people.

Loading of lifeboats: crew

A prerequisite for effective use of lifeboats is that there are sufficient members of the crew to prepare, lower and operate them. To achieve this boats must be routinely checked, the crew trained and boat drills carried out. On almost all counts there were shortcomings with *Titanic's* organisation, due in part to a failure by the Board of Trade to lay down adequate requirements for boat drills.

The boats had been checked in Belfast prior to sailing but there is no record of a full load test having been carried out. One had, however, been conducted in *Olympic* a year earlier. Captain Smith and his chief and first officers had served in the *Olympic* and might be expected to have been familiar with the test and the proven ability of the lifeboats to be lowered fully laden. If they did know it, they evidently did not impart this information to any of the other officers, who remained unaware how many people a boat could safely take while being lowered. This was a significant factor in explaining why the boats were not loaded to their full capacity.

No full boat drill was ever exercised. The pre-sailing Board of Trade boat drill in Southampton, involving just two boats, was witnessed by a surveyor and judged to have met the requirements. The surveyor admitted in evidence that the test was not really satisfactory but it was 'the custom' to conduct and approve it. The drill was not attended by firemen, who did not believe it was a matter for them.

It was also customary for ships of the White Star Line to hold a boat drill when at sea on a Sunday and, following this practice, it would have been conducted on Sunday 14 April. It was not, and the reasons are not known. It is judged that had the drill been conducted, those members of the crew who had not previously discovered which boat they had been allocated to would have taken the trouble to find out. The evidence indicates that many did not know to which lifeboat they had been allocated, nor was there a system to ensure they knew where that boat was.

From the moment the order to clear away the lifeboats was given in the early hours of 15 April, the level of competence, expertise and availability of the crew became a crucial factor.

Of equal significance was the management and direction of the passengers.

Loading of lifeboats: passengers

Passengers, like the crew, were alerted to some form of trouble by the initial impact or the sudden stopping of the engines. Many people, mainly men, decided to find out for themselves what the problem was and made their way to the upper deck. Nobody really knew what had happened. Members of the crew did their best to reassure passengers that there was no danger.

Third-class passengers accommodated forward on G and F decks needed no further alerting to the presence of flooding. Within 20 minutes of the collision water had reached F deck in the bow section.

From the outset it was evident that no satisfactory organisation existed on board *Titanic* for handling passengers in an emergency.

The evidence reveals that little thought had been given to the handling of passengers in an emergency by the Board of Trade, the White Star Line and, ultimately, by those on board *Titanic*.

Once the decision had been taken to load the lifeboats at around 0030, the most frequent observation made by the officers in charge of filling and lowering them was that so few women and children were on hand on the boat deck. Although some, but by no means all, passengers had been told to go the upper deck, few, if any, realised the seriousness of the situation. This position was not helped by the officers, who were equally ignorant. Nobody realised the vessel was sinking, and few thought that putting people into the boats was anything other than a precautionary measure. It would appear that in the very early stages of the embarkation process passengers were being invited to board the lifeboats rather than being directed.

At least one officer was greatly concerned that the boats, if fully laden, would buckle and, having decided it would be better to embark the passengers at a lower level or even via a gangway door on D deck, directed the bosun and six hands to open it. The seven men despatched to open the doors never returned, and remain unaccounted for. Their absence added to the delays in preparing and lowering the lifeboats.

Several female passengers were greatly concerned at boarding a lifeboat so far above the waterline, while others found the prospect of being sent away in a boat on such a bitterly cold night unappealing and chose to remain on board. Many sought refuge in the warmth and sanctuary of the gymnasium which accessed the upper deck on the starboard side. Conspicuously missing from the arrangements was any organisation to ensure passengers were guided to the waiting lifeboats. With one or two conspicuous exceptions no member of the crew took it upon himself to direct passengers to the point of embarkation.

There were no signs, no directions and no thought given to how best to communicate with passengers who may not have understood English. There was no one person in a position to understand what was happening and take adequate action to give positive directions.

Even when passengers were available, a range of other reason conspired to delay loading. The enforcement of a women and children rule produced its own problems. Several women refused to be parted from their husbands and others found boarding the boats difficult. A number of men had to be ejected from the boats. There was confusion as to where best passengers should board. It had been forgotten by at least the second officer that, unlike on the *Olympic*, the forward part of A deck was enclosed and steps had to be taken to open the outer windows and then find a means of climbing through them to reach the boats.

At no stage was there any apparent discrimination between the classes of passengers, but those from first and second class had unobstructed access to the lifeboats whereas those from third class, by virtue of the deck space allocated to them, did not access the boat deck. This greatly inhibited the ability of the third-class passengers to reach the upper deck in time, and it was not until the last minutes that a large number of them suddenly appeared.

There were several instances when some male passengers instinctively gave way to the needs of female passengers, and equally, cases when precisely the opposite applied. Evidence from third-class passengers was not easily obtainable but the culture of the day might suggest that having come from backgrounds where everything depended on being told what to do to survive, they may have waited below expecting the same treatment to apply. By the time it became evident that they had to take matters into their own hands it was too late.

In the later stages of the evacuation the order that had previously prevailed began to break down as a growing number of people began to crowd round the remaining lifeboats.

Discipline at one stage needed to be maintained by using firearms. A number of passengers became tangled in the falls.

Although there is no specific evidence on which to draw, a number of passengers on board, especially among those travelling in third class, did not fully understand English and would have relied on watching how others reacted before they did so themselves. This may help explain why so many third-class passengers did not appear on the upper deck until very late in the evacuation process.

Women and children first

From the moment the decision was taken to load the lifeboats the instinctive thinking among most was that priority should be given to embarking women and children. When he felt the moment had come to begin putting passengers into the lifeboats, the second officer, Mr Lightoller, went to find the captain to ask whether he should start getting the women and children into the boats. Because the noise of escaping steam prevented effective dialogue, the captain gave his assent by nodding. It was, in effect, the order to begin loading.

It was interpreted in different ways by those in charge of loading the lifeboats. Mr Lightoller, on the port side, insisted it meant women and children only, whereas Mr Murdoch on the starboard side imposed a more relaxed women and children first regime.

Nobody questioned the justification for giving priority to the women and children. It was variously described as being the natural order or the rule of human nature. No such law or other regulation exists. Its adoption reflected the culture of the day, and nothing else.

Notwithstanding the intention to give priority to the women and children, of those who eventually survived 338 were men and only 316 were women. Well over 400 places in the lifeboats remained unfilled.

Given the impossibility of allocating places in the lifeboats to everyone, some form of priority had, in all probability, to be devised. Whilst a women and children first policy was one way, given the circumstances, its implementation and the associated delays greatly contributed to the loss of life.

Despite its ramifications, the imposition of the policy was helpful in one important respect. In enforcing it the officers were able to convey a degree of discipline that encouraged order when it was most needed.

Command and control

The organisation for alerting both crew and passengers was piecemeal. There was no general alarm system, and the only means of communicating was by word of mouth. There was no system in place for mustering passengers. Stewards made their way around most of the accommodation spaces in the first-, second- and third-class sections to rouse people and tell them to put on warm clothing and life preservers. There was no drill as such, nor did the Board of Trade regulations lay down a requirement to drill passengers about what to do in an emergency. White Star Line procedures fared little better; there were no company procedures indicating what should be done or practised.

It is reasonable to assume that as soon as the captain realised the *Titanic* was going to sink, he instinctively knew there were insufficient lifeboats for all on board. He would have known from the outset that a large number of people for whom he was responsible were unlikely to survive unless help was forthcoming.

In such circumstances the predicament he faced was almost overwhelming. He was faced with an impossible dilemma for which he was totally unprepared. Sudden stress on individuals can be devastating and can lead to near-paralysis. The ability to absorb information, make decisions and, in the worst situations, even speak can be adversely affected. There is no medical evidence to indicate how Captain Smith reacted on this occasion but it must have been a tremendous shock. People trained to deal with sudden trauma are infinitely better placed to deal with it, but no such training existed for merchant seamen or had ever been considered.

There is nothing to suggest that Captain Smith behaved irrationally but, in my opinion, the leadership qualities for which he was renowned seemed to desert him once he knew the ship was going to sink. Whilst he very evidently did his utmost to encourage both women and children to board the boats, he gave little positive direction to his officers and showed few signs of being in control of the situation. Notwithstanding a natural wish to avoid inducing panic by telling passengers too much too soon, he could have done more to ensure a greater number of people would survive. As far as can be established he spent the time between midnight and the sinking either in the vicinity of the bridge and the forward end of the boat deck, or in the Marconi office. It is hard to believe that he failed to notice that at least some of the lifeboats were only partially full as they pulled away from the ship, that the numbers assembling on the boat deck fell far short of what was required and, possibly, the absence of third-class passengers. There is no evidence to show he took any measures to ensure passengers were escorted to the lifeboats and then loaded so that each one was filled to capacity. Given the extremely calm conditions that still prevailed he might even have taken a risk and told his officers to overload the boats.

In my opinion few things determine the successful outcome of an emergency where it becomes necessary to abandon ship, more than the conduct and example of the captain. The training and preparation for such an eventuality had never been envisaged or planned for, and Captain Smith was the victim of the system that prevailed.

Examination of the syllabus for the Certificates of Competency for either masters or mates makes no reference to the handling of emergencies except in terms of seamanship. It is apparent that masters and mates were expected, without formal training, to know exactly what to do. Such expectations make no allowance for the mental stress likely to exist at such a time. The situation on this occasion cannot have been helped by Captain Smith having only been on board for two weeks and not having time to weld his team together. There is little to suggest that any of his officers, particularly the chief officer, were supporting him in the command functions as *Titanic* slowly began to fill with water in the early hours of that Monday morning.

The officers were never briefed on the gravity of the situation, nor were they informed about the need for haste. No check was made to ensure that all the officers had been called: the fifth officer slept through the initial actions. The officers in charge of the lifeboats were never given directions as to the overwhelming importance of loading them to their full capacity. No instructions were given on the action to be taken by those in charge of the boats once they had been lowered. Such decisions were taken individually by the officers concerned, and the evidence indicates that the process of filling and loading the boats was quicker and more efficient on the starboard side of the boat deck than on the port. Nobody appeared to spot this and establish the causes.

So far as can be ascertained no orders were given to remove the barriers dividing third-class passengers from the rest of the ship. Members of the crew standing by some of these barriers had no instructions to waive the normal restrictions required by the US immigration authorities. They, like others in junior positions, only knew how to receive orders, and nothing in their nature led them to use their initiative.

There is no evidence to indicate that stewards in charge of third-class passengers were given any orders as to what they should do. Stewards would have been totally reliant on instructions and, lacking any, would fall back on custom and take no action until ordered to do something different. No drill had ever been conducted to practise such an eventuality.

There is no evidence to indicate that measures were taken to maintain the ship's watertight integrity. No steps were taken to check that portholes and side doors were shut. It is known that attempts were made to operate the manual watertight doors but uncertainty remains as to the result.

Despite so much that did not go well during the loading of the lifeboats, two features greatly aided the measures that did take place. The first was that by and large *Titanic* sank on an even keel. Evacuating people from any vessel that takes on a heavy list is fraught with difficulty and danger. Had the list been any greater than the maximum recorded of, at the most, 10 degrees to port, the numbers losing their lives might have been greater.

The second feature that made the evacuation procedure more successful than it might have been was the ability of the engine-room staff to maintain lighting for as long as they did. The lights did not finally go out until a few moments before *Titanic* foundered. The commitment of the many engine-room staff, and particularly the officers, who remained at their posts until it was too late, is to be commended.

Throughout the lifeboat loading process the ship's orchestra continued to play music, and this contributed to the lack of undue anxiety by many on board in the later stages. They too are to be commended.

Distress messages: wireless

From shortly before midnight both *Titanic*'s Marconi operators were awake and assisting each other as events unfolded. Mr Bride was due to relieve Mr Philips at 0200 but had made the conscious decision to come on watch two hours early to enable his senior colleague to catch up on sleep. With both operators still awake following the handover, the captain alerted them to the need to send a distress message. From that moment onwards both men dedicated themselves to meeting the captain's requirements.

The first distress message was transmitted at 0027 and was

immediately picked up by the steamships *La Provence* and *Mount Temple* and the shore station at Cape Race, Newfoundland. The ability to intercept a transmission at that time of night was entirely dependent on the receiving station being operational, manned and within range. Those with more than one operator, able to maintain 24-hour cover and within wireless range were in a position to do so. Ships without wireless or with only a single operator who was off duty were not. Single operators tended to stay up late to benefit from the longer ranges obtainable at night but would start to retire either shortly before midnight or soon afterwards. *Titanic*'s first distress signal went out at about the time the single operators were shutting down for the night. Some were still up and listening, others had just turned in.

Over the next one and three-quarter hours *Titanic*'s two operators worked tirelessly to summon help. Following the repair work done on the previous evening the equipment worked well.

The signal used initially was the Marconi CQD: 'all ships – distress'. It was widely recognised as a distress signal but was not the internationally agreed distress signal SOS. The letters have no specific meaning but are very easily recognised; dot, dot, dot, dash, dash, dash, dot, dot, dot. There is no evidence to indicate that use of the incorrect CQD inhibited the ability of the receiving stations to understand what was meant.

The operators remained at their station until released by the captain shortly before *Titanic* foundered. They are to be commended for their diligence and commitment.

Distress signals: visual

Between about 0045 and 0130 on 15 April, *Titanic* fired at least eight socket rockets as distress signals but almost certainly more. The precise number fired has never been established, but it could have been a dozen or more.

To be effective, a distress signal system must have four

complementary ingredients. The regulations must clearly state that the characteristics cannot be mistaken for anything else. Ships must carry the signals, the means to use them, and in sufficient quantities. The operators must know how to use them. And ultimately the most important is that an observer must instinctively recognise distress signals for what they are and take the appropriate action. Failure in any one of these essentials can lead to misunderstanding or confusion.

It is therefore appropriate to test these requirements in the context of the signals carried and used in *Titanic*.

The regulations laid down two types of rocket signal for use by ships in distress at night. The first was a 'gun fired at intervals of about a minute'. The second stated 'rockets or shells bursting in the air with a loud report and throwing stars of any colour or description, fired one at a time at short intervals'.

Among the distress signals carried by *Titanic* in accordance with Board of Trade regulations were 36 socket signals in lieu of guns, and 12 ordinary rockets. The regulations also required the socket signals be fired from approved sockets and that there should be two of them, one forward and one aft on different sides of the ship. As these requirements would have been checked by the Board of Trade surveyors prior to sailing it is taken that *Titanic* met the requirements.

Whether by choice or chance, the distress signals selected to signify a ship in distress were the socket signals in lieu of guns. There is evidence to indicate that once the decision to fire them had been taken the fourth officer was tasked to do so. It is assessed that the first socket signal was fired shortly before 0045, at about the time the first lifeboat took to the water.

The firing interval has never been established, nor is there any evidence to indicate that a specific interval was planned or aimed for. They were fired over a period of about an hour and at intervals of, perhaps, five minutes. There is nothing to suggest they were fired at the correct interval of one per minute and there is at least a suspicion that many of the rockets carried were never fired at all. This means that a number were never used on the one occasion when they were most needed. The captain would not only have been aware the rockets were being fired at intervals over nearly an hour but personally supervised the firing of the last one or two rockets himself after the fourth officer had been released to take charge of lifeboat No. 2 at 0045. As an experienced ship master, he should have been totally familiar with the regulations for using them, and he may have noticed they were not being fired at the correct intervals. Whether he did so or not, the fact remains that the rockets being fired did not comply with the international regulations, and it appears he did nothing to correct the error. The extended firing interval may have confused anyone observing them.

The key element in any distress signal is that it cannot be mistaken for anything else. The pyrotechnics carried by many vessels could also be used as a means by which ships could communicate with each other. The concept was perfectly legitimate and regulations concerning their use were clear. The signals, known as company signals, had many different characteristics but very little in common with distress signals. They were not, however, so uniquely distinctive that their function could not possibly have been mistaken for anything else. Had they been a colour, such as red, that was not used for company signals it is unlikely they could have been mistaken for anything else.

Those fired from *Titanic* contained a detonator that made a loud bang in lieu of a gun, but for this feature to be effective they required the observer to be within earshot. Although another ship reported seeing about eight rockets being fired by a vessel at times very similar to those fired from *Titanic* no sound was heard, indicating that she was at some distance away.

The interpretation of these signals will be examined in greater detail when analysing the role of SS *Californian*, a ship that was believed to be stopped and within sight of *Titanic* following her collision with an iceberg.

Sighting of lights

Several people on board *Titanic*, including officers, members of the crew and passengers, said they saw the light, or lights, of another ship in the 90 minutes or so before she sank. This unknown vessel was judged to lie between 3 and 10 miles away.

They could have been mistaken. It could have been a star or a planet or even a figment of the collective imagination and 'seen' because so many people *wanted* to see the lights of a ship coming to their rescue. If, however, it was another ship, it was important to identify it, establish how far off it was, and reach some conclusion as to what it was doing.

To totally dismiss all the sightings as figments of the imagination ignores the fact that several different people reported seeing much the same thing. Some saw a single white light while other saw two, together with coloured lights thought to be red and green sidelights.

It is possible that a bright star or planet on or near the horizon could have been taken for a ship's light, but this is thought unlikely. Jupiter, rising in the east, was by far the brightest object in sight that night and would have been seen rising in the east but would have risen steadily thereafter. It might have been mistaken for a ship's light initially, but its subsequent movement would have been evident to an observer and this explanation is discounted as a result.

It is also extremely difficult for anyone, including the most experienced ship master, to accurately estimate the range of a single light at sea at night without some form of reference. There is a temptation to form a judgement based on what the range should be rather than what is possible. The regulations state that a steaming light should be 'of such a character as to be visible on a dark night with a clear atmosphere, a distance of at least 5 miles'. Given no other clue, an inexperienced mariner might be tempted to think that such a light cannot be seen at ranges much in excess of the stated 5 miles. In practice, navigation lights, including a well-tended oil lamp, can be seen at far greater ranges on a dark clear light.

The assessment at this stage is that the lights observed were of another ship whose identity remains unknown.

Titanic's foundering

Titanic displaced 52,310 tons. Her total pumping capacity was 1700 tons per hour but the water was pouring into the ship far faster than her ballast and bilge pumps could manage. It is not possible to accurately assess the rate at which the water was entering the ship through the damaged hull but it was several times faster than the ability of the pumps to contain it.

It is assessed that the damage extended from the fore peak tank, through cargo holds Nos. 1, 2 and 3, No. 6 boiler room and just into the coal bunker within No. 5 boiler room. It has been estimated that the damage extended over about 300 feet (91 metres) but the opening itself was not continuous.

The initial flooding was biased towards the starboard side and caused the ship to list, initially in that direction. The main flooding was contained initially by bulkhead E separating boiler rooms Nos. 5 and 6, but as it became more extensive it began to make its way aft via the passageways on E deck.

Over the first hour a bow-down angle of about 4 degrees developed as the fore part of the ship began to fill. It is not known how many manual watertight doors remained open, but the possibility exists that some were, to ease access to the aft part of the ship. As the water continued to make in the fore part of the vessel and the passageways became fully flooded, the initial list to starboard decreased and an upright position was eventually achieved.

Over the second hour the increasing bow-down angle was less marked and only grew by a further degree as the bow section continued to flood. At about 0045 the bulkhead between boiler rooms Nos. 5 and 6 probably gave way, allowing boiler room No. 5 to flood and lower the bow section even further. Flood water

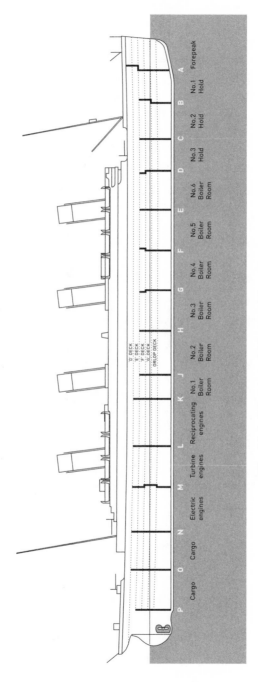

Titanic's bulkheads and 16 watertight compartments

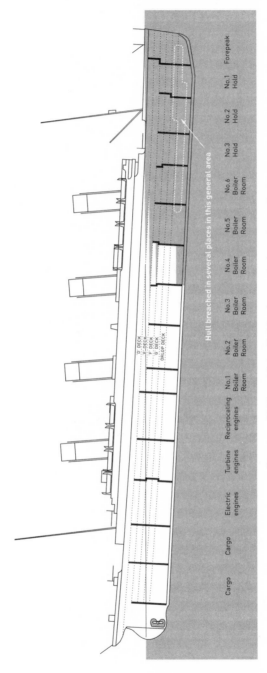

Cargo Cargo Electric engines Turbine engines Reciprocating engines No.1 Boiler Room No.2 Boiler Room No.3 Boiler Room No.4 Boiler Room No.5 Boiler Room No.6 Boiler Room No.3 Hold No.2 Hold No.1 Hold Forepeak

D DECK
E DECK
F DECK
G DECK
ORLOP DECK

Hull breached in several places in this general area

Titanic at 0200 on 15 April, 20 minutes before the end

progressively filled the fore part of the ship, began to spread aft through the various passage ways, spilling over the forward bulkheads and downflooding the next watertight compartment. The flooding process was greatly aided by having a number of portholes and at least one gangway door open to the sea, and these expedited the rate at which water was able to pour into the ship.

The forward well deck submerged soon after about 0150, allowing sea water to flood through more openings on the weather deck forward. The forward pitch angle grew further to about 4 degrees and matched the list to port. At about 0210 boiler room No. 4 suddenly flooded, and this initiated the sequence that eventually led to *Titanic* sinking. From now onwards the water ingress was rapid. The bridge began to dip into the sea moments later, the pitch angle increased to about 8 degrees and accelerated thereafter. The stern began to rise out of the sea at about 0213 and the forward funnel collapsed as the water engulfed its base a minute or two later. The forces acting on the hull at about 0217 were such that it broke in the vicinity of No. 1 boiler room and the engine room, allowing the fore part of the ship to continue its descent to the seabed at about 28 knots and the after part to settle momentarily on a near level keel. The watertight doors that might have prevented at least some of the water from entering the after part had been opened earlier to enable hoses to be passed through. The openings now facilitated the rapid flooding of the stern section, and very shortly afterwards it too pitched forward, hovered momentarily and then began to sink. It was not possible for the whole section to flood before it left the surface. Large quantities of air trapped inside would have led to an implosion of the hull shortly after leaving the surface, at a depth of no more than 40–50 feet (12–15 metres).

The taffrail at the stern was the last part of the ship to go under. She went down shortly after 0220.

As *Titanic* sank there was almost no suction.

Other ships

From the moment the first CQD message was sent at 0027 a number of other ships became involved in the overall picture. They, and their relationship with the *Titanic*, are now examined in more detail.

SS *Californian*

Following the collision many on board *Titanic* saw the lights of one other vessel ahead. The direction is believed to have been north. A least one of these lights was observed by a number of the occupants in the lifeboats once they had taken to the water. Were these the lights of the stopped, but swinging, *Californian*, or some other vessel whose identity has never been established?

Watchkeepers and others on board the SS *Californian*, lying stopped and surrounded by loose ice on the evening of 14 April, saw another ship pass by to the south of her, stop, and then apparently steam away. The timings of the various observations made could equate with many of the features associated with *Titanic*'s final four hours. Was the vessel observed by those on board *Californian* the westbound *Titanic*, both before and after she collided with the iceberg, or another ship?

◀ *This may be a suitable moment to interrupt the analysis to share with the reader the thought process of an accident investigator confronting evidence that is conflicting, ambiguous and thoroughly confusing. The role of the* Californian *is by far and away the most contentious and divisive feature of the entire* Titanic *story and needs to be explored in greater depth than other aspect of the tragedy.*

Nearly everyone who gives any thought to the part played by the Californian *on the night that* Titanic *hit an iceberg and sank, does so with the benefit, or as some would have it the curse, of hindsight. Hindsight is a feature of human nature and will always influence our thinking, but it can equally distort careful analysis. Linked to it is the* human tendency to adopt a view and stick with it. When some piece of evidence doesn't fit a particular theory, we either ignore it or, as Lord Mersey did, declare it as being unreliable. Some have gone further and readily accuse witnesses of lying.

A marine accident investigator does not have the luxury of choosing the evidence to suit his favoured hypothesis but has to look at everything and change the story line every time something he judges important doesn't fit. He endeavours, furthermore, to see things through the eyes of those present at the time and will remember the human tendency to make sense of what they think they saw. Unless they have good ground to think otherwise, a view once formed by a witness tends to remain in place.

Most people addressing the evidence in connection with the Californian believe that parts of it cannot be right, and to an extent the judgement is fair, as some statements made in 1912 describe things that cannot possibly have happened. Investigators have, however, to allow for the frailties of human memory and will be aware of how difficult it is to recall time and the correct sequence of events. The experienced mariner will also know how incredibly difficult it is to judge the distance of a light at sea on a dark night and may know that in certain, rare, conditions it is possible to see lights at extreme ranges. Another feature of memory is the inability to remember the number of times something happens when repeated. This is very evident when trying to establish how many rockets were fired by Titanic. I am prepared to state with a degree of certainty that nobody recalled exactly how many were fired and that the figure of eight is almost certainly on the low side.

My personal approach was to do something slightly different and believe, for a moment, that every witness on board both Californian and Titanic did his very best to tell the truth as he saw it. If you separate the raw facts from the expressed opinion as to what was being seen, a much more coherent version of events begins to emerge.

What follows pursues that philosophy and, in my opinion, explains what probably happened that night. ▶

A number of things are known. The visibility was exceptional. The *Californian* encountered ice at around 2220 and stopped. She remained in the same position throughout the night and, having initially been pointing in a northeasterly direction, swung slowly to starboard over the next few hours. She had two steaming lights and sidelights and there is no reason to think they were not burning brightly throughout.

Her dead reckoning position at the time she stopped, based on earlier observations of the sun with the latitude established by a Pole Star sight taken at 1930, was 42° 05' N, 50° 07' W. A dead reckoning position takes no account of other influences such as wind or current. There was no wind that night.

From sunset on the same night *Titanic* had been steaming on a heading of S 86° W at about 22 knots. Star sights had been taken at around 1930 and there is no reason to think the result-ant position was anything other than accurate. She had a single masthead light at a height of about 150 feet (46 metres) above the waterline and sidelights at 70 feet (21 metres).

She collided with the iceberg at 2340 and, by the time all way had fallen off, was lying in a direction believed to be just east of north. She slowly settled and finally foundered at 0220 on the morning of 15 April. *Titanic* estimated her position as being 41° 46' N, 50° 14' W, or 19½ miles from where the *Californian* thought she was lying stopped.

The *Californian* saw one ship that night and only one ship. She first detected a single white light to the east followed a little later by a green light, almost certainly a starboard navigation side light, and some accommodation lights. The precise times are not known, as it seems the first white light may, initially, have been confused with a star or planet on the horizon. The bearing move-ment was observed to be slowly right and the range judged to be, variously, between 4 and 10 miles. The view by some on board the *Californian* was that it was another vessel of similar size. Others thought she was a passenger vessel and further away. No matter what her identity, this other vessel was observed to stop at about 2340 and put her lights out. At about 0045 rockets were observed to come from her direction, but their height above the horizon was such that those watching them thought they must have come from a ship at a greater distance on a similar bearing.

The sighting of these rockets was reported to the captain sleeping in the chartroom below at 0115. He did not come to the bridge but asked if they were company signals. The officer of the watch did not know and was instructed to call her up on the Morse lamp. The fact that the captain had to ask whether they were company signals suggests they could have been something else. An effective distress signal should be so distinctive as to be unmistakable. It wasn't. The captain meanwhile would have been under the impression that the ship being reported was relatively close.

Later on, *Californian's* bridge watchkeepers thought the angle of the lights was a bit unusual but believed the single white light left was the stern light of a vessel steaming away. When it eventually dipped below the horizon it conformed to their assessment that it was a ship steaming away on a southwest heading. She was last seen on a compass bearing reported as SW $^1/_2$°W. In my opinion the accuracy of this bearing is doubtful. The rest of the watch was uneventful.

Come the first light of dawn two hours or so later, a ship was seen on a very similar bearing to the south. She had four masts and two masthead steaming lights and was therefore judged by *Californian's* master to be another vessel. The earlier ship had only a single masthead steaming light. This new ship was at such a distance that at least part of her hull was above the horizon and clearly visible. Although it is impossible to make any firm judgement from such a rudimentary description the indications are that she was probably no further than 10 miles away and quite possibly closer. In my opinion there is no doubt this other vessel was the *Carpathia*.

The events of the night are now analysed in more detail. The starting point is that from 2220 *Californian* lay stopped. All the evidence indicates that only one other, unknown, ship was seen from her bridge throughout the night, and her single white light was seen to approach from the east at about 2300. In all probability it was the single masthead steaming light of *Titanic*. If so, and given the quite exceptional visibility that prevailed that night, it would have been seen by an observer on the bridge of the *Californian* at a range of about 22 miles. The sidelights could be seen at about 15 miles and the accommodation lights marginally less. Precise distances are not used in these calculations and no latitude is given for conditions known as super-refraction or superior mirage. It was therefore perfectly possible for those on board the *Californian* to observe *Titanic*'s navigation lights as soon as they appeared over the horizon. The evidence supports this hypothesis. It is judged that *Titanic*'s masthead steaming light was first observed by those on board the *Californian* shortly after 2300. Her starboard navigation light came into view some time later at a range of about 15 miles. Different people on board the *Californian* saw the lights at different times and made their interpretation of what they saw accordingly. Had *Titanic* passed the *Californian* at a range in excesses of 22 miles she would not have been seen at all. Had she, as some infer, passed the *Californian* at a range of no more than 3–5 miles, it is inconceivable that her identity as a large passenger ship would not have been obvious to all. A passenger ship passing at such close range is very, very distinctive.

To an observer watching from the north *Titanic*'s bearing movement was right. One witness claimed to have seen this other ship's port side light but this does not tie in with any other evidence and is discounted. *Titanic* was also steaming at 22 knots. Whatever the identity of this new ship she needed to be steaming fast to cover the ground from the eastern horizon to a position south of the stopped *Californian* in the time available, and the speed needed was probably in excess of 20 knots. A slower ship would not cover so much ground in the same time and would still have been well to the east of south when she

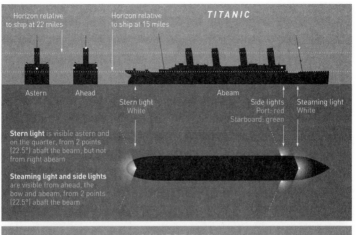

Navigation lights on *Titanic* and *Californian*, each seen from the other's bridge. From within a little under 15 miles, lights from *Titanic*'s upper accommodation could also have been visible to *Californian*.

came to stop. Only a few ships could steam at this high speed, and *Titanic* was one of them. She was the only such ship in the vicinity at the time.

The one thing that nearly all observers on board the *Californian* misjudged was, in my opinion, the range at which this other vessel was seen. It is extremely difficult to judge distances of lights at sea unless one has some form of yardstick by which to measure it. The perfect visibility that prevailed on the night of 14/15 April was such that even the most experienced officer would have underestimated the range and made his judgement as to the other's identity based on seeing a much smaller ship, going much more slowly, at a much closer range.

The evidence suggests that *Californian*'s master, having asked his Marconi operator what other ships were around that

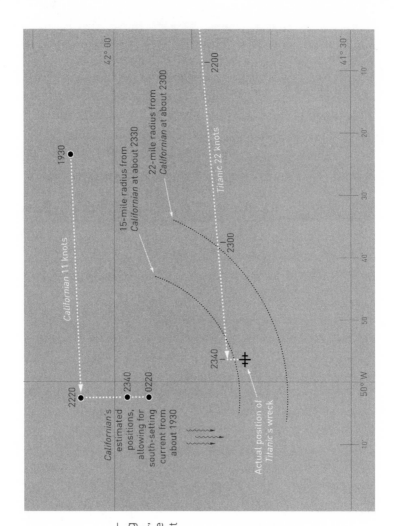

42° 00'

1930

Californian 11 knots

15-mile radius from
Californian at about 2330

22-mile radius from
Californian at about 2300

2200

Titanic 22 knots

2300

2220

2340 0220

Californian's
estimated
positions,
allowing for
south-setting
current from
about 1930

2340

Actual position of
Titanic's wreck

50° W

41° 30'

Titanic and *Californian* –
relative movements during
the night of 14/15 April,
showing the effect of the
south-setting current

evening, knew that *Titanic* was in the area. There is less evidence to indicate that he ever passed this information to any of his officers on the bridge. They therefore would have remained ignorant of *Titanic*'s presence throughout. Had they known, the second officer in particular might have been more positive about the identification of the vessel seen to be passing, known it would have been travelling fast and therefore at a range much further than first thought. Had he, in turn, shared this information with the master there might have been a greater understanding as to the likely identification, speed and range of this unknown ship. The failure to share such basic information was a contributory cause of those on board *Californian* not assessing more fully what they might have been looking at.

It is judged that the ship seen by *Californian* steaming past to the south on a near westerly course at speed was the *Titanic*. Her closest point of approach was in the order of 13 miles, and this is also the distance she was from the *Californian* at the time she foundered.

The question now arising is whether this hypothesis matches the situation from the perspective of the *Titanic*.

Nobody on board the *Titanic* appears to have seen the lights of any vessel in the hour or so before the collision with an iceberg. It is quite possible her lookouts were preoccupied with looking out for ice ahead and were not specifically concerned with what lay on either beam. It is also possible that *Titanic* lay outside the arc of visibility of the *Californian*'s masthead and starboard navigation lights. With *Californian* pointing in a northeasterly direction and the arcs extending two points (22 degrees) abaft the starboard beam this is indeed possible. Had this been the case *Titanic* would have been within the arc of visibility of *Californian*'s stern light, which, at a height above sea level of some 30 feet (9 metres) would have been visible for a maximum range of about 16 miles. At the same time, had the *Titanic* passed the *Californian* as close as 5 miles, someone on board would have seen at least one of her lights. Nobody did, and it is judged that her closest point of approach was at least 12 miles.

The first time a light, or lights, from the other vessel were observed on board *Titanic* was about 0030. Thereafter her lights were seen to indicate a ship closing and altering course as she did so. Those in the lifeboats a bit later were less certain as to what they were seeing but the consensus view is that they were looking at a single white light of a ship not very far away. The estimated range of this other ship was between 3 and 7 miles.

The key to almost everything that happened that night concerning both the *Titanic* and the *Californian* was, once again, the exceptionally good visibility. The two things that prevented the navigation lights of both ships being sighted by the other were not the intensity of the lights but the curvature of the earth and the arcs of visibility of the lights themselves.

If the other ship was the *Californian* then her lights would, coincidentally, be seen at almost the same range as *Titanic*'s were from *Californian*. *Californian*'s aft steaming light was approximately 105 feet (32 metres) above the waterline, the lower forward one was about 90 feet (27 metres) and the sidelights about 40 feet (12 metres). The stern light was the lowest one at some 30 feet (9 metres) above the waterline. Their lower heights were almost precisely compensated for by the greater height of the observers on *Titanic*'s bridge or boat deck. The aft masthead light would have been seen at just under 22 miles and the sidelight at between 16 and 17 miles. Significantly, an occupant in one of *Titanic*'s lifeboats would be able to see the highest steaming light at a range of about 14 miles.

Several observers on board *Titanic* hazarded guesses as to how far off the lights of the other ship were. Estimated ranges varied between 3 and 10 miles, but only one hypothesis fits all circumstances. A vessel stopped but swinging to starboard, and some 13 miles from *Titanic*, would look almost exactly as described by the witnesses who saw the lights.

The failure of anyone to see any lights initially can be

attributed to the fact that this other vessel was pointing away from *Titanic*. As she continued to swing to starboard her steaming lights would have become visible as well as her green starboard light. A little later one observer saw both steaming lights and then just her port light. The swing, and a natural interpretation that this other ship must have been closing, would have create an impression of movement.

Once embarked in the lifeboats several occupants said they could see a single white light on the horizon, and this would match the sighting of a masthead light. Had the distance between the two ships exceeded 14 miles it is unlikely to have been seen.

I have no doubt that the unknown vessel seen by those on board *Titanic* was the *Californian* at a range of about 13 miles. I am equally convinced that no other vessel was involved.

This analysis, however, fails to satisfy three other features of the conundrum that night. Looked at in purely relative terms the two ships are probably only 13 miles apart, but the actual positions, as derived from the evidence, suggest the distance between them was much greater. The second factor seeks to explain why neither ship could see the Morse light of the other as they attempted to communicate with each other over a period that lasted an hour or more, while the third attempts to reconcile the positions of the various ships that found themselves in sight of one another during the early hours of the next morning.

In trying to resolve the apparent dichotomy of the mismatching evidence with regard to position, the starting point is to consider the accuracy of the positions involved. There are three: the dead reckoning (DR) position of the *Californian* once way had been taken off her at 2220, the corrected position of the *Titanic* contained in her SOS message, and the position of the wreck following its discovery in 1985. In my opinion, one of these positions is extremely accurate, one was almost certainly good and the third was almost certainly not.

The mean position of the wreck has been determined within inches. The nature of the debris field on the sea bed confirms my view that the wreck lies almost vertically beneath the spot where she foundered. The wreckage may have 'glided' in any direction as it descended but, because it is so closely grouped, I am satisfied that any such movement was limited. The position of the wreckage may not equate to the precise position where the collision with the iceberg occurred, as *Titanic* would have drifted some way following the impact and she may also have got under way for a few minutes afterwards. It is also likely that she too drifted with a current but at a rate less than that experienced by the *Californian* on the edge of the icefield. For the purposes of resolving the basic position issue these movements are not considered. They may have been accumulative or they may have been self-cancelling. The indisputable fact remains that *Titanic*'s navigators thought she was some 13 miles from where the wreck was eventually discovered. In my opinion, therefore, the position contained in the SOS message was in error by a substantial margin. This is also borne out by the *Carpathia*, who found *Titanic*'s lifeboats in a position much more aligned to the wreck position than to the one given in the distress message.

When the *Californian* stopped after encountering ice, her DR position was calculated as being 42° 05' N, 57° 07' W. In my view this position, based on earlier sights was reasonably accurate and put the position contained in *Titanic*'s SOS message 19½ miles distant and bearing 197°. Although not known at the time, it meant the actual wreck bore 160° at a range of 23 miles. *Californian*'s DR position did not, however, make any allowance for any other influence on her movement such as a current. Once any such allowance has been made the resultant position becomes her estimated position (EP).

An analysis of the evidence, based largely on the position of the wreck, indicates that *Titanic* did not travel as far to the west as her navigators had estimated. There is furthermore no evidence to indicate she steamed through the ice barrier with its eastern extremity being on a longitude of about 50° W. Assuming for a moment that her calculated position from stellar observations was more or less correct, it means her speed over the ground during her final hours was less than expected. It is therefore probable that she encountered an east-setting current during the final hours. If this applied to *Titanic* then the same applied to *Californian*. This does not, however, fully explain the discrepancy in the position between *Titanic*'s SOS position and that of the wreck, and it may be that no entirely satisfactory explanation will ever be forthcoming.

The key to understanding what happened that night lies with four things: the undisputable position of the wreck; the narrow but long tongue of the icefield and icebergs that formed a north–south barrier to the west of where most of the action took place; the fact that *Californian* swung gently to starboard throughout much of the night; and *Carpathia*'s sighting of the *Californian* at a much closer range the next morning. Add to this *Californian*'s position from observations the next day, which placed her over 30 miles south of her dead reckoning position the night before, suggesting that she had moved far further to the south overnight than in the hour she had spent steaming in that direction earlier that morning. Everything indicates a significant drift to the south overnight.

The accumulation of ice in the area, which embraced ice floes, growlers and icebergs, extended north and south over many miles but was only 2–3 miles wide in many places. Its shape was analogous to a river of ice in the open sea, with the majority of the icebergs, with their deeper keels, lying to the east of it. Some unknown factor must therefore have existed to give it this shape, otherwise the ice would have been spread over a much wider, and broader, area. The driving force must have been a relatively strong and very narrow surface current, probably exceeding 1 knot, pushing the ice on a narrow front southwards. Any vessel caught within its influence would be similarly affected. The only ships to fall within this category were the *Californian* and, to a lesser extent, the *Titanic*.

As *Californian* approached the icefield the influence of this south-setting current would have begun to take effect. It probably started soon after passing the icebergs reported to *Antillian* at 1830 and reached its maximum rate by the time *Californian* stopped on the edge of the icefield at 2220. There was no wind that night and yet we know that the *Californian* swung slowly to starboard over the next few hours. Ships do not swing unless under some external influence, and the judgement made is that it was a localised current with its swirls on the edges that created the circumstances to swing a ship. In my opinion this is precisely what happened to the *Californian* as she lay stopped and swinging from about 2220 on the Sunday evening. During her approach to the ice edge she was being pushed towards the south by an unknown amount and then stopped to drift at a faster rate over the next seven hours. It is impossible to judge how far she was set to the south but it was probably at least 7 miles and maybe even more. The swing was caused by the effects of the current so close to the edge of the icefield.

The bias of the icebergs to the east, meanwhile, might suggest they were being influenced by some other current pushing them further to the east than the smaller bits of ice within the icefield.

One question remains: why did neither ship detect the use of the Morse lamp by the other? They were both omni-directional and were not, as such, anywhere near as powerful as navigation lights. Operated by a Morse key positioned on the bridge, such lights are surprisingly difficult to see by an observer unless the two ships are relatively close together. Even when only 2–3 miles apart they are not as clear as one might expect. Evidence at the inquiry that suggested they can be used at ranges of up to 10 miles may indeed be true but, in my opinion, the chance of them being effective at ranges in the order of 13 miles is not good. I believe it is very unlikely that the officers on either the bridge of *Titanic* or *Californian* would have seen the other's Morse light.

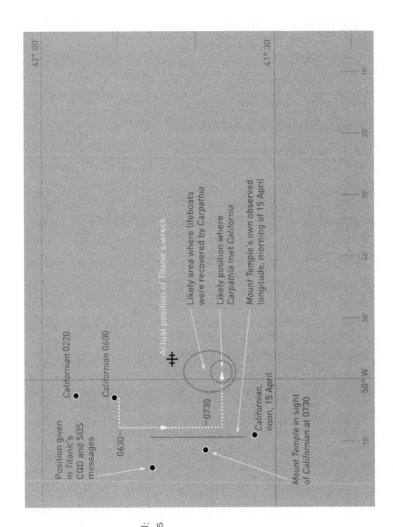

Position given
in *Titanic*'s
CQD and SOS
messages

Californian 0220

Californian 0600

—0730—

0630—

Actual position of *Titanic*'s wreck

Likely area where lifeboats
were recovered by *Carpathia*

Likely position where
Carpathia met *California*

Mount Temple's own observed
longitude, morning of 15 April

Californian,
noon, 15 April

Mount Temple in sight
of *Californian* at 0730

15 April, 0200–0800:
Californian's movements

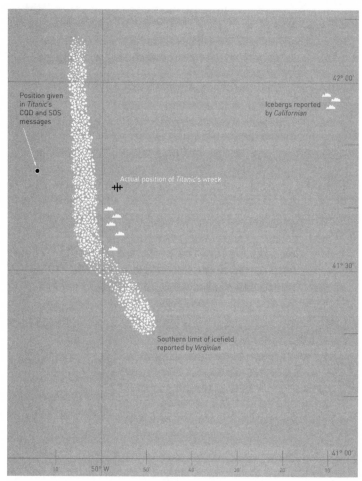

The location of the icefield on 14/15 April, based on various reports, relative to *Titanic*'s SOS position, and the actual position of her wreck.

The final point that needs to be addressed is to assess the significance of the relative positions of the various ships that found themselves in sight of one another the next morning. There is no doubting that the *Californian* remained stationary overnight and only got under way soon after 0600 on a course for the position given in *Titanic*'s SOS message. She had, however, already seen another steamer to the south on a very similar bearing to the one on which the disappearing vessel had been earlier that morning. She was described as being a vessel with four masts, two steaming lights and a yellow funnel. No range was given but the detailed nature of the description suggests it was sufficiently close to discern some colour in the first light of daybreak as well as the basic characteristics of the vessel. Whilst difficult to assess a range from such sparse details, it is likely to have been between about 8 and 10 miles. It should be said, however, that determining the colour of a funnel with any accuracy so early in the day would not have been easy at such a range.

In the meantime the *Carpathia*, having steamed towards *Titanic*'s SOS position from 0040, had stopped in what she believed was the correct position. It is assessed that she had not covered as much ground as she had estimated, having never reached the speed she had allowed for. She actually stopped in the vicinity of where the wreck was eventually discovered in 1985 and close to where the lifeboats found themselves as dawn broke. She began recovering survivors soon after 0410 and whilst doing so a bit later noted another steamer to the north at a range estimated to be about 10 miles.

I have no doubt that the vessel seen by the *Californian* to the south was indeed the *Carpathia*, and that one of the vessels observed by the *Carpathia* was the *Californian*. It comes as no surprise that those on board the *Carpathia* were not paying that much attention to other ships between 0400 and 0830 the next morning.

Californian's position on leaving the wreckage was 41° 33' N, 50° 01' W, some 32 miles almost due south from his estimated overnight stopped position. This confirms a significant movement south overnight, not all of which is explained by her being under way heading south after about 0600.

Californian and distress messages

Californian had the means to detect two types of distress message from *Titanic*: wireless and visual.

Wireless

Titanic transmitted wireless distress messages almost continuously from 0027 until a few minutes before she foundered at 0220 on 15 April. *Californian*'s ability to receive these messages was entirely dependent on her wireless equipment being available for use and switched on, and an operator listening in.

There was no requirement for ships to maintain a listening watch for 24 hours a day. *Californian*'s single watchkeeper ceased keeping his watch at about 2325 and turned in. He had previously been in communication with *Titanic* and had attempted to inform him that *Californian* was stopped and surrounded by ice. *Titanic*, however, told him to 'keep out.' He did.

There was no reason for *Californian*'s wireless operator to remain awake, and his decision to turn in was both lawful and legitimate.

When *Titanic* first started sending wireless distress messages at 0027 on the 15th nobody on board the *Californian* was maintaining a watch. There was no requirement to do so.

The lack of provision for 24-hour-a-day watchkeeping for wireless operators was a factor in ships being able to respond to *Titanic*'s distress calls for assistance.

Visual

Titanic fired rockets as distress signals between about 0045 and 0115 on 15 April.

Officers keeping watch on the bridge of the *Californian*, lying stopped a number of miles to the north of *Titanic*, saw rockets being fired from the direction of a ship stopped, seemingly, on the horizon some miles to the south. *Californian* did not appear to identify them as distress signals and ignored them.

It is judged that the rockets observed by the *Californian* were those fired by the *Titanic,* in which case the reasons why they were not recognised as distress signals requires examination.

Everyone who reads, or hears, what happened that night knows the outcome. *Titanic* fired rockets. *Californian* saw rockets, ignored them and remained where she was. After a while *Californian* saw the lights disappear and only heard that *Titanic* had sunk the next morning. Surely, the argument goes, it should have been very obvious that the rockets seen by *Californian* were distress signals and she should have reacted.

The officer keeping the middle watch on board *Californian* was the second officer, accompanied by the apprentice. On coming on watch shortly after midnight his attention had been drawn to a ship, believed to be about 5 miles away, lying, apparently, stopped. She was showing a single white masthead steaming light, a port side light and some indistinct accommodation lights. The captain had instructed the second officer to keep an eye on this other vessel and let him know if it came any closer. From about 0045 white rockets were observed above this vessel, and at 0115 the second officer informed his captain, who, assuming she was close by, told him to contact her by Morse lamp. He also asked if they were private signals. The second officer did not know, and was told to keep trying to make contact. The captain did not come to the bridge. The port sidelight of this other vessel vanished, her accommodation lights had taken on an unusual angle, and eventually her remaining white light, judged to be her stern light, vanished. To someone who knows what actually happened, it is clear that the disappearing stern light was *Titanic*'s steaming light getting lower in the water and that the unusual angle of the lights matched the bow-down angle in the minutes before she sank. Those on the *Californian* thought they were looking at a ship about five miles away that had turned to the southwest and steamed away until her stern light had dipped below the horizon. In the observer's opinion almost nothing unusual had happened. But what about those rockets?

On seeing the rockets, *Californian*'s officer of the watch would have relied on three factors: his knowledge, his experience and his interpretation of what he was seeing. As the holder of a Mate's Certificate of Competency, and having been at sea for eight years, he should have been fully aware of the regulations that covered distress signals. He would also have been familiar with company signals, whereby ships communicated with each other using rockets and candles.

Distress signals at sea are unusual, and many mariners will enjoy a full career without ever seeing one. There is nothing to indicate that either the second officer or the apprentice had seen any in their respective careers, but the second officer may have seen company signals. To be effective, a distress signal must be so distinctive that anyone who has never seen one before cannot possibly mistake it for anything else, and yet those on board *Californian* saw white rockets but failed to recognise them instantly for what they were. Why not?

The regulations that covered distress signals had been drafted for the user of the rockets. They were not nearly so well drafted for anyone seeing them. Much was made of socket signals in lieu of guns being fired at intervals of one minute, and yet an observer out of audible range would have had no idea what type of rocket was being fired, would not hear the detonation and would only have seen a rocket. The only characteristics he could count on to signify the purpose of the rockets would be their colour and the intervals at which they were fired.

The colour of *Titanic*'s rockets was white. It is very easy to assume that any rocket, no matter what its colour, would automatically be recognised as a distress signal in all circumstances. No such assumptions can, however, be made if there is any possibility, no matter how remote, that it might be interpreted as something else. *Californian*'s captain specifically asked if it was a private signal and sought an answer rather than join his second officer on the bridge to see what was happening. No such question should ever have been necessary, nor should the officer of the watch have had any doubt as to what he was seeing. But the question was asked and the second officer did not know instinctively what he was looking at. Hindsight clearly shows that both the captain and his watchkeepers onboard *Californian* were wrong in their assessments. Hindsight is, however, no substitute for clarity when drafting regulations.

There is no evidence to indicate that anyone on board *Californian* was timing the interval at which the rockets were being fired. Had they been sent up at the intervals required by the regulations, which required 'short intervals' or 'intervals of one minute', they would have been recognised regardless of anyone needing to time them. The actual interval being used was almost certainly far in excess of this and would have done very little to alert an observer that they were distress signals. What was evidently missing that night was a signal that could not, under any circumstances, be mistaken for anything else. The judgement is made that the regulations failed to meet the most fundamental requirement of any distress signal: to be instantly recognisable.

There is, however, another dimension that cannot be overlooked: the seeming failure of anyone on board *Californian* to react positively to the rockets. Even if nobody realised they were distress signals, the reasons for not doing anything about them requires further examination.

Those on the bridge thought the vessel they could see was a relatively small steamer lying stopped and not very far away. They had not been informed that the *Titanic* was likely to be in the area and it had never occurred to them that they might be looking at a much larger vessel at a far greater range. Unless anything happened to make them change their minds about what they could see they had no reason to do so. The one thing that did not fit their perception was the very low height of the rockets being fired. Whether it was this or the mere fact that rockets were being fired at all, the second officer was evidently uneasy about what he was seeing, as was the apprentice. The captain knew nothing about it until about 30 minutes after the first rocket had been fired.

Perhaps in keeping with his position, the second officer did not appear to take a view as to what he was seeing but chose to inform the captain and leave him to decide what to do. Whether he had an opinion or not is not known, but he seemed to be content for the captain to act on what he was being told. That the captain did no more than acknowledge the reports and seek further information appeared to satisfy him. There is no evidence to indicate that the second officer had it in mind to wake the Marconi operator to get him to set a watch to see if anything was amiss. It is possible the thought never occurred to him, or that it was not his place to take such a decision, or he might have been concerned that any such action would attract derision or criticism from the captain. It is known that *Californian's* junior officers were in some awe of their captain, and such a relationship is not conducive to the making of reports. It is quite probable that the second officer lacked the confidence to use his initiative and take decisions without reference to someone more senior. The deference given to senior officers and the reluctance of junior officers to act without being given specific orders was a feature of life in merchant ships of the era. It is possible that the culture of life afloat at the time played a part in the failure of anyone to call the Marconi operator just as soon as it became clear that more than two rockets had been fired. On the other hand, he may have thought, as the captain may have done, that, with the other vessel so close, there was nothing to be gained by using the wireless when the Morse lamp was so readily available. The second officer stated that the ship he had been watching was last observed on a bearing of SW $1/2°$ W. This does not tie in with any other evidence and, because it is very similar to the true bearing of *Titanic's* transmitted CQD/SOS position from *Californian*, it is at least possible that it was calculated retrospectively. The position of the wreck indicates that *Titanic* sank further east than *Californian's* position.

SS *Mount Temple*

The Canadian Pacific Railway steamer *Mount Temple* was on passage from Antwerp to Saint John, New Brunswick, in mid April 1912. Her master was under instruction from his company to avoid any encounter with ice and had adjusted his westbound course to avoid it. He sailed further south than originally intended and, having done so on the evening of 14 April, altered course back again to make for his destination when *Titanic's* wireless distress message was intercepted at about 0030. This indicated she had struck an iceberg some 40 miles to the east and was sinking. Course was altered towards *Titanic's* position and speed increased.

Some on board reported seeing the lights and rockets of another ship to the east but, given the distance apart of the two ships, it is unlikely that *Titanic's* lights were seen. It is however possible that *Mount Temple* did see rockets, either from the sinking *Titanic* after 0100, or from the *Carpathia* in the hour or so before dawn. The distances apart of the ships involved made this possible.

Whilst steaming east towards the sinking *Titanic*, *Mount Temple's* wireless operator listened to the many transmissions between the White Star liner and other ships but did not break in on the grounds that he should not interfere. This was not unreasonable.

Having reached *Titanic's* distress position and found nothing, *Mount Temple* judged the *Titanic* to have sunk and searched the area without success. It had occurred to the master that the *Titanic* had been further to the east than indicated in her SOS message but he did nothing about it and did not share his thoughts with other vessels. He made no attempt to proceed through the icefield to the east of him, and it was only later that he discovered the survivors from the *Titanic* had, indeed, been picked up on the far side of the barrier. This supports the contention that the *Titanic* never penetrated the ice barrier and sank several miles further to the east than she had calculated.

There is no evidence to indicate that *Titanic* saw *Mount Temple* at any stage.

Other ships

The judgement is made that no other ship was in sight of *Titanic* when she foundered.

Lifeboat action after the sinking

Because the estimates varied so widely it is not possible to judge with any certainty how far away the lifeboats were when *Titanic* finally foundered. As people tend to overestimate distances when afloat it is very possible that no boat was more than half a mile away. Some were undoubtedly very close, within 200 metres. Handling a boat in good conditions with an experienced crew at the oars is one thing; trying to do the same with inexperienced or novice rowers at night in a crowded, heavily laden boat is an entirely different matter. That many heard the cries of victims struggling in the water after *Titanic* sank confirms they were never far away. It can also be reasonably assumed that the occupants of the lifeboats had just witnessed something so traumatic that it is unlikely to have left them unaffected. It is also almost impossible for anyone who was not there on the night to have any concept as to what the survivors were going through in the first hour after seeing *Titanic* sink. Not only had they been witness to an appalling sight, and heard the cries of people in the final minutes of life, but they had no idea what their own fate was likely to be. It was also extremely cold.

The evidence suggests that only one boat made any real attempt to row in the direction of where the victims were thought to be with a view to picking up any survivors. That some attempted to do so is commendable. Other boats were in a position to do so but, for a number of reasons, did not. It is no part of this analysis to criticise those that chose not to, but the difficulties of recovering people from the sea should never be underestimated. People swimming or floating are hard to find in the dark, are extremely heavy when trying to recover them and are rarely able to help themselves. It requires strength and space to recover a person from the water. With every passing minute the effects of the ice-cold water would have been taking their toll and people would have been dying. The important thing is to give consideration to how best to increase the chances of recovering people from the sea in the minimum time possible should such a situation ever arise again. The task, especially at night, in a high sea state and with large numbers of people, is among the most difficult facing professional mariners. The cold takes a dreadful toll very rapidly.

The rescue

Had *SS Carpathia*'s wireless operator been off watch when *Titanic* began transmitting distress messages, the outcome of the night might well have been very different.

Carpathia's immediate response to the call for assistance was exemplary and in the finest traditions of good seamanship under positive direction. The preparations for the reception of passengers were good and the ship was well handled. Her captain was, like *Titanic*'s master, taking a risk in proceeding at speed into waters known to contain both ice and icebergs but had taken the precaution of increasing the lookout capability and remained on the bridge himself. Once it was evident that the *Carpathia* was steaming in waters where icebergs were lying and not being seen until relatively close, speed was reduced.

Carpathia based her course to steer and the distance to run on the position given in *Titanic*'s distress message. Approaching this from the southeast, she found the survivors in almost the position she had predicted, but analysis reveals she was several miles short by the time she found the boats. There were three reasons. The first was the error in the initial position sent out by *Titanic*. Assuming the lifeboats were reasonably close to where

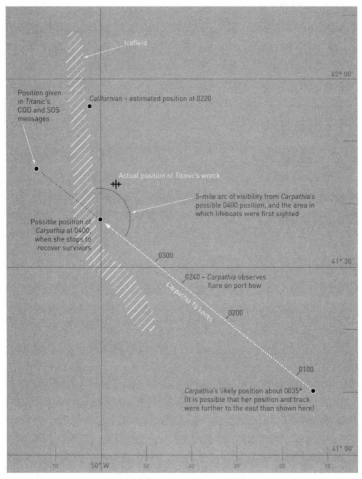

Carpathia's movements on 15 April

she foundered the position of the wreck indicates she must have been much further towards the direction from which the *Carpathia* was approaching than was at first thought. The second was that *Carpathia* was not making the speed over the ground she had originally estimated and did not, therefore, steam as far as she thought; in my opinion her maximum speed that night was little more than 15 knots, and far less than the 17 knots she was estimating. The third was the decision by *Titanic*'s fourth officer to place a box of green flares in his lifeboat before leaving the sinking ship. By firing these flares he was able to draw attention to the presence of the lifeboats as the then unknown rescue ship approached. It was a fortunate string of circumstances that the accumulative errors in determining the position of both *Titanic* and *Carpathia* almost exactly cancelled each other out. Had *Carpathia* been approaching the estimated distress position from any other direction, the outcome would almost certainly have been very different.

She manoeuvred alongside the first of *Titanic*'s lifeboats, No. 2, at 0410, about 1 hour 50 minutes after the ship had foundered. Once there was sufficient light to see where the other lifeboats were it became evident they all lay within 2–4 miles of each other.

At 13,500 tons *Carpathia* was a relatively small vessel, but even so the freeboard and the distance between the waterline and the gangway doors made the boarding of cold and tired survivors far from easy. Some of the children and others were hoisted on board using mail bags. Although the wind and sea state was beginning to pick up as dawn broke, the fine conditions made the recovery process relatively straightforward. Even so it took about four hours to recover all 700 survivors. Had the recovery been conducted during the night it would almost certainly have taken longer. Had the sea state been much higher the rescue would have taken much longer, the lifeboat occupants would have been more distressed and, very possibly, the number of fatalities would have been much higher. To assume that similar conditions might prevail in any future emergency is both naive and short-sighted.

The victims

It has not proved possible to establish the precise numbers of those who were killed in the accident, but it is assessed that the final figure was just over 1500 souls.

Apart from those whose bodies were recovered from the sea several days after the accident, and on whom post-mortems were carried out, it is impossible to state the cause of death for the majority. Although some may have been killed by falling debris, ship fittings and collapsing funnels as the *Titanic* took on an ever-increasing bow-down angle in the moments before she finally foundered, the precise cause of death for all the others is unknown. Some may have drowned, but the more likely cause was hypothermia. The wearing of lifejackets and the donning of warm clothing were, ultimately, of little help in saving the lives of anyone unable to find a place in a lifeboat. The life-jackets did however provide the survivors in the lifeboats with a degree of protection against the bitter cold of the night and almost certainly contributed to the saving of life.

One month later the White Star SS *Oceanic* came across one of *Titanic*'s collapsible lifeboats still afloat with three dead men onboard. Two were members of the crew and the third a male passenger. On the balance of probability it is most likely that they were the three souls that had died during the night in collapsible boat A before the survivors had been transferred to lifeboat No. 14 and taken to the *Carpathia*.

Casualty figures

It has proved impossible to determine with any accuracy the precise number of people who were embarked when *Titanic* sailed from Queenstown. It is equally uncertain how many survived and how many lost their lives.

According to the emigration officer who cleared *Titanic* from Queenstown on 11 April there were 2208 people were on board when she sailed. They consisted of 892 crew and 1316 passengers. The actual number of people on board that day was eventually assessed at 2201: 1316 passengers and 885 crew. The *Carpathia* rescued 711 survivors on 15 April, indicating that 1490 souls lost their lives. Uncertainties, however, remain.

A breakdown of survivors reveals that 499 were passengers, of whom 296 were women and 57 were children. 212 were crew members, of whom 20 were female.

PART 3

Conclusions, causes and recommendations

Introduction

This chapter draws together the threads of the *Titanic* disaster. It summarises her conformity, or otherwise, with the regulations of the day, identifies the causes of the accident and touches, very briefly, on the recommendations. As this is not an official investigation I do no more than remind the reader what the original recommendations were and very briefly describe how they were implemented.

The causes of the accident fall into three categories: the single action that initiated the sequence of events that led to the *Titanic*'s collision with the iceberg, the three fundamental reasons that underpinned the entire tragedy, and the many underlying causes that contributed so much to everything that went wrong. Although many of them did receive a mention in some form in the original inquiries, particularly in the recommendations, they were never identified in quite the same way.

As in the majority of other accidents the initiating cause was something entirely innocuous but one that had tragic consequences. The three fundamental, or root, causes, answer the three key questions posed at the outset: why did *Titanic* hit the iceberg; why did she sink; and why did do many people lose their lives?

Contributory causes lie at the heart of any marine accident investigation. Less obvious than the root causes and sometimes overlooked or misinterpreted, they provide the material from which the most fruitful, far-reaching and effective safety recommendations can be made.

No new recommendations are made, but the original ones made in 1912 are summarised together with a brief update on how they were implemented.

The conclusions, causes and recommendations are presented in the format adopted for use in a marine accident report today.

Findings

It is concluded that:

(a)   When *Titanic* sailed from Queenstown on 11 April 1912 she complied with all the requirements of the Merchant Shipping Acts of 1894–1906, and the rules and regulations pertaining to passenger steamers and emigrant ships.

(b)   *Titanic* complied with all the regulations with regard to manning and the certification of both officers and ratings.

(c)   *Titanic* was properly equipped with a full outfit of charts, sailing directions and appropriate instruction for the conduct of a safe passage across the North Atlantic.

(d)   Both charts and sailing directions contained adequate warnings about the possible extent of ice in the vicinity of the Grand Banks of Newfoundland during the month of April.

(e)   *Titanic* carried both lifeboats and lifesaving apparatus in excess of those required by the regulations.

(f)   Once *Titanic* had stopped in the water following her collision she remained stationary up until the moment she foundered. During this time the lights of another vessel were observed. She was the Leyland Line steamship *Californian*.

(g)   Lying stopped and surrounded by ice from 2215 on the
        evening of 14 April, the Leyland Line steamship *Californian*
        in approximate position 42° 05' N, 57° 07' W, saw the lights
        of another, unknown, steamer pass by some miles to the
        south of her, stop, and subsequently disappear. That vessel
        was the *Titanic*. The *Californian* remained stopped in her
        position until about 0600 the following morning.

(h)   The Cunard Line steamship *Carpathia* responded imme-
        diately to the distress signal transmitted by the *Titanic*,
        steamed towards the position given and was able to
        rescue all those who had survived the sinking and were in
        the lifeboats. She proceeded with the survivors embarked
        to New York, where she arrived on the evening of 18 April.

The initiating cause

A single action triggered the entire sequence of events that resulted in the loss of the *Titanic*. It was the order given at approximately 1750 on Sunday 14 April 1912 to alter course to starboard
to a new course of S 86° W. The order probably consisted of two
words such as 'port 10' followed by a course to steer. It is likely to
have been given by either the captain or the officer of the watch
with the intention of taking the ship to the next alteration of
course off the Nantucket Shoals light vessel before making for
the Ambrose Channel light vessel and New York. The order was
perfectly legitimate but led to the *Titanic* steering a course that
took her into an area where ice was expected, and proved to be
when she hit the iceberg at 2340. No further order to change this
course was given until a matter of seconds before impact. By
then it was too late.

The root or key causes

The prime reason for *Titanic* colliding with an iceberg was the
decision to steer a course that would take her towards an area
where ice was known to exist on a dark night and with no

thought being given to the consequences of not seeing any hazard in time to take avoiding action. Had the decision been taken to shape a course that ensured she passed well to the south of the known presence of ice, the accident would not have happened. Had she maintained her original course to the southwest and delayed altering to the west until she had intersected the 50th meridian some 75 miles further south, she would have added about 25 miles to her passage, cleared all the reported ice by a significant margin, and extended her passage time by less than an hour and a half. She had more than enough time in hand to enable this to be achieved without affecting her timely arrival in New York.

The root cause of *Titanic*'s sinking after colliding with an iceberg was that the damage she sustained was more than her design and build allowed for.

The key factor that led directly to the extensive loss of life was the failure to update the 1894 regulations concerning the provision of lifeboats in steamships and the decision by the British Board of Trade to base its rules for the carriage of lifeboats on the gross tonnage of the vessel concerned rather than the number of people being carried.

Underlying and contributory causes

The underlying reasons for *Titanic* disaster were:

General

(1) Scheduling the maiden voyage so soon after completion of build.

(2) Appointing ship's officers so late in building that they were given insufficient time to absorb the technicalities of their ship, to know their away around, to check their areas of responsibilities and find out what tests had been carried out and the results.

(3) Allowing insufficient time for comprehensive sea trials to be undertaken.

(4) The White Star Line's decision to appoint the master at such short notice and without giving him adequate time to settle down before the hour of sailing.

(5) The White Star Line's decision to change the senior navigating officers around on the morning of departure.

(6) The culture of 'custom' that dictated the Southampton-based Board of Trade surveyor to approve the conduct of the boat drill on board *Titanic* when his instincts told him it was not unsatisfactory.

(7) The lack of internationally agreed requirements on stability.

(8) The lack of internationally agreed provision for lifesaving apparatus to be carried on board ships.

Collision with an iceberg

(1) The lack of any system on board for collection, collation and dissemination of navigation warnings.

(2) The arrangement whereby the great North Atlantic steamship companies agreed to implement lane routes to ensure outward and homebound ships were separated and kept clear of ice by using fixed tracks.

(3) The failure of the great North Atlantic steamship companies to agree a system with the relevant hydrographic offices to agree arrangements whereby tracks could be changed when ice extended beyond the charted extremities.

(4) The lack of any system to ensure that effective priority was given to the handling of any message containing navigational information.

(5) The failure of some ships to prefix their ice warning messages with the prefix MSG.

(6) The employment of wireless operators at sea without ensuring they had sufficient training to recognise the significance of navigational warnings, including ice reports, in the area of interest.

(7) The introduction of wireless at sea without making provision to ensure that operators could monitor the receipt of distress messages at all times.

(8) The lack of any integration between wireless operators and navigating officers and the lack of any means by which the wireless room could be in direct communication with the bridge.

(9) A defect to the wireless overnight on 13/14 April that required both operators to remain up for much of the night repairing it, which meant that their performance throughout the next day was not as effective as it should have been.

(10) The failure to plot all ice warnings on the chart in use by the navigating officers.

(11) The failure to collate all ice warnings into a coherent picture.

(12) The lack of any procedure on board to ensure that all navigating officers were routinely kept updated on potential hazards likely to affect ship's safety.

(13) The lack of a system to plot all ice reports on a chart that was readily available and seen by all navigating officers.

(14) The lack of any review of the alternatives to maintaining the planned track on approaching the 'turning point'.

(15) The acceptance by *Titanic*'s senior officers of shaping a course to leave only 4 miles between the planned track and the reported position of ice; this was poor seamanship.

(16) The lack of any system to ensure that officers new to the North Atlantic were appraised of the potential hazards, and the methods used on board for handling them.

(17) The culture extant on board that ensured no officer would undertake any responsibility other than what he was expected to do for his rank.

(18) The widespread culture within the mercantile marine of unquestioning acceptance of the most senior officer's interpretation of a situation despite the experience and qualifications of those in subordinate positions. Many such officers held at least a Master's Certificate of Competency and were perfectly capable of offering sensible and seamanlike advice.

(19) Insufficient attention being given to where a lookout in a high-speed transatlantic steamship could most effectively keep a watch regardless of the prevailing weather conditions.

(20) The inflexibility of a watchkeeping system that failed to ensure that sufficient watchkeeping officers were actually keeping a lookout when potential hazards existed.

(21) The failure to ensure all three officers of the watch were on the bridge keeping a lookout at the time the ice was expected.

(22) The lack of any command briefing on the measures to be adopted to ensure the ship's safety in the anticipated conditions.

(23) The failure to post additional lookouts when approaching an area where ice was known to exist.

(24) The unjustified assumption by senior officers that, given the exceptional conditions that existed on the night of 14 April, the anticipated ice would be sighted in good time to take the necessary action.

(25) The unjustified assumption that those keeping watch would recognise 'haze' ahead as ice.

(26) The very cold air temperature and corresponding 22-knot apparent wind speed, which adversely affected the keeping of an efficient lookout.

(27) Failure to provide better protection for those required to maintain a lookout in the windswept crow's nest in very low temperatures.

(28) The speed of the ship, which generated the higher apparent wind speed.

(29) The speed of the ship, which reduced the reaction time needed to take avoiding action in the event of a late sighting of ice.

(30) The limited brief to the lookouts in the crow's nest by the officers on watch at around 2130.

(31) The failure to alert the lookouts to look out for and report any sighting of 'haze'.

(32) The inexperience of the lookouts in recognising ice at night under a starlit sky.

(33) The decision by the master to leave the bridge during the time the anticipated ice was expected to be seen.

(34) The failure of the bridge to alert the engine room to the possibility of the ship having to slow down as it approached an area where ice was know to exist.

(1)　The assessment that the risks a ship such as *Titanic* would face would never include damage extending over five watertight compartments or more.

(2)　The decision to limit the upper limit of watertight bulkheads to the top of F deck and no higher.

(3)　The inadequate provision of watertight subdivisions on board.

(4)　The lack of any system on board the *Titanic* to assess the extent of the underwater damage and how it might be contained.

(5)　The lack of any consideration being given to how best to reduce the rate of flooding.

(6)　The inability to pump the maximum amount of water out of compartments without having to run hoses through watertight doors.

(7)　The lack of any system to ensure the maximum watertight integrity of the vessel once the initial assessment of the damage had been made.

(8)　The decision to open a gangway door to facilitate the embarkation of passengers into lifeboats.

(9)　The lack of any procedure to ensure that all manually operated watertight doors were shut and kept shut.

(10)　The lack of any organisation to ensure that all portholes, shell doors and other openings were fully shut and secured.

(11)　The possible weakening of a watertight bulkhead in the vicinity of a coal bunker at the aft corner of boiler room No. 6, where a fire had been burning for several days before being extinguished on 13 April.

(1) Lack of knowledge among the navigating officers as to the number of people who could be embarked safely in the lifeboat.

(2) The lack of an effective lifeboat drill at any time.

(3) The lack of any regulation requiring lifeboat drills to be held.

(4) The failure to ensure that every member of the crew was aware of his or her allocated lifeboat.

(5) The lack of urgency to prepare, fill and launch the lifeboats.

(6) Lack of familiarity by many in *Titanic*'s crew with launching and handling the lifeboats.

(7) Having insufficient numbers among the crew who were sufficiently competent, trained and practised to clear away, prepare, launch and handle the lifeboats

(8) The delay in the decision to abandon ship.

(9) The failure of effective command and control of the lifeboat loading and lowering process.

(10) The failure by the command to ensure that all lifeboats were loaded to their maximum capacity.

(11) The lack of any means to alert everyone to an emergency.

(12) The lack of any procedure for effectively informing crew and passengers on the gravity of the situation without inducing undue distress or panic.

(13) Having lifeboats that did not readily permit speedy preparation.

(14) The lack of any procedure or organisation for mustering passengers, looking after them, bringing them forward and embarking them in the lifeboats in a timely and expeditious manner.

(15) The lack of any organisation to bring steerage passengers to the lifeboat embarkation points in a timely manner.

(16) The officers' lack of knowledge as to the capacity of the lifeboats.

(17) The lack of a coherent lifeboat loading strategy and awareness among officers as to where passengers should embark.

(18) The failure to ensure that barriers designed to separate steerage class passengers from the other two classes were removed once the implications of the damage had been assessed.

(19) The delay in transmitting a wireless distress call.

(20) The failure of the international maritime community to ensure that all vessels equipped with wireless telegraphy equipment carried sufficient wireless operators to ensure a monitoring watch could be maintained at all times when at sea.

(21) The lack of any discernible organisation to monitor, organise and control events as the ship settled.

(22) The decision to observe a 'women and children first' rule. No such rule exists.

(23) The decision to enforce a 'women and children only' rule. No such rule exists.

(24) The decision to send away several lifeboats before they had been fully loaded.

(25) The high noise level on the boat deck caused by the steam valves lifting. The noise made communications difficult during the early part of the evacuation process and may have deterred some people from proceeding to the waiting boats.

(26) The inadequacies of the regulations to have a visual means that was immediately and unmistakably recognisable as a distress signal.

(27) The failure of the International Regulations for Preventing Collisions at Sea to include a distress signal that was sufficiently distinctive that it could not, under any circumstances, be interpreted for something else.

(28) The inadequacies of the regulations to clearly stipulate the interval at which rockets should be fired.

(29) The failure to conform to the regulations to fire rockets at 'short intervals'.

(30) The inadequacies of the life preservers to save life among those who found themselves in the water. The judgement is made that many of those who died did so from hypothermia and not from drowning.

(31) The inability of the lifeboats to provide any form of protection against the elements.

(32) The placing of collapsible lifeboats on top of the officers' accommodation.

(33) Whilst acknowledging that *Carpathia* found *Titanic*'s lifeboats at almost the precise time that had been anticipated, the inaccuracy in the position transmitted in the CQD message could have had serious consequences. They were, fortunately, never tested.

The actions of the Californian

(1)   The failure of the international regulations for distress signals at night to be so distinctive as to remove any possible grounds for doubt as to their purpose.

(2)   The failure of those in charge of SS *Californian* to set a wireless watch once a number of rockets had been seen.

(3)   The failure of the master to help his officer of the watch identify the significance of the rockets seen.

(4)   The lack of a free exchange of basic information between the captain and his junior officers whilst lying stopped on the night of 14/15 April.

(5)   The failure, even reluctance, of the officer of the watch to call the captain more forcefully when he was in doubt as to the significance of the rockets observed.

(6)   The reluctance or inhibition that prevented the second officer using his initiative during his watch on the bridge of *Californian* once rockets had been observed.

(7)   The failure of the master to respond more responsibly to reports from the bridge

The rescue

(1)   *Carpathia*'s rescue was well planned and executed. It was, however, greatly helped by the relatively calm conditions, and by the facts that the majority of it was carried out during daylight and her freeboard was low.

(2)   The task would have been infinitely more difficult had the task been conducted during the night, in poor weather and by a ship with a much higher freeboard.

Recommendations

The 1912 Wreck Commissioner, Lord Mersey, made 24 recommendations in his report of the Formal Investigation. They covered matters such as watertight subdivisions in ships, lifeboats and rafts, the manning of lifeboats, boat drills and a number of general topics.

The most obvious shortcoming was the shortage of lifeboats, and recommendation No. 6, 'That the provision of lifeboat and raft accommodation on board such ships should be based on the number of persons intended be carried in the ship and not upon tonnage,' had in fact started to be implemented within days of the accident. The need for additional lifeboats was so obvious to all that measures to correct the deficiency were implemented without having to wait for any official report to publish its findings. It seems strange that this very obvious shortcoming was not identified in the original report as the main reason for the loss of life.

Included under the heading of 'General' the list recommended that lookouts should undergo sight tests at reasonable intervals; that there should be proper control and guidance of all on board in times of emergency, and that there should 'be an installation of wireless telegraphy, and that such installations should be worked with a sufficient number of trained operators to secure a continuous service by night and day.' There were also recommendations to steamship companies to instruct their ships to either moderate their speed when ice was reported in or near their track or alter course so as to go well clear of the danger zone. He also recommended that the Board of Trade remind masters of vessels that it was a misdemeanour not to go to the relief of a vessel in distress when possible to do so.

By far the most far-reaching of Lord Mersey's recommendations was his last, No. 24. To quote it in full he said:

That (unless already done) steps should be taken to call an International Conference to consider and as far as possible to agree upon a common line of conduct in respect of (a) the subdivision of ships; (b) the provision and working of lifesaving-appliances; (c) the installation of wireless telegraphy and the method of working the same; (d) the reduction of speed or the alteration of course in the vicinity of ice; and (e) the use of searchlights.

This recommendation alone was to result in the most enduring legacy of the *Titanic* tragedy, the International Convention for the Safety of Life at Sea (SOLAS). This was preceded, however, by two preliminary actions, the passing of the US Federal Government's Radio Act of 1912, and deployment of two US Navy cruisers to the area of the Grand Banks to monitor and report the presence of ice.

The 1912 Radio Act initiated the process whereby ships were required to carry two wireless operators so that a constant watch could be maintained as well as ensure that absolute priority would be given to distress signals.

The deployment of the two cruisers to report the locality of ice was maintained for the rest of the 1912 season, but responsibility for the same task the following year was passed to the United States Revenue Cutter Service, the predecessors to the United States Coast Guard.

Thirteen nations gathered in London in November 1913 for the first SOLAS Convention and concluded their work within two months. The treaty was signed on 20 January 1914 and took account of the recommendations and lessons from the *Titanic* disaster as well as laying down internationally applicable rules for the first time. It addressed such issues as the safety of navigation and the setting up of the North Atlantic ice patrol; the requirements for watertight bulkheads; radiotelegraphy and the requirement for a continuous watch on radio frequencies while at sea; life-saving appliances and fire protection and the need for ships to obtain a safety certificate. It also addressed the problem of insufficient numbers of lifeboats aboard *Titanic*. Article 40 of the new convention states: 'At no moment of its voyage may a ship have on board a total number of persons than that for whom accommodation is provided in the lifeboats (and the pontoon lifeboats) on board.' There was also provision for life-jackets, the allocation of duties to the crew in the event of an emergency and lifeboat drills.

It had been the intention for the SOLAS convention to enter into service in July 1915, but the war years intervened. Several individual nations adopted the provisions straight away, but it was not until a second London conference was convened in 1929 that further progress was made. Eighteen countries attended and, basing the new convention on the one agreed in 1914, adopted it with several new provisions included. Since then the SOLAS convention remains at the heart of all safety measures at sea, and it is administered by the only United Nations agency to be based in the United Kingdom, the International Maritime Organization, which has its home on the Albert Embankment in London. Diagonally opposite it, and on the other side of the River Thames, lie the British Houses of Parliament.

As a consequence of the 1914 agreement, and in accordance with the SOLAS convention, the International Ice Patrol continues to monitor the movement of icebergs and oceanographic conditions in the region of the Grand Banks to report the position and drift of icebergs. Since the 1940s, however, aircraft have replaced ships as the means by which the patrols are mounted. Responsibility for undertaking the ice patrol today lies with the United States Coast Guard. Every year, during the iceberg season, HC-130 aircraft flying from Newfoundland continue to monitor and report the presence of the ice. It is a testament to the effectiveness of the patrol that no vessel that has heeded the Ice Patrol's published iceberg limit has ever collided with an iceberg.

The 1912 inquiry recommendations and the subsequent SOLAS convention covered almost all the shortcomings identified as a result of the *Titanic* disaster. The fact that there could be ambiguity in interpreting the firing of rockets to indicate a vessel in distress was recognised during the original inquiries, but no specific recommendation was made to overcome the problem entirely. What was needed was a signal that was instantly and unambiguously recognisable as a distress signal, but the rules governing distress signals in 1912 did not meet this criterion. When the first SOLAS convention was agreed there was an acknowledgement that some distinction was necessary. The 1929 SOLAS convention stated: 'The use of an international distress signal, except for the purpose of indicating that a vessel is in distress, and the use of any signal which may be confused with an international distress signal are prohibited on every ship.' This effectively banned the use of rockets as 'company signals', but it was not until 1948 that specific provision was made that the stars released by a distress rocket must be red. Had this very obvious assessment been made by Lord Mersey in lieu of his attack against the *Californian* in 1912, he would have made an even greater contribution to the safety of life at sea.

There is very little I would wish to add to these recommendations, with, perhaps, one exception. It has a relevance to almost every accident involving passenger ships in the many years since the *Titanic* sank, including the very recent capsizing of the *Costa Concordia*. It is not a new idea, and I am well aware that shipping companies have looked at it before and are, I'm sure, looking at it again. It concerns the need for the command team to keep both crews and passengers informed.

The problem arises when it comes to managing passengers (and crew) in an emergency without inducing panic. Analysis of several serious accidents involving passenger ships in recent years reveals that the failure to keep both crew and passengers informed about what is happening is a recurring theme. Time and time again it seems that passengers felt they were not being told what was happening, that information was disseminated too infrequently or was grossly inaccurate.

It is never up to the marine accident investigator to provide answers to all the identified problems, but, to give a flavour of what a recommendation today might look like, the following could be added to those made by the Wreck Commissioner in 1912:

It is recommended that the White Star Line produces guidelines to its masters for use in emergencies on how best to inform crew and passengers about what is happening, and how to deliver it without inducing fear or panic. Such information must be timely, frequently updated and true. It should not attempt to disguise the severity of the situation but must give positive and clear directions to both passengers and crew to ensure that there is no confusion. Guidance should also be given on how best to inform people whose first language is not English.

For many passengers today, and indeed members of the crew, lifeboat drill is too often a tiresome and boring ritual to be endured on the first day of a cruise. I sometimes wonder if, after all these years, we have got it right. Having participated in many such drills, and trained others to use the equipment, it seems to me that passengers would benefit by being given some idea as to what to expect should a genuine emergency arise. Few passengers, for instance, expect the deck to tilt, the lights to go out, and the main public address system to fail when most needed. Should any of these unexpected situations arise the average passenger is, more often than not, totally unprepared for them and reacts accordingly. A prepared passenger is far more likely to react positively and correctly when the need arises. Experience indicates that in an emergency people seek three things: to have accurate information and clear instructions as to what to do, to be with their families, and to recover at least one essential item from their cabin below. It could be their lifejacket. Several hundred people going the wrong way is unlikely to be that helpful when time could be the most valuable asset available.

It is not the task of a marine accident investigation organisation to recommend solutions to an identified problem. They rarely have the means or competence to do so, but on the other hand they do have the ability, and the duty, to identify areas where shortcomings exist and make recommendations to have them resolved by organisations better placed to do so.

Among the more crucial features of the *Titanic*'s loss is the fact that she sank after incurring damage that affected too many watertight compartments and led to a rate of flooding beyond the capacity of the pumps to handle. I make no claim to being a naval architect or to possessing the skills or experience necessary to offer any advice for preventing such a loss arising from similar circumstances in the future. What I do know is that no ship is unsinkable and, in passing, merely state that no such claim was ever made about the *Titanic*.

Since I started writing this book, the world has indeed been reminded yet again that ships do sink. It was only the fortuitous grounding of the unfortunate cruise ship *Costa Concordia* in shallow water off the Tuscan island of Giglio in January 2012 that prevented her from sinking with, very possibly, greater loss of life.

It was not as if the event was unique. Only five years earlier another cruise ship, the Greek-flagged *Sea Diamond* sank after four watertight compartments were breached in circumstances that had some similarities. She too was very close inshore in what she thought was deep water, and it seems that some rocks off the island of Santorini in the Aegean may not have been charted correctly. Such an explanation does little, however, to identify the many other factors that must have had a bearing on what happened both before and after the hull was damaged. So far as I have been able to ascertain the Greek authorities still have not published their report into the accident, so it is impossible to make any judgement as to whether any of the lessons that may have arisen about stability and evacuation had a bearing on what happened with the *Costa Concordia* incident.

Until such time as the accident report is published I make no observation about the *Costa Concordia* other than to mourn the terrible loss of life. It would seem, however, that there are several important issues at stake, not least with the stability of modern cruise ships, evacuation procedures and the way both passengers and crew are directed in such circumstances. I very much hope that improvements will be made in a number of areas so that in the event of something going badly wrong in the future, everyone on board can be evacuated safely, that any list can be contained, that in the event of a complete power failure those on board are not kept in the dark as to what is happening, and that the accident is properly investigated and the report made public.

Which brings me back to *Titanic* and the question as to whether a modern marine accident investigator, having taken a fresh look at the evidence, would be tempted to make any new recommendations. It could be argued that even after a hundred years we still find ourselves seeking better stability rules, better evacuation procedures and better direction of crew and passengers. And making sure ships don't head directly towards known danger. Perhaps after all this time we aren't as good at learning lessons as we should be!

Epilogue

Perhaps the three most thought-provoking questions I'm sometimes asked after lecturing on the *Titanic* are:

- whether I think Mr J Bruce Ismay, the Managing Director of the White Star Line, deserved the vilification he received in the aftermath of the sinking

- whether Captain Lord of the *Californian* was unjustly treated by the two inquiries

- whether, after all these years, there are still lessons to be learned.

Mr Bruce Ismay

The straightforward answer to the first question is no. Whilst I'm not at all sure I would have warmed to Mr Ismay as a person, I find the various charges against him both unfair and unjustified. He is widely accused of two misdemeanours: putting pressure on the captain to use excessive speed to arrive in New York early, and boarding the last lifeboat to leave *Titanic* instead of going down with his ship like a hero.

There is no credible evidence to support the charge that he ever influenced the captain to use excessive speed as the voyage drew to an end. By the Sunday he would have known the ship was ahead of schedule and would, no doubt, have been pleased with the progress being made. He almost certainly knew the ship was in a position to arrive in New York on the Tuesday evening or even earlier without him having to influence the captain in any way whatsoever.

With regard to his actions in the aftermath of the collision late on the Sunday night, Mr Ismay was one of the very few people on the boat deck who, from the outset, knew the ship was going to sink. By remaining there and eschewing the warmth and comfort of the well-lit accommodation spaces he probably did more than anyone to ensure the lifeboats were fully manned and sent away. None of the officers supervising the launching of the lifeboats knew of the ship's predicament, and they and found his presence on the boat deck both irritating and irksome. Dressed in no more than pyjamas and a coat, he did his best in circumstances that must have been challenging to even the most experienced seafarer let alone someone whose life had been spent ashore and in the board room of the White Star Line.

We will never know the precise circumstances of how he boarded the last lifeboat to be launched, but there is no evidence to suggest that his action prevented anyone else from doing so. Had he stayed on board and 'gone down with the ship' he would no doubt have been seen by some as a hero and had his name added to the depressingly long list of casualties. The judgement that he was a coward is, in my opinion, a harsh one.

It was not all. Many accused him of lying when, in giving evidence, he claimed he was facing away from the sinking ship whilst helping to row away from it. There is a natural assumption that if he was rowing he must have been facing the *Titanic*. This is not necessarily the case. He may well have been seated facing away from the sinking ship and pushing the oar while someone else was sitting opposite and pulling it. Although unusual, it is entirely feasible in the confines of a crowded lifeboat.

Once on board the *Carpathia*, and in a degree of shock, he also attempted to look after the crew of the *Titanic* by attempting to make arrangements for them to return home to Great Britain at the earliest opportunity after they arrived in New York. He had no idea that steps were being taken to convene an inquiry in the United States and assumed that any such inquiry would be held in the United Kingdom. It was not an unreasonable line of thinking.

The gravest charge against Mr Ismay is that he overruled any decision to fit additional lifeboats on board *Titanic* and, against strong recommendations to do otherwise, sanctioned the 20 she was carrying at the time of the accident. This is an accusation easily made with the benefit of hindsight. His decision would have been dictated by a number of factors, but the one that influenced him most was what the regulations required. He met them in full.

Captain Stanley Lord

My answer to the second question is yes, he was unfairly treated. There is no doubt in my mind that both he and his officers could, and should, have done far more as they lay stopped surrounded by loose ice on the night of 14/15 April 1912, but for the *Californian* to be castigated in the way it was by both inquiries was too easy and totally unjustified.

Sober analysis of what happened the night the *Titanic* sank shows that Lord did much that was thoroughly professional and seamanlike. During the day of 14 April he specifically asked ships ahead of him to report the presence of any ice. As darkness fell he doubled the number of people keeping a lookout and remained on the bridge himself. He saw the ice in time to take avoiding action and take the way off his ship and, very reasonably, decided not to proceed until he could see where he was going. He would have earned no favours had he pressed on at night and damaged his ship without good cause.

He attempted to inform other ships that he was stopped and surrounded by ice, and it was not his fault that *Titanic* failed to listen to the one message the *Californian* tried to send her to pass on this information. He ensured the engines would be available for use should they be required. He maintained a full bridge watch throughout the night even though the ship was stationary in a flat calm sea and chose, furthermore, not to sleep in his cabin but in the chartroom immediately below the bridge. He made himself immediately available should anything untoward arise, and his officers were well aware that they had to call him should they be in any doubt. He is criticised for not responding to reports made to him during the night but I, too, have known moments when a report made to me as captain and fast asleep after many hours awake failed to make the impact it should have. It falls to the officer of the watch to make sure his captain has understood the full implications of what he has been told. I have no means of proving it, but it is possible that today's young officers are more likely to use their initiative than was evident in 1912.

From the comfort of my study at home I sometimes ask myself why the *Californian*'s second officer, who saw the rockets being fired from an unknown ship in the early hours of 15 April, did not wake Captain Lord with a report such as 'Captain sir, I've just seen a distress signal from rockets going up to the south of us and on the horizon. I've called the wireless operator to see if he can find out what is happening, I've alerted the chief [engineer] to go on standby, and I have just sent for the chief officer. Would you please come to the bridge, sir.' I wonder, just wonder, how Captain Lord would have reacted. As we know only too well no such report was ever made and it is pointless to speculate on the outcome had it been. Rather than blame the second officer for any perceived failures, the good marine accident investigator will dig deep to find out why not, and it is the answers to that question that will lead to genuine steps being taken to improve marine safety.

I do not point the finger of blame at any one person on board the *Californian*. The problem lay not so much with the performance of individuals but with the culture that prevailed in Edwardian England. Subservience, deference, fear, lack of confidence and the inbuilt instinct that the senior officer is always right were factors that were all too evident that night.

To be blamed (as the *Californian* has been) for the large loss of life on board the *Titanic*, and without being informed by anyone that the ship was to be criticised in advance of the report being published, was a gross injustice as well as a misrepresentation of the mistakes that were undoubtedly made by the ship and her crew that night and afterwards. I personally think Captain Lord was gravely at fault for a number of things, not least for not reporting what he knew sooner than he did, and for not ensuring the rough log was carefully preserved for further scrutiny. He could furthermore have helped restore his reputation had he expressed some sorrow at the loss of so many lives. Even allowing for these mistakes he did not, in my opinion, deserve to be made the scapegoat for the severe loss of life when the *Titanic* sank.

I think it is a tragedy that no procedure exists to clear Captain Lord's name. He was never, as such, blamed for anything personally whereas his ship the *Californian* was. His name will forever be linked with his ship.

Lessons to be learned: could it happen again?

The final question I am sometimes asked is, could it happen again and have we, after all these years, learned all the lessons from the loss of the *Titanic*?

The honest answer to the first part of the question must be that while it is extremely unlikely we will ever see another *Titanic*-type accident, there is always the possibility there will be others due to unforeseen circumstances. We only have to reflect on the capsize of the *Costa Concordia* in 2012 to realise that even in this day and age, and despite the very safety-conscious cruise-ship industry, accidents do happen from time to time. The overriding priority every time must be to learn whatever the lessons are.

In response to the question as to whether we have learned all the lessons from the *Titanic* after 100 years, I believe there are at least two issues that still remain: the use of large rudder angles when under way at relatively high speeds, and how one rescues large numbers of survivors from a sinking ship if, for any reason, it is not possible to use all the available lifeboats and life rafts.

Rudder angles

One of the more curious thoughts that has occurred to me since taking an interest in the *Titanic* is that when Mr Murdoch attempted to avoid the iceberg he ordered hard a starboard with the ship still propelling at about 22 knots. When ships turn at speed they tend to tilt away from the direction of the turn but, given her design, construction and displacement, *Titanic* barely listed (heeled) at all when she began to alter course.

Had it been necessary to give the same order in a modern cruise ship, with its high freeboard and relatively shallow draught, the vessel would have reacted very differently. In April 2010, almost exactly 98 years after the *Titanic* wheel order had been given, the cruise ship *Carnival Ecstasy* was at sea in the Gulf of Mexico one afternoon when she made a sudden turn and took on a heavy list. She had, it seems, taken action to avoid a large buoy that 'was adrift and mostly submerged, thereby preventing it from being detected by the ship's radar.' Over 60 passengers were injured and the incident made headline news.

I have no idea what the causal factors were in this incident, or how much wheel was applied, but it seems to me that any unexpected list on board modern high-sided cruise ships caused by applying a large rudder angle, and with swimming pools full of water on the upper deck, will have three consequences: injuries to personnel, headline news coverage and massive compensation claims from passengers. Such instances, while fortunately rare, do not help the image of the cruise industry, and it comes as no surprise to me that those held responsible for the wheel going hard over are in every case disciplined for what is invariably described as human error.

Accident investigators, however, try to probe more deeply

into the causes beyond just 'human error', and may well reveal some more fundamental shortcomings.

Operating procedures on board modern cruise ships do in fact minimise the risk of excess rudder ever being applied, but I can't but help wonder what might happen should an unexpected emergency arise. It is very simple to declare that the situation cannot possibly happen but things can go wrong from time to time. If something did suddenly appear close ahead, would today's ship's officer instinctively follow Mr Murdoch's actions and seek to use full wheel, or would he be more concerned by the onset of a heavy and unexpected list, people being injured, emptying swimming pools, bad press coverage and a threatened career?

Mass rescue operations

My second thought about unfinished business from the *Titanic* disaster concerns the rescue of large numbers of people from any ship in distress far from land and in bad weather. Apart from it happening at night, the *Titanic* disaster occurred in almost perfect conditions. What, I ask myself, if tomorrow's big accident involves a ship listing badly, far from land, in a gale and at night?

The *Titanic* foundered in conditions that were near ideal for launching and handling lifeboats and, indeed, for recovering the survivors. The rescue by the *Carpathia* was superbly planned and executed but the calm conditions, and the daylight, made it look deceptively easy. It may not always be that straightforward in future.

There was an assumption by the authorities in 1912 that, when a vessel was in distress, another ship would quickly come to her aid and rescue survivors, either by going alongside the stricken ship or by plucking them from the sea. To an extent this philosophy was borne out by the actions of the Cunard liner *Carpathia*, who successfully embarked the survivors from 19 lifeboats in just under 4 hours.

This impression of simplicity and ease was further demonstrated by the Wreck Commissioner Lord Mersey who observed in his 1912 report that the SS *Californian* 'could have pushed through the ice to the open water without any serious risk and so have come to the assistance of the *Titanic*. Had she done so she might have saved many if not all of the lives that were lost.'

Ignoring for a moment the special circumstances that applied to the *Californian*, he implies, in just a few words, that rescuing survivors from a sinking ship is straightforward. When it comes to learning the lessons from the *Titanic*, no such assumption of simplicity should be made. Rescuing a small number from a ship in distress using helicopters or a shore-based lifeboat can be extremely difficult and frequently demands bravery and skill of a very high order. To project the concept to the need to rescue hundreds if not thousands from a sinking ship is something entirely different and raises a number of questions. To adopt a *Titanic* analogy, 'It can't happen' is being naive. It could. One has only to recall the difficulties facing the search and rescue authorities when the ferry *Estonia* foundered in a storm in the Baltic in September 1994. The accident occurred in appalling weather conditions and many of those on board were unable even to reach the upper deck when the ship began to list heavily. The high winds prevented the effective use of many of the lifesaving facilities, while the ships and helicopters standing by found the task extremely difficult. 852 people died in what was one of the most awful marine tragedies of recent years. Factors that can complicate any such rescue might include fire on board, a heavy list, a high sea state, appalling weather, night time, badly injured or elderly personnel, and insufficient members of rescuing crew.

Statistically, sea travel is among the safest of all modes of transport and cruising continues to be a singularly rewarding and enjoyable way of taking a well-earned holiday. I have no doubt that recent accidents will lead to some far-reaching improvements to both the stability of modern ships and evacuation procedures, but I also hope that those charged with improving safety at sea will expedite their work in finding a workable solution to rescuing large numbers of people when it all goes wrong.

The zeal with which people over the years have criticised Captain Lord for ignoring the rockets from the *Titanic* has allowed attention to divert from learning the lessons into a never-ending argument that gets us nowhere. Had Lord Mersey spotted this in 1912, and recommended that steps be taken to examine the problem of saving people from a foundering ship, then many people who have died in subsequent marine accidents might have been saved. Identifying where the real problems are at sea, rather than trying to find someone to blame, places a heavy responsibility on those who are tasked to carry out independent investigations into the things that do, unfortunately, go wrong from time to time.

The last word

Had this been a real-life investigation many people would have been involved in collecting the evidence, analysing the results and compiling the report. It would then have been sent to anyone whose reputations might have been affected by the findings to enable them to comment on judgements made before it was published. The closest next of kin of any victim would be treated in exactly the same way and every consideration would be given to any view they may have had. The conclusions drawn in this book are not derived from a new investigation or great technical expertise, and no others are involved. As I said at the outset, I am not a *Titanic* expert but have drawn heavily on my experience as a seafarer and a former Chief Inspector of Marine Accidents to analyse what I think happened that night in April 1912.

I started this book by reflecting on how the loss of the *Titanic* has managed to capture people's imagination over the years and how it continues to fascinate and intrigue. It is, however, more than just another maritime story. It was, first and foremost, a tragedy in which over 1500 people lost their lives. Communities such as Southampton in southern England and Addergoole in County Mayo in the west of Ireland were particularly badly affected by the number of their own who were killed. There were many other places in the British Isles, the United States of America and about 26 other nations where victims were mourned. A marine accident investigator never forgets that the real losers in any accident in which there is loss of life are the families of the victims. Some seek only to find someone to blame but, in my experience, most would far rather the accident be properly investigated with the sole aim of seeking ways to prevent the same thing happening again. For all its awfulness, *Titanic* did achieve something. It was the catalyst for bringing the maritime nations of the world together to agree the first Safety of Life at Sea convention in 1914. Since then SOLAS in various guises has set the standard for safety at sea today. Whether you embark in a ship as a member of the crew or as a passenger, you owe it to the many over the past 100 years who have worked hard to draw up and enforce regulations that have their origins in a tragedy played out on the ice-cold waters of the North Atlantic when a brand new four-funnelled liner called *Titanic* hit an iceberg and sank.

Titanic should however serve to remind us about something else. For many people it is the only ship they have ever heard of, and yet, in this age of the internet, international air travel and 24 hours a day news coverage we forget the importance and relevance of the sea and shipping. We forget that international trade is the lifeblood of the world economy and that over 90 per cent of all goods are still carried by sea. Few of us today know anything about ships, seafarers and the world of merchant shipping. There was a time when a London commuter would cross the River Thames via London Bridge and look down on ships loading and discharging at their riverside berths. The ships have long since gone from this part of the river and so have the sailors, the stevedores and the trades that supported them. There was a time when readers in the United Kingdom would look at the front page of the Times and see details of future sailings of ships bound for the Far East, Australia, the Cape, Rio de Janeiro and New York. In some instance the names of the captains would be included.

It is all so different today. The only names that anyone remembers are *Titanic* and Captain E J Smith. I just hope, perhaps forlornly, that this book will do something to stimulate renewed interest in this forgotten, but vital, industry. Remember *Titanic*, but also the ships and seafarers of today who do so much to ensure our forecourts are topped up with petrol, our supermarkets and high-street shops are stocked with goods and the wheels of industry are kept turning.

Glossary of terms

Many of the terms given below will be strange to those unfamiliar with the sea, but there are good reasons for nautical terminology. Many of the words, terms and expressions are derived from practices and customs developed over the centuries. To be effective, the mariner must have instant and unambiguous understanding of the terminology being used regardless of the ship he is serving in. Whilst a landsman may, very reasonably, refer to left or right, upstairs or down, in front or behind, such simplistic language will lead to confusion at sea. Even the most straightforward expression such as 'to the left' can depend on which way one is facing whereas 'to port' can only mean one thing: on the left hand side of the ship.

Abaft	'Behind', or 'nearer the stern than', something else on a ship.
Abeam	At right angles to the line of a ship and on either side.
Aft	Towards the back of the ship; can be both relative and absolute: e.g. 'Go aft' is an order to proceed towards the stern; the 'aft end' means the stern of the vessel or the end furthest away from the bows.
Amidships	The position on board a vessel that lies at or near the middle of the ship between bow and stern.
Amplitude	The bearing of the sun (or other heavenly body) in relation to true east or west at the time of its rising or setting. By taking a bearing of e.g. the sun when it is just above the horizon (to allow for refraction) it is possible for the navigator to compare this with a simple calculation derived from tables to establish error, if any, of the compass being used.
Astern	Behind. To look back or in the wake of a moving ship.

Azimuth

The true bearing of a celestial object such as the sun, moon, planets or stars. From an azimuth it is possible to determine any error in the accuracy of a compass so that a correction can be applied to either bearings taken and plotted, or courses to be steered.

Beam

The measure across the width of a ship, or the direction at right angles to its keel.

Bearing

The direction measured in angular terms between the ship's head and an object, or between the meridian and an object. An object bearing northeast would be 45 degrees to the east of north, while an object bearing red 30, or about three points on the port bow, would be seen about 30 degrees to the left of where the bows are pointing.

Binnacle

Usually made of varnished wood and situated immediately in front of the wheel used for steering, it contains the steering compass and the compensating magnets. It is viewed from the top, with that part of the compass card required for steering illuminated by lamp.

Bosun

A contraction of boatswain, the title traditionally given to the senior deck rating on board who is responsible for the care and upkeep of sails, rigging, anchors, cables and ropes, and, under the first mate or chief officer, has charge of all deck ratings for the general upkeep and running of the ship.

Bow

The front end of a ship or boat.

Brace

The rope attached to the boom or yardarm onto which a sail is attached to enable the sail to be trimmed. In a square-rigged ship, the braces trim the yards horizontally.

Brig

A sailing vessel with two masts carrying square sails but the aft one also has a gaff-rigged mainsail.

Bulkhead

An upright partition on board a ship. At their strongest they are watertight, but they can also be of light construction and do no more than separate one compartment from another.

Bunker   The compartment or space in which coal to fuel
                      a steamship's boilers is stored.

Bunkers   The fuel used to power a vessel.

Calm   No wind at all. The sea is flat and mirror-smooth.
                      Force zero on the Beaufort scale.

Chart   A nautical map showing a wide range of
                      information of value to the navigator. The scale
                      of the chart varies on the requirement. Whereas
                      a single small-scale chart might suffice for the
                      crossing of the Atlantic, an approach to a coastline
                      would require a larger-scale version showing more
                      detail. A navigator lining up to enter a harbour
                      entrance would require the chart to be on an even
                      larger scale and showing as much relevant detail as
                      possible.

                      Charts show the outline of coasts, key
                      topographical features, navigational marks
                      including the light characteristics of buoys and
                      lighthouses, depths of water and submerged
                      hazards such as wrecks, rocks, sandbanks and other
                      underwater obstructions. Distances are measured
                      using the latitude scale on the side of the chart, and
                      compass variation will be given for a certain date
                      and the annual change to be applied. A key feature
                      of any chart is that it must be kept up to date as
                      details required for safe navigation change. This
                      is achieved by a variety of means but primarily
                      by a publication known as a Notice to Mariners.
                      It is published weekly. The British Admiralty
                      Hydrographic Office produced its first Notice to
                      Mariners in 1834.

                      A chart outfit is the collection of charts issued to a
                      ship for the route or trading area being used.

Compass   An instrument whereby the ship's direction, or
                      the bearing of an object from the ship, can be
                      determined. The units of measurement are either
                      degrees (of which there are 360) or, in the days
                      before degrees became commonplace, points (of
                      which there were 32 but broken down further into

half or quarter points). The four cardinal points are north, east, south and west.

In the early years of the twentieth century compasses were dependent on the earth's magnetic field to provide direction In theory the reference point, due north, would point exactly towards the north pole but it actually pointed towards the magnetic north pole, which would lie some distance from the pole and would vary from year to year.

Ships would carry two types of compass. The standard compass provided the main reference source and would invariably be placed in a position as free from the ship's own magnetic field as possible, with special magnets placed in its immediate vicinity to reduce local ship-borne anomalies as much as possible. *Titanic's* standard compass, mounted on gimbals, was positioned on top of a deckhouse between the second and third funnels.

The second type of compass, known as the steering compass, was positioned immediately in front of the helmsman to provide a reference for him to steer by. It too was provided with magnets to remove magnetic anomalies. At night the compass card was lit with a small light.

Compass cards were in practice notated so that both points and degrees would feature. The helmsman would be given a course to steer in either points or degrees.

Compass error The compass is liable to error. Gyro compasses today very rarely feature errors more than 1 to 2 degrees, and often much less or none at all, but the magnetic compass has two inherent errors, both of which were present in *Titanic* variation and deviation (see below).

Ships' navigating officers, the mates, will take bearings of the sun or other stellar bodies, known as an azimuth (or an amplitude), to determine the error from nautical tables where the true bearing can be calculated and then compared with those actually taken from the ship's magnetic compass (usually the standard compass). The difference will give the compass error for whatever heading the ship is on at this precise place.

Providing cloud cover permits, the taking of an azimuth will usually be undertaken every watch.

Commutator　　The term features frequently in *Titanic* literature. It is attributed to an instrument positioned at the front of *Titanic's* bridge to give a visual indication of pitch and roll.

No such term exists in the context of a ship's movement. Ships do have an instrument, known as an inclinometer or clinometer, to measure the degree of list or heel. It does not measure pitch. The expression 'commutator' seems to stem from the evidence given by the quartermaster, Mr Hitchins, to the American Senate Inquiry. Whether Mr Hitchins used the wrong term or it was misheard by the stenographer recording the testimony is not known, but the word 'commutator' in the context in which it is being used is incorrect.

Course　　The direction in which a ship is being steered. Except when steering using landmarks, a helmsman will steer a course by watching the compass card in front of him and keeping the ship's head aligned to the direction ordered. Given a course of S 86° W, the helmsman will steer a course 86 degrees west of south, i.e. 4 degrees to the south of due west.

Crimps　　People who would accommodate sailors and others in seaports, board them, find them ships and then rob them of all they possessed.

Crow's nest　　Sometimes known as the 'cage' or 'nest'. An enclosed platform but open at the top in which one or more lookouts are stationed to keep a lookout for other ships and objects. It is normally placed on the leading edge of the foremast and at a height above the level of the vessel's bridge. It is accessed either by a ladder inside the mast and an opening into the nest or by climbing an external ladder.

Davits Small crane-like structures fitted on the upper decks of ships to handle the lowering and hoisting of lifeboats. The davits fitted in the *Titanic* were manufactured by the London-based Welin Davit Company, and were Welin quadrant davits.

Dead reckoning (DR) The position of a ship derived purely from the course made in a specific direction and the distance covered. No allowance is made for the effects of tide, currents or wind.

Departure A ship takes her 'departure' when proceeding out of sight of land. It is usually the last position taken with any accuracy from fixed positions ashore. It is from this position that both direction and distance are subsequently determined.

Derelict A ship drifting without human life on board. A derelict is unlikely to have any power or show lights. As such they are hazards to safe navigation.

Deviation The difference between the heading of a ship's compass and the true magnetic pole due to the influence of local magnetism. It can be removed, or nearly removed, by the strategic placing of iron magnets in the near vicinity of the ship's compass and any residual error calculated and allowed for.

Drift To be carried by the tide, wind, stream or current alone. There is an implication that the vessel is not under control.

Dunnage Matting or lengths of timber used to keep a cargo in position in a ship's hold, to keep it dry or separated from other types of cargo.

Elder Brother (of Trinity House) The term given to a member of the Court of the Corporation of Trinity House, the lighthouse authority for England, Wales and the Channel Islands. There are currently about 35 Elder Brethren and they must first have been admitted as Younger Brethren. Many hold, or have held, positions of influence but most are current or former trustees of the Trinity House charities or directors of the lighthouse service.

The expression Elder Brethren is derived from the Royal Charter granted in 1514 by King Henry VIII when he tasked his 'trewe and faithfull subjects, shipmen and mariners of this Our Realm of England' to 'begyn of new and erecte and establish a Guild or Brotherhood of themselves or other persons as well men as women, whatsoever they be ...'

Falls
A fall is that part of a rope which you pull. The plural 'falls' refers to the complete set of ropes (or wire) used to hoist or lower a lifeboat from the davits.

Fatigue
Fatigue is a condition brought on by excessive physical exertion, stress, disrupted or lack of sleep, and interruptions to the circadian rhythm. It manifests itself in a number of ways including lethargy, an inability to absorb information or make rational decisions, forgetfulness and a marked reduction in mental agility. It also leads to marked physical weariness and weakness. It can often be found among seafarers who work long and irregular hours.

Flag
A banner depicting a ship's nationality, ownership, or a letter (or numeral). Flown from masts, yards or a flag pole. Several flags flown together one above another can form a code word for interpretation by an observer.

The flag state of a ship is the term used to describe the nationality of its registry. A British-flagged vessel is registered in a British port. *Titanic* was registered in Liverpool and flew a British flag.

Foc's'le
The foc's'le or forecastle is the foremost part of the vessel on the upper deck. It derives its name from the old sailing-ship days when it was that part of the ship's structure between the fore mast and the bow where a castle-like structure was built. In the

age of steamships it referred to the raised part of the structure right forward where the deckhands were accommodated.

Founder	A ship founders when she finally sinks
Freeboard	The distance between the waterline and the upper deck level in the centre of the ship.
Great circle	A great circle is a straight line on the surface of a sphere, the shortest distance between two points, and its plane will pass through the sphere's centre. When plotted on a Mercator chart a great circle course will appear as a curve bulging towards the nearest pole
Gunwale	Pronounced 'gunnel': the topmost part of the hull into which the holes to accept rowlocks are placed. The oars are then placed in the rowlocks.
HMS	His (or Her) Majesty's Ship. The prefix given to the name of a British warship belonging the Royal Navy.
Heading	The direction of travel, usually expressed in compass points or degrees based on north.
Heavenly body	The sun, moon, any star or planet that can be used for astronavigation.
Helm	The process by which a ship is steered to follow the desired course.
Helm orders	The orders given to a helmsman to steer or alter course. Prior to 1933 helm orders followed the practice adopted in the days of sail whereby an order to alter course one way or another was given by ordering the helmsman to turn the wheel in, apparently, the opposite direction. This conformed to the traditional practice of putting the tiller in the opposite direction to the way the ship's head was required to go. The practice was changed in 1933 and since then all helm orders follow the more natural practice whereby an order to alter course to, say, port results in the wheel being turned in the same direction. When in 1912 the iceberg was sighted *Titanic's* officer of the watch

ordered 'hard a starboard'. This resulted, quite correctly, in the wheel being turned hard to port.

<table>
<tr><td>Ice terminology</td><td>

Glacier – a mass of compressed snow and ice formed over many hundreds of years and continually moving from higher to lower ground. At its lowest edge the ice of the glacier either melts into fresh water or breaks off as icebergs, bergy bits or growlers.

Iceberg – a massive piece of ice which has broken away from a glacier. It may be afloat or aground and its shape varies greatly. It protrudes more than 5 metres above sea level but only about an eighth of its mass is visible. It is made of fresh water and the whole becomes unstable over time when floating in water where the temperature is above freezing. The warmer water melts the underwater mass, resulting in the entire edifice toppling over.

Bergy bits – a large piece of floating glacier ice generally showing between 1 and 5 metres above the surface. It normally covers between 1 and 300 square metres in area.

Growler – piece of ice smaller than a bergy bit and less than 1 metre above the surface of the sea. Can be ice that has turned over and can appear transparent, translucent green or even black or dark blue. Is less than 20 square metres in area and is very difficult to see at night.

Pack ice – ice normally formed by frozen water rather than a glacier, covering wide areas in polar waters. May be formed of many individual pieces of ice pushed together or 'packed' by the wind and current.

Floe – any relatively flat piece of sea ice of 20 square metres.

Field ice – the term given to frozen seawater floating in a form looser than in pack ice.

Icefield – an area of floating ice consisting of any size of floes where the area is greater than 10 kilometres across.

</td></tr>
</table>

Ice blink – a whitish glare that appears on the horizon and on low clouds above an accumulation of distant ice.

Iceberg keel – the bottom of an iceberg, which can, if the water is sufficiently shallow, scrape along the seabed. If the iceberg capsizes as it melts then the keel may well land up at the top and out of the water.

Knot

A measurement of speed. One knot is one nautical mile per hour. It is never 'knots per hour'. It derives its name from the practice whereby a vessel's speed was measured by knots being tied in a rope at specific intervals (47 feet 3 inches) and then the end of the rope was dropped into the sea attached to a wooden board. The rope was then allowed to pay out over the stern for a known number of seconds (28) and the number of passing knots would be counted. The number would equate to the speed.

Latitude

One of the two coordinates used to indicate a position on the earth's surface. It is the distance north or south of the equator measured in degrees and minutes of arc. One degree of latitude (or one degree of longitude at the equator) equates 60 nautical miles.

Lloyd's List

One of the world's oldest newspapers, founded by Edward Lloyd, the proprietor of Lloyd's Coffee House in London in 1734. Its function has been to provide news and intelligence on shipping matters, and it is still used by merchants, marine insurance agents and the shipping industry as an essential source of information.

Log
(for measuring speed or distance covered)

A device for measuring a ship's speed. *Titanic* was fitted with a Walker's taffrail log that consisted of a small brass cigar-shaped body with angled fins on it that, when towed behind a ship, would rotate. This rotation would be transmitted by a line that turned in sympathy to operate a wheel connected to a readout dial that measured the distance covered. It was read hourly.

Log *(for recording events)*	The ship's log is the official record for everything significant that happens on board. Navigational information, weather, embarking and disembarking of the pilot, draught and a range of other activities are recorded. The practice in most merchant ships is to maintain two logs, the official one and a rough log. The rough log is the one kept contemporaneously, the official one is usually written up later and in neater handwriting. Ship owners and regulators require the official version, whereas marine accident investigators will always be more interested in the rough log.
London River	The sailors' name for the seaward end of the tidal River Thames.
Longitude	One of the two coordinates used to indicate a position on the earth's surface. It is the arc at the pole between the prime meridian (Greenwich) and the meridian of the position being referred to. In other words, it describes position east or west of Greenwich.
Marconigram	A message transmitted by a wireless operated by Marconi's Wireless Telegraph Company.
Mercator	Gerardus Mercator was a Flemish geographer and cartographer who, in 1569, presented a way of showing the curved surface of the earth on a flat chart. This is achieved by making the meridians (lines of longitude) parallel and increasing the scale of latitude as it moves away from the equator. Mercator charts are widely used by mariners.
Meridian	Taken that the earth is a sphere, the meridians are the lines (circles) on the surface that pass through both the north and south poles. They derive their name from the Latin *meridies*, midday, and have the characteristic that they mark all places which have noon at precisely the same instant.
Navigation lights	Ships carry lights at night to indicate their presence, their ability to manoeuvre and their rough direction of travel. These are known as navigation or running lights, and only three

colours are used: white, red and green. Carried on the centre line of the vessel, or on either side in a position where they can be clearly seen by another ship, they are an essential ingredient in the prevention of collisions at sea. The main ones are white steaming lights, which are carried only by power-driven vessels, high up on masts, funnels or some other suitable structure, to indicate rough direction of travel; red and green sidelights to indicate which side of the ship an observer is on; and a white light aft known as the stern light or overtaking light, analogous to the red rear light of a car. Each light has a specific arcs over which it can be observed, and a minimum distance at which it can be seen. There are a number of other light combinations that convey different types of specialist activity.

Noon
The instant when the sun is on the meridian of the observer.

Orlop deck
The lowest deck in a ship. Derived from the term 'over-lop'.

P&O
An established British shipping company, the Peninsular and Oriental Steam Navigation Company, trading between Britain, India, the Far East and Australia.

Passage
A passage is the voyage a vessel is engaged when travelling from her port of departure to the one of arrival. 'She made a good passage' refers to a voyage made at a fair speed and without mishap.

Point
As in 'two points on the bow'. Merchant seamen's terminology for an angle of horizontal measurement. Derived from the 32 parts into which the magnetic compass card is divided, a single point is $11^{1}/_{4}$ degrees and is simple to estimate when describing the relative position of a light or object relative to ships head.

Port
The left-hand side of a ship when facing forward.

Pratique
The official approval given by a health authority to

enable a ship to enter a port having satisfied the authority that the vessel concerned is free from contagious disease.

psi　　　　A measurement of pressure: pounds per square inch.

Quartermaster　　　　The sailor whose primary task is to steer the ship. When not steering he may be used for other tasks around the ship including maintaining a watch in the vicinity of the aft docking bridge, where he is answerable direct to the officer of the watch. In harbour he usually keeps watches at the head of the gangway.

Rhumb line　　　　A line on the earth's surface that cuts all the meridians at the same angle. A rhumb line that represents a ship's track on a Mercator chart will appear as a straight line. If, however, this same track is transferred to a sphere, or gnomonic projection, it will appear as a curve and will be longer. At the time of the collision with an iceberg *Titanic* was following a rhumb line from the 'turning point' to a position to the south of the Nantucket Shoals light vessel.

RMS　　　　Royal Mail Steamer. The prefix to the name of a British ship contracted to carry mail. It is never prefixed by the definite article.

Rubbing strake　　　　A beaded bit of wood on the outside of a small boat just beneath the gunwale (the top) to provide a measure of protection against jetties, piers and other boats.

Rudder　　　　The means by which the direction of a ship's travel is controlled. Situated underwater, it is normally positioned at the aft end of the vessel and is controlled by mechanical, hydraulic or electrical links to a tiller, wheel or steering control in the cockpit of a small vessel or the bridge of a large one.

Sailing directions	The Admiralty Sailing Directions carried by the *Titanic* were textbooks published by the Hydrographic Office designed to supplement the chart outfit. They contain valuable information gleaned over the years by mariners to assist masters and ships' officers to navigate their ships safely. The Directions appear in a number of volumes, with each one covering a specific area. They are kept up to date by the periodic issue of Supplements and Notices to Mariners. Sailing Directions are often referred to as Pilots.
Schooner	A vessel with fore-and-aft sails on two masts. The main mast is the higher of the two and topsails will be carried on the fore mast. Schooner nowadays may have more than two masts and no topsails.
Screw	Propeller.
Ship rigged	A vessel is ship rigged when she has a bowsprit, three masts, each with a topgallant and topsail masts, all of which carry square sails.
Slip	A vessel slips when she lets go of all her mooring lines on departing a dock.
Socket signal	A rocket with a distinctive sound component that can be used in lieu of a gun for attracting attention. They have to be fired from specially approved sockets mounted on either side of the bridge, or the docking station aft, and of such a design that they are fired at least 20 degrees off the perpendicular to prevent them falling back onto the vessel's deck.
Soul	Rather than use expressions such as people, crew and passengers, or hands, the word soul is used when describing a person on board a vessel involved in an accident. This eliminates any confusion as to the age, race or status of anyone on board. It is still used today.
'Sounding' the ship	The process whereby a line or chain with a weight on the end of it is lowered into a pipe that accesses the bilges, a tank or other space in the lower parts of a ship to determine whether water exists, and

if so, how much. Some tanks are designed to hold water, in which case the quantity held will be sought but other spaces should be dry. Any sounding of a tank that reveals water when it should be dry may indicate an ingress of unwanted water or, at the worst, flooding, meaning it will have to pumped out.

Speak As in 'speak' by light. The process of communication between ships. Traditionally this involved signalling by flags but also with a dedicated signal lamp using Morse code.

Specie Coins and bullion money, as opposed to currency notes.

Starboard The right-hand side of a ship when facing forward.

Stellar observations Star or planet sights taken shortly before dawn or shortly after sunset when both the object and a clearly defined horizon could be seen. The 'window' for taking such sights was limited, and it involved using a sextant to measure the angle between the horizon and the heavenly body at a precisely recorded time. Using nautical tables and an almanac it was possible to work out an accurate position for the time the sights were taken. Navigators would, if possible, try to observe a number of stars at right angles to each other to establish both latitude and longitude.

Taffrail The rail at the very stern of the ship. It derives its name from the word 'tafferal' used to describe the intricately carved wooden top of the stern of sailing ships in the age when it was feature of construction.

Telegraph The engine-room telegraph is the means by which the master, pilot, or officer of the watch conveys engine orders to the engine room. It is a pedestal-mounted instrument with a moveable handle attached to a pointer that is repeated in the engine room.

Tingle	A temporary patch put over a hole or damage to a ship's hull, and applied from the outside. Traditionally of wood or even metal they can, in extremis, be made from canvas. They serve to prevent, or reduce, flooding until permanent repairs can be made.
Tonnage	Ship's tonnage is given in four basic ways: gross registered tonnage, net tonnage, deadweight and displacement. Each has a different function. The word tonnage normally refers to a measure of volume and not weight and is often the basis on which taxation or other charges are levied. A ton is 100 cubic feet (2.83 cubic metres)..
	Gross registered tonnage (grt) is the total internal, and usable, volume of a ship.
	Net tonnage is the total internal volume of the ship that can be used for carrying cargo.
	Deadweight is the number of tons that a vessel can transport of cargo, stores, and bunker fuel.
	Displacement is the total weight of the vessel at a specific draught, equating to the amount of water displaced.
Tween deck	Derived from 'between deck': the space between the upper deck and the hold. It can be used for storing cargo or for the accommodation of both crew and passengers. Where accommodation features it would be built into the tween deck space.
Variation	The difference in the direction of the earth's magnetic pole and the geographic pole. Depending on the ship's position the difference can be substantial. It varies from year to year as the position of the magnetic pole changes. The charts in use will indicate both variation and the rate of change to be used. The magnetic north pole in 1904 was in position 70° 31' N, 96° 34' W, some 1930 miles from the geographic north pole.

Voyage data recorder (VDR)	Today's VDR, the maritime equivalent of the aviation industry's 'black box,' is capable of recording a wide range of data drawn from many sources on board a ship including course, speed, radar parameters, GPS and electronic chart data, radio communications and speech picked up by one of the strategically placed microphones on board. When downloaded afterwards the stored information enables the investigator to work out what happened with a high degree of accuracy. Establishing why it happened is more difficult and is only possible after carefully analysing all the available evidence.
Way	The word way in phrases such as 'under way' or 'making way' refers to movement through the water due to the vessel being propelled. Head way means going forwards, and stern way is the opposite.
Weigh	The process of lifting the anchor from the seabed. To 'weigh anchor' means to heave in the anchor using the capstan so that the ship is no longer tethered to the ground by it. When the anchor finally breaks free from the seabed it is 'aweigh'.
Well deck	The spaces on traditional merchant ships between the fo'c'sle and the amidships superstructure and between that same structure and the poop deck right aft.
Wind chill	The temperature felt by exposed skin caused by the wind. It is invariably lower than the actual air temperature. Given an air temperature of 31 °F (−0.5 °C) and a wind speed of 22 knots the wind-chill temperature on exposed skin would be in the order of 2 °F (−17 °C).
Yard	A spar hung from a mast on which a sail is attached.